Advance Praise for *Classified*

"The nation urgently needs what David E. Bernstein here provides: a lucid explanation of the long and tangled intersection of racial classifications and the law. With the intellectual boldness and clarity that he brought to *Rehabilitating Lochner*, he points to a path from today's tensions to a less angry, more sophisticated future."

–George F. Will, *Washington Post*

"A thorough, careful, magisterial work on a subject that's both of great practical and great theoretical importance in modern American law; highly recommended."

–Eugene Volokh, Gary T. Schwartz Distinguished Professor of Law, UCLA School of Law

"Chief Justice John Roberts has called our racial sorting system a 'sordid business.' In *Classified*, David Bernstein provides the sordid details. What began as a government effort to combat discrimination now serves mainly to advance political agendas and stoke racial resentment. Well-researched and clearly written, *Classified* explains how we got into this mess and why a rethinking of official racial and ethnic categories is long overdue."

–Jason L. Riley, *Wall Street Journal* columnist, and author of *Maverick: A Biography of Thomas Sowell*

"David E. Bernstein's excellent book—*Classified: The Untold Story of Racial Classification in America*—exposes the full extent of what we all should have known: When governments dispense benefits based on race and ethnicity, the conflict over which groups should receive those benefits and which individuals qualify as members of those groups will be never-ending."

–Gail Heriot, Professor of Law, University of San Diego, and member, U.S. Commission on Civil Rights

"David Bernstein has written an illuminating, thoughtful, and often troubling book about the history of racial classifications in American law. This history underscores the validity of Oliver Wendell Holmes's dictum that 'experience,' rather than 'logic,' dictates the actual development of law, for Bernstein demonstrates the extent to which the adoption of racial (or, more commonly 'ethnic') classifications has been responsive far more to systematic political pressures rather than the application of a coherent overarching theory. Even (or especially) supporters of 'affirmative action,' as I ambivalently continue to be, will benefit enormously from confronting the material that Bernstein carefully presents. It truly deserves a wide readership and, just as importantly, respectful discussion."

–Sanford Levinson, W. St. John Garwood and
W. St. John Garwood, Jr. Centennial Chair,
University of Texas Law School, and author of
Wrestling with Diversity

"We mock the racial-classifications schemes of the Jim Crow south, of Nazi Germany, and of Apartheid South Africa. But as David Bernstein ably demonstrates, our own racial classification system is just as risible, and no more scientific."

–Glenn Reynolds, Beauchamp Brogan Distinguished
Professor of Law, University of Tennessee, founder of
Instapundit.com

"David E. Bernstein proves ably and conclusively that the familiar legal classifications for racial and ethnic groups used by the federal and state governments, census-takers, medical regulators, racial-preference dispensers, and others are arbitrary to an extreme."

–Stuart Taylor, contributing editor, National Journal, and coauthor, Mismatch: How Affirmative Action Hurts Students It's Intended to Help, and Why Universities Won't Admit It

☑ Classified

☐ The Untold

☐ Story

☐ of Racial

☐ Classification

☐ in America

David E. Bernstein

BOMBARDIER
BOOKS

Published by Bombardier Books
An Imprint of Post Hill Press
ISBN: 978-1-63758-173-5
ISBN (eBook): 978-1-63758-174-2

Classified:
The Untold Story of Racial Classification in America
© 2022 by David E. Bernstein
All Rights Reserved

Cover Design by Matt Margolis
Interior Design by Yoni Limor

BOMBARDIER
BOOKS

Post Hill
PRESS

Post Hill Press
New York • Nashville
posthillpress.com

Published in the United States of America
1 2 3 4 5 6 7 8 9 10

For Natalie, Eden, and Ben

TABLE OF CONTENTS

INTRODUCTION
The Modern American Law of Race

O fficial American racial and ethnic classifications are arbitrary and inconsistent, both in how they are defined and how they are enforced. The categories are socially constructed and historically contingent. They evolved from older racist categories and have barely been updated since the 1970s.

Consider the government's official Asian American classification. This classification derives from a racist category used before the modern civil rights era to exclude those classified as Asian from immigration and citizenship. People in the Asian American category are extremely diverse in appearance, culture, religion, and ancestry. "Asian American" includes people with ancestry anywhere from Pakistan to Indonesia and Japan but excludes all people of western Asian origin. Most people who come within the Asian American category do not identify with that label.[1] Nevertheless, they are classified as if they are part of a monolithic group.

This has real-world consequences. Kao Lee Yang, a Hmong American neuroscience PhD student, was recently nominated for a prestigious fellowship for students who are members of "groups historically excluded from and underrepresented in science." The fellowship committee determined that because Yang is Asian American, she is not a member of an "underrepresented" group. The committee therefore refused to even consider her application.

---

1. "The Rise of Asian Americans." June 19, 2012. Pew Research Center. http://www.pewsocial-trends.org/2012/06/19/the-rise-of-asian-americans.

Yang took to Twitter to vent: "While some Asian Americans are academically successful, others like the Hmong are underrepresented in STEM and academia in general...name me just one Hmong American woman you know who is a neuroscientist." She added, "I am an example of the consequences resulting from the continued practice of grouping people with East/Southeast/South Asian heritages underneath the 'Asian American' umbrella."[2]

Yang blamed her predicament on the "model minority myth" that Asian Americans are all successful. Her ire would have been better targeted at the federal Department of Education. For over forty years, its Office of Civil Rights has required educational institutions to collect and report demographic data about "Asian Americans," with no differentiation among the many national origin groups. The educational establishment, in turn, has grown accustomed to treating Asian Americans as a uniform racial group.

America's official racial and ethnic classifications can be particularly troublesome for people who immigrate to the United States from other countries, where America's unique system of racial and ethnic classification is unknown. My wife, for example, is an olive-complexioned American citizen born and raised in Israel. She is of Sephardic and Iraqi Jewish descent. She does not think of herself in American racial terms. Instead, she considers herself to be "Jewish," "Sephardia" (Sephardic), and "Mizrahit" (Middle Eastern). None of these categories is recognized by the US government, and none is available to check on forms.

I recently helped a native of Peru of mixed Spanish and indigenous origin apply for a green card. She was mystified by the form asking her to classify herself by one of the standard American racial categories. None of the racial options fit how she perceived herself. The American Indian category on the form, which might otherwise have covered her Inca ancestry, is limited to North American Indians.

Trying to be helpful, I asked, "Eres blanca?" ("Are you white?") She replied, "No, no soy blanca." ("No, I am not white.")

2.   Yang, Kao Lee. October 26, 2021. "A Letter to #AcademicTwitter." Twitter, https://twitter.com/KaoLeeYang1/status/1453210553871110150.

"Pero tú no eres negra." ("But you are not black.")

"No, no soy negra. Soy mestiza." ("No, I am not black. I am a mestiza [Spanish-Indian].") There is no official mestizo racial classification in the United States.

Even when someone comes within the official definition of a category, government officials may or may not accept one's membership. For example, "Hispanic" is officially defined as being of Spanish origin or culture, but things can get much more complicated in practice.

Christine Combs and Steve Lynn applied to the Small Business Administration (SBA) to have their respective businesses certified as Hispanic-owned and therefore eligible for minority business enterprise preferences. Combs's maternal grandparents were born in Spain, she grew up in a bilingual family, was fluent in Spanish, and acted as an interpreter for Mexican and Spanish customers.[3] Lynn's sole claim to Hispanic status was that he was a Sephardic Jew whose ancestors had fled Spain centuries earlier.[4]

The SBA ultimately decided that Lynn qualified as Hispanic, but Combs did not. Combs's SBA hearing officer declared that Combs could not claim Hispanic status for affirmative action purposes because she presented no evidence that she had faced discrimination because she is Hispanic. The officer noted that neither Combs's maiden name nor her married name was recognizably Spanish, and her blond hair and blue eyes did not give her a noticeably Hispanic appearance. On appeal, a judge found that the hearing officer had "reason to question Ms. Combs' status as a Hispanic." The judge therefore upheld the denial of Combs's petition.

An SBA hearing officer also initially denied Lynn's claim to Hispanic status because Lynn had not shown that he had been discriminated against as a Hispanic. But when Lynn appealed, the judge noted that the underlying law defined Hispanic as including anyone of Spanish origin or culture, which includes Sephardic Jews. The judge concluded that once Lynn showed that he had Spanish ancestry, the hearing officer

---

3.   DCS Electric, SBA No. 399 MSBE-91-10-4-26, 1992 WL 558961.
4.   Rothschild-Lynn Legal & Fin. Servs., No. 499 MSBE-94-10-13-46, 1995 WL 542398.

should not have required him to also provide evidence that he had faced discrimination because of that ancestry.[5]

Welcome to the often-surreal world of official American racial and ethnic classification.

Have you ever wondered...

What role tribal membership plays in giving someone the legal status of an American Indian?

Or whether people can lawfully change what box they check on demographic forms based on the results of DNA tests showing they have minority ancestry?

Or whether Armenians and Jews, victims of twentieth-century genocides abroad, are ever classified as members of a minority group in the United States?

Or why an American of mixed-race heritage cannot identify as multiracial on the census and other forms?

Or why US government rules dictate that a family that moves from Latin America is Hispanic but not Asian no matter how many generations they stay in Asia, but a family that moves from Asia to Latin America becomes both Asian and Hispanic?

Or why the government classifies immigrants from India as Asian but their first cousins from Afghanistan as white?

Or why the government may classify a fair-skinned Spanish immigrant as Hispanic, but a dark-complexioned Egyptian, Greek, Iranian, or Italian American is always generically white?

Or why biomedical researchers report their findings broken down by crude racial categories even though the categories are not scientifically valid?

This book addresses those questions and much more.

Debates over racial classification in the contemporary United States almost always involve abstract arguments about justice, equality, and individual and collective rights. These discussions ignore how classifications work in practice. This book, by contrast, explores the complex and sometimes bizarre real world of government-imposed racial classification.

---

5.   See also, Storer Broadcasting, 87 FCC2d 190 (1981). (Accepting Sephardic heritage as evidence of Hispanic status, though it was cumulative of much other evidence.)

Racial classification by law in the United States has a terrible history. We Americans shake our heads when we encounter the absurd and often cruel lengths federal and state government once went to in classifying Americans by race at a time when people's rights depended on how they were classified.

For example, we react with visceral disgust to century-old legal decisions discussing the distinctions between an "octoroon" (one-eighth African by descent) and a "quadroon" (one-quarter African by descent) and how that affected which side of the Jim Crow segregation line people occupied.[6]

We are similarly appalled by century-old cases adjudicating whether Asian Indian and Arab immigrants should be considered white people eligible for naturalization and what blood quantum of Native American ancestry makes one an American Indian for legal purposes.

As Mark Twain said, history does not repeat but it often rhymes. Despite our revulsion at historical examples of government-mandated racial classification, it's more common than ever. Applying for a mortgage, enrolling a child in school, receiving a COVID-19 test or vaccine, applying for a green card, and many other common activities involve checking racial and ethnic boxes dictated by federal agencies.

Modern American racial and ethnic classifications do not reflect biology, genetics, or any other objective source. Classifications such as Hispanic, Asian American, and white combine extremely internally diverse groups in terms of appearance, culture, religion, and more under a single, arbitrary heading. The government developed its classification scheme via a combination of amateur anthropology and sociology, interest group lobbying, incompetence, inertia, lack of public oversight, and happenstance.

Inertia, in terms of extending past practices, has been especially important. As we shall see, many of the legal classifications used in the United States today represent updated versions of racist categories used by the government in the past.

---

6. Gross, Ariela. 2008. *What Blood Won't Tell: A History of Race on Trial in America.* Cambridge, MA: Harvard University Press.

Unlike classification a century or more ago, modern classifications typically are used to try to help minority groups rather than to segregate them from mainstream society. Classifications and the resulting data are used to facilitate enforcement of civil rights laws, identify disparities resulting from discrimination in the hope of redressing these disparities, ensure that minorities are represented as subjects in medical studies, provide aid to Native Americans, and allow for affirmative action preferences.

Nevertheless, there is still debate over how the government should classify Americans of various backgrounds. Indeed, many of historical controversies regarding classification recurred in the post-civil rights era. Some remain unsettled. For example, in a modern version of the octoroon versus quadroon controversy, courts and administrative agencies have debated whether one needs one-fourth or one-eighth minority ancestry to claim minority status to qualify for affirmative action.

The question of how to classify Asian Indians, which bedeviled courts in the early twentieth century, was raised again in the 1970s. The government initially classified them as white before ultimately moving them to the Asian category.

Controversy over whether Arab Americans should be classified as white, an issue decided in the affirmative a century ago, has also returned. Activists have touted a new Middle Eastern and North African racial category. This category came very close to being listed on 2020 census forms.

Meanwhile, American Indian status—federal law almost always uses the term American Indian rather than Native American—often still depends on a person's blood quantum. Indeed, the federal Bureau of Indian Affairs continues to issue to individuals Certificates of Degree of Indian Blood, providing official documentation of one's percentage of Native American ancestry.[7]

But surely, most people think, we no longer have hearings and trials to determine an individual's racial identity, as was common in the

---

7. Bureau of Indian Affairs Certificate of Degree of Indian or Alaska Native Blood Instructions. https://www.bia.gov/sites/bia.gov/files/assets/public/raca/online_forms/pdf/Certificate_of_Degree_of_Indian_Blood_1076-0153_Exp3-31-21_508.pdf.

bad old days.[8] Racial identity is now purely a matter of self-identification, right? Not exactly.

Eligibility for affirmative action preferences depends on one's racial and ethnic classification. As a result, the government finds itself policing claims to minority identity to protect the integrity of its programs. The result is that we sometimes do have hearings or trials to determine someone's proper legal classification.

Racial and ethnic status is left *mostly* to self-identification. Current practices involve first asking whether someone is of Hispanic/Latino ethnicity. Regardless of the answer, the next step is to identify one's race as Asian American, African American/Black, Hawaiian or Pacific Islander, Native American, White, or "other."

While self-identification is the norm, it is not universally respected. If people decline to answer either question, someone else is often required to guess their ethnicity and race and check boxes on their behalf.[9] The Equal Employment Opportunity Commission allows an employer to override an employee's self-identification "where the declaration by the applicant or employee is patently false."[10]

There are also quite a few modern cases, reviewed in this book, in which administrative agencies and courts have considered and ruled on whether someone's claim to a minority identity is valid. Most of these cases are obscure, and many have never been discussed elsewhere.

In the Jim Crow era, in determining whether a litigant should be classified as "Negro" southern courts fluctuated between definitions based on ancestry, appearance, and perceptions by the community.[11] Courts and administrative agencies do the same today in cases involving questions of ethnic or racial identity.

Most of the contemporary cases raise the question of whether someone improperly claimed Hispanic status to be eligible for affirmative action. As we have seen, some decision makers have concluded

8.   Gross, *What Blood Won't Tell.*
9.   For example, Equal Employment Opportunity Commission, EEOC Compliance Manual section 632.3, Violations Involving Advertising, Recordkeeping, or Posting of Notice, CCH-EEOCCM ¶5403, 2009 WL 3608161 (2012).
10. Ibid.
11. Gross, *What Blood Won't Tell*; Kennedy, Randall. *Interracial Intimacies: Sex, Marriage, Identity, and Adoption.* (New York: Pantheon); Pascoe, Peggy. 2009. *What Comes Naturally: Miscegenation Law and the Making of Race in America.* (New York: Oxford University Press).

that anyone with Spanish-speaking heritage can legitimately claim a Hispanic identity. Other courts and agencies have considered such factors as whether the claimant "looks" Hispanic, speaks Spanish, has a Spanish surname, belongs to Hispanic cultural organizations, or has Latin American ancestry traceable to Spain and not (like many South Americans) elsewhere in Europe.

In the not-so-distant past, the United States had a large non-Hispanic white majority, a significant Black minority, and a relatively small number of "others." In 1970, only 5 percent of Americans were Hispanic, and they were generally classified as whites. Less than 1 percent were Asian or Native American. Today, thanks to immigration and intermarriage, Hispanics are by far the largest officially recognized minority. Hispanics, Native Americans, and Asian and Pacific Islander Americans combined are nearly 30 percent of the population. Collectively, they outnumber African Americans by around two to one.

American ethnic diversity goes well beyond these groups, of course. The government, however, reflecting the historical prominence of the black-white divide, classifies everyone else as white, regardless of their appearance, culture, religion, or self-identification.

For example, many Americans with North African, Mediterranean, or Western Asian heritage have dark complexions. Nevertheless, unless they are Hispanic, they have what this book calls "legal whiteness." The government classifies them as part of the general white population, regardless of how others perceive them or how they perceive themselves.

This book raises the following questions about racial and ethnic classification in the US:

Are the standard racial categories coherent?

- Does it make sense to classify all people with Spanish-speaking ancestry within the same category, regardless of their differences in skin hue, race, national origin, and culture?

- Is there a defensible reason to classify European Hispanics—but no other European national or ethnic group—as members of a minority group?

- Do South Asian Americans (such as Pakistanis), East Asians (such as Cambodians), and Austronesians (such as most Filipinos) belong in the same Asian American category?

- Why are Filipino Americans, whose ancestors lived on Pacific Islands and mostly share Austronesian ancestry with other Pacific Islanders, classified as Asian Americans and not as Pacific Islanders?

How should bi- and multiracial people be classified?

- If a parent who identifies as black and his white-identified partner have a child, and that child checks off both boxes on a government form, should the government classify that child as black, white, multiracial, or something else?

- Should that child be classified the same way for affirmative action purposes as someone with two black-identified parents?

- Some laws dictate that anyone with one-quarter "Indian blood" legally qualifies as an American Indian and therefore for programs benefiting American Indians. Is that a permissible classification by political status or an illegal racial one?

- If someone has always identified as white, but a DNA test reveals that he or she has African ancestry, can that individual claim a black identity? Does it matter what percentage of African ancestry the DNA test reveals?

What is the boundary between white status and official minority status?

- Should people with Middle Eastern or North African ancestry continue to be classified as white, or should they have a separate nonwhite legal category? If they were to have a separate category, which non-Arab groups would it include?

- Should Hasidic Jews, who have high rates of poverty and face significant linguistic, cultural, and religious barriers to participating in the general economy, be classified as an official minority group?

- Should Americans of Uzbek descent be classified as Asian American, like Indians and Pakistanis, or white, like Afghans and Iranians?

- If Italian Americans are intentionally excluded from juries in criminal cases involving Italian American defendants, is that illegal discrimination, or is it legal because the government does not classify Italian Americans separately from other whites?

Who is Hispanic? In addition to the issues surrounding Hispanic identity noted previously, this book considers such questions as:

- If Hispanic status depends on having a Spanish surname, can a person claim Hispanic status if he changes his name from Robert Lee to Roberto Leon and claims to have had a Spanish grandparent?

- Should Hispanic status extend to people of Brazilian origin because they are (arguably) "Latinos?"

- If people of Spanish and Brazilian descent may be classified as Hispanic, what about immigrants from Portugal and their descendants?

As we shall see, administrative agencies and courts have resolved some of these controversies, albeit not always coherently or consistently. The answer often depends on the jurisdiction, or on the judge or bureaucrat making the decision. In some contexts, the relevant government officials have ignored or papered over the relevant issue.

Decades ago, Americans had powerful incentives to assert a white identity, given widespread societal prejudices. Indeed, an American's status as a white person was seen, and was sometimes treated by the courts, as a valuable property right.[12] As recently as the 1980s, a Louisiana woman who identified as white but was of 3/32 African descent sued to have her birth certificate changed when she discovered it categorized her as "colored."[13]

Today, discrimination is still a barrier to minorities, but minority status makes Americans eligible for civil rights protections and affirmative action preferences that are not available to those classified as non-Hispanic whites. For example, being classified as a minority makes American business owners eligible for minority business enterprise preferences that influence hundreds of billions of dollars of government spending annually.

One result has been the emergence of identity entrepreneurs—Americans who claim and leverage a minority identity for economic gain, even if that identity has never caused them significant harm.[14] Some individuals tailor their identities to maximize benefit; they claim a white social identity in contexts where they may otherwise face racial discrimination and a nonwhite identity in other contexts where affirmative action preferences are available.[15] In my own world of the legal academy, it's not uncommon for mixed-race individuals to check a

---

12. Harris, Cheryl I. June 1993. "Whiteness as Property," *Harvard Law Review* 106, No. 8: 1707-1791.
13. Trillin, Calvin. April 6, 1986. "Black or White," *New Yorker*, 62.
14. Leong, Nancy. 2016. "Identity Entrepreneurs," *California Law Review* 104:1334; Rich, Camille Gear. "Performing Racial and Ethnic Identity: Discrimination by Proxy and the Future of Title VII. 2005" *New York University Law Review* 79: 1157; Beydoun, Khaled A. and Wilson, Erika K. "Reverse Passing," *UCLA Law Review* 64: 289.
15. Longmire v. Wyser-Pratte, No. 05 Civ. 6725 (SHS), 2007 WL 2584662 (S.D.N.Y. Sept. 6, 2007), for example, involved a man with one white parent and one black parent. When applying to Stanford Business School, he identified himself as black. When working on Wall Street, he primarily presented himself as white.

minority box when they apply to law school and then identify socially
as non-Hispanic white once they matriculate.[16]

Political conservatives have long been skeptical about the logic of
American racial classification. In recent years, the emergence of identity
entrepreneurs has led left-leaning commentators to question the standard government-dictated categories and how they are enforced.

With the emergence of the Black Lives Matter movement, progres-
sives also increasingly question whether lumping all groups other than
non-Hispanic whites together as "people of color" distracts from the
specific plight of African Americans and their centuries-old battle
against state and private violence and discrimination. Existing classifications often wind up assisting mostly post-1965 immigrants and their
descendants, who have only known an America changed by the civil
rights movement and modern civil rights legislation, most prominently
the 1964 Civil Rights Act.

These developments have led activists to increasingly critique
"antiblackness" instead of racism and to substitute "BIPOC" (Black,
Indigenous, People of Color) for the phrase "people of color." BIPOC
is ambiguous, perhaps intentionally so, as to whether it's an acronym
for "Black, Indigenous, or other People of Color," thus including but
downgrading other minority groups, or "Black and Indigenous People
of Color," thus excluding everyone else. Either way, the idea is to center
the African American freedom struggle. Placing African Americans
into the much larger and more amorphous people-of-color category,
by contrast, dilutes the significance of the unique African American
experience.[17]

Other activists go even further. They argue that "ADOS" (American Descendants of Slaves) should be classified separately from African
and Caribbean immigrants and their descendants.[18] Similarly, some

16.   Panter, A. T. et al., 2009. "It Matters How and When You Ask: Self-Reported Race/Ethnicity
      of Incoming Law Students," *Cultural Diversity and Ethnic Minority Psychology*, 15, No. 1:
      58.
17.   Kim, E. Tammy. July 29, 2020. "The Perils of 'People of Color,'" *The New Yorker*.
18.   Brown, Kevin D. 2014. *Because of Our Success: The Changing Racial and Ethnic Ancestry
      of Blacks on Affirmative Action*. Durham, NC: Carolina Academic Press.

Latino activists argue that the Hispanic classification should be limited to Latinos with discernible indigenous or African ancestry.

Meanwhile, most Americans whom the government classifies as Asian Americans reject that pan-ethnic identity.[19] And many Americans of South Asian ancestry, such as Indians and Pakistanis, are uncomfortable being classified with East Asian Americans with whom they have nothing in common. A South Asian student remarks, "Why would anyone [of South Asian background] classify themselves as Asian in the American sense of the word when most Americans think of Japan, Vietnam, Laos, Cambodia, Korea, China as Asian?"[20]

Implicit in America's racial classification scheme is the notion that society will be permanently divided into suspicious or hostile racial groups. Relevant government decision makers implicitly assumed that European, West Asian, and North African ethnic groups would assimilate into mainstream white society. African Americans, Asian Americans, and Hispanics, in contrast, would always be excluded from the mainstream by their origins, each group to approximately the same degree.[21] The data now suggest the contrary possibility that Americans will develop a unique, singular multiethnic and multiracial American identity.[22]

As of 2017, 46 percent of Asian and 39 percent of Hispanic American newlyweds born in the United States married a spouse from a different category.[23] Moreover, many Americans with partial Spanish-speaking ancestry do not identify as Hispanic to begin with.[24]

---

19. Pew Research Center, "The Rise of Asian Americans." http://www.pewsocialtrends. org/2012/06/19/the-rise-of-asian-americans; McGowan, Miranda Oshige. 1996. Diversity of What?" *Representations* 55: 133.
20. Balu, Rekha. Dec. 31, 1996. "Political Issues Unite the Asian-American: But are South Asians Marginalized?" *Masala* 11, No. 5: 24.
21. Lee, Jennifer and Bean, Frank. 2010. *The Diversity Paradox: Immigration and the Color Line in 21st Century America.* New York: Russell Sage Foundation, 27; Hollinger, David A. 2008. "Obama, the Instability of Color Lines, and the Promise of a Postethnic Future," *Callaloo* 31, No. 4: 1033-37.
22. Alba, Richard. 2020. *The Great Demographic Illusion: Majority, Minority, and the Expanding American Mainstream.* (Princeton: Princeton University Press); Lee and Bean, *The Diversity Paradox.*
23. Pew Research Center. June 18, 2017. Trends and Patterns in Intermarriage. https://www. pewresearch.org/social-trends/2017/05/18/1-trends-and-patterns-in-intermarriage.
24. Duncan, Brian and Trejo, Stephan J. *Ethnic Identification, Intermarriage, and Unmeasured Progress by Mexican Americans.* http://www.nber.org/chapters/c0104, 235.

Asian Americans, meanwhile, are increasingly perceived as belonging to the same demographic category as European-descended Americans. One often reads articles about how an American high-tech company employs almost no minority workers, only to discover many of their US-based employees are Asian Americans. For example, an article in the *New York Times* declared that Google's demographic data "offers a stark glance at how Silicon Valley remains a white man's world." Just a few lines later, we learn that one-third of Google's American employees are Asian.[25]

Some sociologists believe that the trajectory of American society is that Americans will divide into two broad groups, a majority of nonblack Americans and a minority of black Americans, the latter perhaps joined by darker-skinned Asians and Hispanics. But even the assumption that African Americans, the most segregated official minority group, will be excluded indefinitely from the mainstream seems much less certain than it used to. Consider, for example, the dramatic rise in intermarriage rates for African Americans. The percentage of African American newlyweds marrying someone from a different group soared from 5 percent in 1980 to 18 percent in 2015.

In short, the time is ripe for a full consideration of the law of racial classification in the United States. This book focuses on how the modern law of racial classification has developed, how the familiar categories and their boundaries were established by government agencies, and how they are enforced.

The book begins by addressing two related issues. Chapter One discusses the US government's post-World War II development of official, uniform racial and ethnic classifications for data gathering and civil rights enforcement. These categories also became the standard determinants for eligibility for affirmative action. Chapter One examines the contours of those categories and then discusses federal and state rules for demonstrating membership in them.

---

25.   Miller, Claire Cain. May 28, 2014. "Google Releases Employee Data, Illustrating Tech's Diversity Challenge," *Bits*. https://bits.blogs.nytimes.com/2014/05/28/google-releases-employee-data-illustrating-techs-diversity-challenge.

The next three chapters examine different ethnic and national origin groups that have been on the borders of legal whiteness. Their success or failure at achieving official minority status has helped to define the boundary of legal whiteness. Chapter Two discusses the development of the Hispanic/Latino category and how administrative agencies and courts have addressed its boundaries when adjudicating claims of Hispanic identity in the context of affirmative action. Chapters Three and Four discuss mostly unsuccessful attempts by other groups to get the government to define them as official minorities distinct from the White category. The upshot of the efforts described in Chapters Three and Four is that of the groups discussed, only South Asians generally lack legal whiteness. By contrast, the government almost always uses the White category for Americans of Armenian, Cajun, Iranian, Italian, Jewish, Polish, and Arab and other Middle Eastern and North African descent.

The last two chapters, Five and Six, address contexts apart from civil rights enforcement and affirmative action in which government racial and ethnic classification have a significant impact on American life. Chapter Five considers the way federal law defines and polices official American Indian identity. Among other things, the rights of criminal defendants and of children whose fates are in the hands of the legal system sometimes depend on whether courts classify them as Indians. Chapter Six discusses FDA and NIH rules requiring biomedical researchers to classify and sort study participants by the standard government-dictated ethnic and racial classifications. These rules exist even though the classifications have no valid scientific or anthropological basis.

In the Conclusion, I propose shifting from vague, ill-defined, and often overly broad and non-specific racial and ethnic categories to more precise, objective categories defined by history, politics, sociology, and, in the scientific context, genetics. While the current categories work reasonably well for monitoring discrimination, sociological and biomedical research would benefit from using much more salient and justifiable ways of classifying research subjects. Universities seeking a truly diverse student body also would benefit from abandoning their reliance on the crude official racial and ethnic classifications.

Moving away from the current official classifications need not entail the government abandoning the goal of bringing previously excluded groups into the American mainstream. Rather, in the affirmative action context the government could use categories that are not coextensive with race. For example, "American descendants of slaves" could be substituted for Black Americans, currently defined as people with "origins in the black racial groups of Africa."

Speaking of affirmative action, this book is about racial classification by law, not affirmative action. However, any discussion of racial classification in modern times will inevitably address the interplay of affirmative action with those classifications, and this book is no exception.

Reform of America's racial classification system is likely to prove elusive. Strong political and cultural forces support the status quo. This book explores that status quo and how we came to our current equilibrium. The book addresses the classifications' history, definitions, boundaries, enforcement, and application. Readers should consider whether and to what extent the results are sensible, and to what extent the United States should abolish its official racial classifications and move toward a separation of race and state.

CHAPTER ONE
The Rise of Modern Racial Classification

Racial classification by the government has been as American as apple pie since the nineteenth century and beyond. Yet it was only in the late 1970s that the federal bureaucracy established five standard official classifications: American Indian or Alaska Native, Asian and Pacific Islander (the latter later spun off to a new category with Native Hawaiians), Black, Hispanic, and White.

There was no inherent logic to adopting these categories, nor to how they were defined. The classifications are not precise, consistent, or comprehensive. Americans with vastly different physical appearances and cultural backgrounds—such as "Asian" Pakistanis and Filipinos, "Hispanic" Spaniards and Mixtecs or "White" Moroccans and Icelanders—share the same category.[1]

Forty-plus years later these classifications seem natural and have been almost universally adopted in our society, albeit with updated nomenclature—African American is a popular and government-sanctioned alternative for Black, and Latino for Hispanic. When the government created the classifications, they came with the caveat that they were for data collection purposes only. Nevertheless, the classifications have been used from the outset to determine which groups are eligible for affirmative action preferences.

---

1. Yanow, Dvora. 2003. *Constructing "Race" and "Ethnicity" in America: Category-Making in Public Policy and Administration*. New York: Routledge, 5; Welch, Ashton Wesley. 2003. "Ethnic and Racial Definitions as Manifestations of American Public Policy," *Ethnic Studies Review* 26, No. 1: 16.

As noted in the Introduction, racial identification for government affirmative action programs is largely based on self-identification. Government agencies and courts do, however, sometimes question and reject an individual's self-identification. Local governments have even fired or otherwise penalized their employees for racial or ethnic fraud— asserting a false racial or ethnic identity.

The most notorious case—indeed, many academic articles incorrectly claim it is the only such case—challenging racial self-identification involved Paul and Philip Malone, twin brothers from Milton, Massachusetts.[2] The Malones applied for firefighter jobs in Boston. On their employment application, they declared their race to be white. They failed the civil service exam and were rejected.

At the time, the Boston fire department had a hiring preference for black applicants resulting from a legal settlement. The brothers retook the exam, this time listing their race as black. Their scores were too low to be accepted as firefighters as whites, but they passed the lower threshold for black applicants and got jobs with the department.

A decade later, fire department Commissioner Leo Stapleton noticed that Philip Malone listed himself as black on a promotion application. Stapleton had interacted with the Malones and always perceived them to be white. He questioned each brother individually about their racial identity. Paul told Stapleton that his father was black; Philip reported that someone in his family was black, but he did not remember who.

This exchange led to disciplinary proceedings against the Malones for fraudulently claiming to be black. The hearing examiner concluded that there were two ways the Malones could defeat the racial fraud charge and keep their jobs.

First, the Malones could show they had a good faith belief that they could claim black status. The hearing officer found that the brothers had made no effort to verify they had black ancestry. They also never inquired as to what standards existed for asserting minority status. The hearing examiner concluded that they did not act in good faith.

2.   Malone v. Civil Serv. Comm'n, 38 Mass. App. Ct. 147, 147-48 (1995); Malone v. Haley, 2 Mass. Civil Service Rep. 1014 (1990).

Second, the brothers could establish that they met one of three objective criteria for being black: by visual observation of their features; by documentary evidence, such as birth certificates, that established black ancestry; or by evidence that they or their families hold themselves out to be black or are considered black by the community.

The hearing examiner found that both men had fair skin, fair hair coloring, and Caucasian facial features, and concluded that "they do not appear to be black." Moreover, the Malones, their parents, and both sets of grandparents had been identified as white on their birth certificates. Finally, the hearing officer found that there was no evidence that the Malones had identified themselves or were identified by others as black, except in the context of their job applications.

The Malones protested that until their disciplinary hearing, racial status in the fire department had always been solely a matter of self-identification. The hearing examiner rejected their plea and ruled against the brothers, costing them their jobs.

As we shall see, the Malones are not the only people whose self-identification as a racial or ethnic minority eligible for affirmative action preferences has been challenged. Claims of Hispanic identity have been especially contentious.

Meanwhile, we can get a sense of the official racial and ethnic classifications by considering how government bureaucracies would resolve recent public controversies over individual Americans' racial and ethnic identities.

Elizabeth Warren

Senator Elizabeth Warren has been criticized for identifying herself as Native American based on family lore that she has Cherokee ancestry. The federal Bureau of Indian Affairs would not classify Warren as an Indian because she does not have either tribal membership or one-quarter Indian ancestry. On the other hand, the federal government's definition of American Indians for statistical purposes includes individuals with Native American ancestry who "maintain cultural

identification through...community recognition."[3] Perhaps the fact
that Warren was invited to provide a recipe for the book, Pow Wow
Chow: A Collection of Recipes from Families of the Five Civilized
Tribes, is evidence of community recognition.[4] And in some states, oral
history plus self-identification is likely enough for the government to
recognize someone as an Indian/Native American.

Tiger Woods

Golf star Tiger Woods has European, African, Thai, and Chinese ancestry;
Woods calls himself a "Cablinasian." Critics in the African American
community have argued that Woods's failure to identify as an African
American is "a sign of naiveté, cowardice or even betrayal."[5]

Under federal contracting rules, Woods could claim Asian American or African American status based on his partial East Asian and
black African ancestry. He would need to affirm that he holds himself
out as a member of the group he chose. Whether Cablinasian counts as
holding oneself out as black or Asian is not clear.

There is, of course, no official Cablinasian classification. Nor
is there an official Thai or Chinese identity Woods could assert. He
would be able to mark one or both ancestries on the decennial census
form. In reporting racial statistics, however, the Census Bureau aggre-
gates all people of South Asian and East Asian descent into the Asian
American category.

George Zimmerman

When George Zimmerman was charged with murdering Trayvon
Martin, people debated whether the media should describe Zimmerman
as Hispanic, half Hispanic, mixed-race, white Hispanic, white, or

3.   Directive No. 15, Race and Ethnic Standards for Federal Statistics and Administrative
     Reporting, 43 Fed. Reg. 19, 260 (May 4, 1978).
4.   "Elizabeth Warren Claimed Native American Heritage in 1984 Cookbook Called Pow
     Wow Chow." May 17, 2012. Daily Mail.
5.   Fletcher, Michael A. May 30, 2017. "Tiger Woods Says He's 'Cablinasian,' but the Police
     Only Saw Black," The Undefeated, https://theundefeated.com/features/tiger-woods-dui-
     arrest-police-only-saw-black.

something else. Zimmerman's father is of European descent, and his mother is a native of Peru. Given his mother's background and his self-identification as Hispanic on voter registration forms, Zimmerman generally qualifies as Hispanic. However, as discussed in Chapter Two, in some affirmative action contexts authorities might question whether Zimmerman "counts" as Hispanic given his German-sounding last name and ambiguous features.

Zimmerman also claims to have had an Afro-Peruvian great-grandfather. Whether he could successfully claim African American status based on this ancestry is unclear. Read literally, the standard legal definition of African American includes anyone with any black African ancestry, so long as the individual self-identifies as a member of the category. However, a federal court recently upheld Washington State's conclusion that distant African ancestry is insufficient by itself to qualify someone as a member of the Black/African American category. The court did not specify how far into the past a claimant may go.[6]

Some states rely on the National Minority Supplier Development Council (NMSDC) for certifying people's racial and ethnic identification. The NMSDC requires that a person be one-quarter African American to claim that status. It's not clear what NMSDC's policy would be if Zimmerman's grandparent, though only half-African by ancestry, identified as Afro-Peruvian; it might make Zimmerman one-quarter African American and thus qualify him to assert a black identity; alternatively, it might make Zimmerman one-eighth African American, limiting him to claiming a white or Hispanic identity. The NMSDC would also demand documentation, such as a driver's license or birth certificate, listing Zimmerman's race as black or African American.

States have their own idiosyncratic rules. In some contexts, for example, California would require three letters from certified ethnic organizations attesting to Zimmerman's group membership. A few states recognize a multiracial classification.

---

6.   Orion Insurance Group v. Washington State Office of Minority & Women's Business Enterprises, 754 Fed. Appx. 556 (9th Cir. 2018).

Rachel Dolezal

Former NAACP official Rachel Dolezal adopted an African American identity as an adult even though she has no African ancestry. Many people accused her of racial fraud; others argued that it was acceptable for her to sincerely adopt an African American persona, given that race is socially constructed. Federal and almost all state laws would classify Dolezal as white based on her European heritage. Under the *Malone* precedent, in Massachusetts Dolezal could have nonfraudulently claimed an African American identity because she held herself out to be black and was considered black by the community.

Kamala Harris

Some of Vice President Kamala Harris's political opponents, primarily on the ideological extremes, have questioned her black identity. Harris is the child of an Indian immigrant mother and a father of mixed-African and European heritage from Jamaica. She has identified as black her entire adult life. She attended a historically black university, others identify her as black, and she has African ancestry. Given those facts, no government authority would reject her claim to black status. The only caveat is that it's not clear how the NMSDC would address her father's mixed-race heritage. Meanwhile, if Harris preferred to claim an Asian American or a white identity, she also meets the legal definitions of those categories.

*   *   *   *

The controversies discussed above were debated solely in the court of public opinion; no courts or government agencies were asked to make a ruling. Most Americans undoubtedly prefer it that way, rightly recoiling at the idea of having the government, at any level, dictate the boundaries of ethnic identity. Such determinations are reminiscent of

Nazi Germany's and South Africa's racial obsessions and America's own sordid past.

As noted previously, however, legal rules may dictate whether someone can claim a particular minority status for affirmative action purposes. This comes up most often when a company applies for minority business enterprise status for government contracts, and the government demands evidence that the owner is a member of an official minority category.[7]

Affirmative action in university admissions, which gets far more public attention than affirmative action in contracting, typically has a sliding preference scale. African American applicants get the biggest boost, while Asian Americans generally get no preference and sometimes are penalized for being "overrepresented."

Minority business enterprise preferences, by contrast, give members of all eligible minority groups the same preferences. A company owned by a white individual with a grandparent from Spain who successfully claims Hispanic status gets the same contracting preference as a company owned by an African American descendant of enslaved Americans. This increases the incentive for those with marginal minority background to claim a minority identity.

In short, Americans are generally free to adopt their preferred identity. No one is going to police what box someone checks off on a census form or a mortgage application. But American law has established racial and ethnic categories with official definitions that set legally enforceable boundaries on racial and ethnic identity in the context of affirmative action preferences.

All this raises two questions, addressed below: How and why did the standard, familiar racial classifications emerge as they did? What evidence must individuals offer to show membership in these categories?

---

7.   SBA's Role in Government Contracting, Small Business Administration. https://www.sba.gov/contracting/what-government-contracting/sbas-role-government-contracting.

Pre-1964: Official Minority Categories Emerge

The story of the development of modern racial and ethnic classifications begins in 1946. That year, President Harry Truman appointed a President's Committee on Civil Rights. Until then, combatting discrimination against Catholics and Jews had been a priority of pioneering state and local civil rights agencies, especially in New York.[8]

The President's Committee, however, focused on racial discrimination. The committee explained that "[g]roups whose color makes them more easily identified are set apart from the 'dominant majority' much more than are the Caucasian minorities."[9] This focus reflected an emerging consensus in civil rights circles that antidiscrimination efforts should focus primarily on combatting racial discrimination.

Truman's successor, Dwight Eisenhower, created the President's Committee on Government Contracts (PCGC) to implement an executive order banning discrimination by government contractors.[10] Through 1958, over one-quarter of complaints of discrimination sent to the PCGC involved discrimination based on religion, mostly against Jews.

In 1958, the PCGC published compliance guidelines requiring contractors to report how many "Negro" workers they employed. Employers were encouraged to use a supplemental form to report other minority workers, including "Spanish-Americans [a euphemism for Mexican Americans], Orientals, Indians, Jews, and Puerto Ricans." Mexican American groups and legislators later persuaded the PCGC to add a "Spanish-American" ethnic category to the main form.[11]

8. Graham, Hugh Davis. 2002. "The Origins of Official Minority Designations," *The New Race Question: How the Census Counts Multiracial Individuals*, Joel Perlmann and Mary C. Waters, eds. (New York: Russell Sage Foundation), 290.
9. The President's Committee on Civil Rights. 1947. *To Secure these Rights: The Report of the President's Committee on Civil Rights* (Washington, D.C.: United States Government Printing Office), VIII–IX.
10. Exec. Order No. 10479, 18 Fed. Reg. 4899 (Aug. 18, 1953); Thurber, Timothy M. Jan. 2006. "Racial Liberalism, Affirmative Action, and the Troubled History of the President's Committee on Government Contracts," *Journal of Policy History* 18(4): 446–476.
11. President's Committee on Government Contracts. 1958. *Five Years of Progress, 1953-1958: A Report to President Eisenhower* 23 (Washington, D.C.: Government Printing Office).

President John F. Kennedy established a new, more active committee to monitor federal contractors' compliance with antidiscrimination rules, the President's Committee on Equal Employment Opportunity.[12] Japanese and Chinese civil rights advocates, assisted by the new State of Hawaii's Congressional delegation, successfully lobbied for an "Oriental" category to be added to the main equal opportunity form.[13] As of the 1960 Census, Japanese and Chinese Americans together numbered less than one-half of percent of the country's population, and less than one-twentieth of the African American population. The addition of the Oriental category to the form therefore did not attract attention or controversy.

The committee also added the category of American Indians, population 546,000, to the main form. Jews as a category were dropped from the relevant forms altogether at the insistence of African American groups and with the assent of Jewish organizations.[14]

Thus, by the early 1960s contractors were required to report on how many "Negro," "Oriental," "Spanish-American," and "American Indian" employees they had. We now generally call these groups Black or African American, Asian American, Hispanic or Latino, and Native American, respectively. Aside from the name changes, the Kennedy-era precedent established the United States' official minority categories, minus the Hawaiian and Pacific Islander category that was established decades later.

White ethnic and religious minorities were lumped into the general white, nonminority category. All this was decided with very little public debate about, or explicit justification for, which groups were included and excluded in minority classifications.[15]

Indeed, there was little public debate as to whether the government should be in the business of tracking race at all; in the wake of Nazi racist horrors, Canada stopped tabulating race in 1951. It had

12. Exec. Order No. 10925, Establishing the President's Committee on Equal Employment Opportunity, 26 Fed. Reg. 1975, 1977 (Mar. 8, 1961).
13. Orlans, Harold. 1989. "The Politics of Minority Statistics," *Society* 26, no. 4: 24.
14. Skrentny, John D. 2002. *The Minority Rights Revolution,* Cambridge: Harvard University Press, 101-02.
15. *Ibid,* 100-02.

been widely expected that the United States would follow. The federal bureaucracy's need for data for civil rights enforcement sent things in the opposite direction.[16]

The 1964 Civil Rights Act and Its Aftermath

When the 1964 Civil Rights Act was enacted, the focus in the legislative history was squarely on the plight of African Americans. Virtually no attention was paid to which other groups, if any, would attract the resources of the Equal Employment Opportunity Commission, which was charged with enforcing the act's ban on racial discrimination in employment.

Although the act also banned discrimination based on religion, the EEOC quietly resolved that its focus should be on race discrimination. It included African Americans ("Negroes"), Hispanics ("Spanish-Americans," defined as Americans of Mexican and Puerto Rican descent), and Native Americans ("American Indians") on its reporting forms because those groups were thought to face the worst employment discrimination. The EEOC also included Asian Americans ("Orientals") for no documented reason beyond that they had been included on previous civil rights reporting forms.

As Hugh Davis Graham explains, the "EEO-1 form, by isolating for minority groups that corresponded to the racial color coding of American popular culture—black, yellow, red, and brown—reified a cluster of assumptions about American society that agency officials, shielded from public debate by their closed process, simply took for granted."[17]

The EEOC also grappled with the question of how employers required to report workforce statistics to the agency should determine their employees' race. One possibility was to have employees self-identify. The NAACP and other civil rights groups vigorously and successfully opposed that option.[18] The EEOC instead decided to rely

16.   Wright, Lawrence. "One Drop of Blood."
17.   Graham. *Collision Course.*
18.   Skrentny. *The Minority Rights Revolution*, 108; Bean, Jonathan J. 2001. *Big Government and Affirmative Action: The Scandalous History of the Small Business Administration.* (Lexington, KY: University of Kentucky Press), 43-44.

on visual identification by the employer. Employer visual identification remained the preferred mechanism for employers to identify race until 2007, when the EEOC began encouraging employers to rely on employee self-identification.[19]

In practice, visual identification meant that if an employee "looked black" to any degree, the employer would report the employee as "Negro." Apparently, the EEOC intended for employers to identify all minority employees this way.

This was especially problematic for Hispanics and Native Americans, who are usually of mixed heritage and have a wide range of appearances. Anthony Frederick, Vice President of Universal Studios, complained to Congress, "I couldn't tell you a Mexican American if I were to look at him. We are not permitted to ask a person his nationality, his national origin, in [California], and we don't, and you cannot tell by surname."[20]

The issue of identifying Hispanics and Native Americans turned out to be largely moot. In the early years of the Civil Rights Act the EEOC ignored groups other than African Americans. This was partly for ideological reasons and partly because the agency received few discrimination complaints from members of other groups.[21] By the time the agency turned its attention to Hispanics and other groups, employers were allowed, though not yet encouraged, to rely on employee self-identification.

In 1967, Herbert Hammerman, the first chief of the EEOC's Reports Unit, proposed removing the Oriental and American Indian categories from two new government reporting forms that covered union apprenticeships. He argued that both groups were very small, that statistics showed that discrimination was not posing a barrier to Asian American economic success, that American Indians living on reservations were not covered by the underlying civil rights law, and that many

19. Rich, Camille Gear. June 2014. "Elective Race: Recognizing Race Discrimination in the Era of Racial Self-Identification," *Georgetown Law Journal* 102: 1520-21.
20. Equal Employment Opportunity Commission, Hearings Before the United States Equal Employment Opportunity Commission on Utilization of Minority and Women Workers in Certain Major Industries.1969. 130.
21. Skrentny. *Minority Rights*, 110, 119.

American Indians living off reservations were of mixed ancestry and were not easily identifiable as Indians by employers.

According to Hammerman, no one at the EEOC disagreed with his analysis. The chairman nevertheless declined to follow his suggestion because he feared political backlash.[22]

The Nixon Administration:
The Philadelphia Plan, the Small Business Administration, the Interagency Commission, and the Origins of the "Hispanic" Category

In 1969, the Nixon administration created the "Philadelphia Plan," which required federal construction contractors to use "goals and time-tables" to increase minority employment.[23] While the focus of the plan was on widespread exclusion of black construction workers, nonblack minorities—"Orientals," "American Indians," and "Spanish Surnamed Individuals"—were also included. The administration thought that including them might win political support from those groups.[24]

In 1971, President Nixon issued an executive order meant to assist minority-owned business enterprises.[25] This was the first such order to define which groups counted as minorities; it applied to businesses owned by "Negroes, Puerto Ricans, Spanish-speaking Americans, American Indians, Eskimos, and Aleuts." Asian Americans, who had high rates of business ownership, were not included.

---

22. Hammerman, Herbert. 1988. "Affirmative-Action Stalemate: A Second Perspective," *Public Interest*, No. 1: 131.
23. US Department of Labor, Office of the Assistant Secretary, Arthur A. Fletcher, Assistant Secretary of Wage and Labor Standards, Memorandum To: Heads of All Agencies: Revised Philadelphia Plan for Compliance with Equal Employment Opportunity Requirements of Executive Order 11246 for Federally-Involved Construction, June 27, 1969, reprinted in The Philadelphia Plan: Congressional Oversight of Administrative Agencies, Hearings before the Senate Committee on the Judiciary. Subcommittee on Separation of Powers, on The Philadelphia Plan and S. 91, 91st Cong., 1st Sess., Oct. 27–28, 1969, at 26, 30.
24. Skrentny, John D. May 2006. "Policy-Elite Perceptions and Social Movement Success: Understanding Variations in Group Inclusion in Affirmative Action," *American Journal of Sociology* 111, No. 6: 1775.
25. Exec. Order No. 11625, Prescribing Additional Arrangements for Developing and Coordinating a National Program for Minority Business Enterprise, 36 Fed. Reg. 19,967 (Mar. 8, 1971).

Meanwhile, the SBA was working on regulations for its Section 8(a) program for disadvantaged business enterprises (DBEs).[26] Section 8(a) was created in the late 1960s to encourage African American entrepreneurship. In 1973, the SBA defined DBEs as including minority business enterprises owned and controlled by "Black Americans, American Indians, Spanish-Americans, Oriental Americans, Eskimos, and Aleuts."[27]

Nevertheless, the program continued to focus on African American-owned businesses. A. Vernon Weaver, Administrator of the SBA during the Carter administration, reported that when he arrived at the SBA in 1977, Section 8(a) "had been operating largely as an African American program."[28]

In 1973, the US Commission on Civil Rights, a federal advisory agency, issued a report urging the federal government to create a racial and ethnic data collection system. Such a system, the report argued, was needed to facilitate enforcement of antidiscrimination rules.[29] The report noted that in deference to that goal, groups like the NAACP and the ACLU no longer opposed the government asking individuals about their race and ethnicity.

The report discussed the "major" ethnic and racial classifications: Asian American/Oriental, Native American/American Indian, Spanish Surnamed/Spanish Speaking/Spanish Origin/Spanish American, Negro/Black, All Other Minority Groups, and White. The authors identified several issues with these broad classifications.

First, each Asian American nationality group had "unique" problems. For example, while Chinese and Japanese Americans had incomes above the American median, Filipino Americans had the lowest median income of all ethnicities in California.

26.   Bean, *Big Government and Affirmative Action*.
27.   38 Fed. Reg. 13,729 (Jan. 3, 1973).
28.   National Advisory Commission on Civil Disorders. 1988. *The Kerner Report: The 1968 Report of the National Advisory Commission on Civil Disorders*. New York: Pantheon Books, 21; La Noue, George R. and Sullivan, John C. 2000. "Gross Presumptions: Determining Group Eligibility for Federal Procurement Preferences," *Santa Clara Law Review*, 41, No. 1: 138; Letter from Ambassador A. Vernon Weaver to Dr. Jonathan Bean (Feb. 26, 1998).
29.   Cynthia Norris Graae, et al. 1973 *To Know or Not Know. Collection and Use of Racial and Ethnic Data in Federal Assistance Programs* (Washington, DC: US Government Printing Office).

Second, the American Indian category was extremely internally diverse. American Indians are members of dozens of distinct tribes with different languages, cultures, problems, and opportunities. Classifying them the same way obscured these differences and inhibited efforts to address unique tribal issues.

Third, the lack of separate statistics for various subgroups with Spanish heritage "presented problems for each of them." Cubans, Mexican Americans, and Puerto Ricans, by far the three largest subgroups, had different cultures, different levels of socioeconomic success, and were concentrated in different parts of the country. As a result, federal officials working with different Hispanic groups consistently requested separate data for each group. The report also raised the unresolved question of whether any or all Spanish heritage groups should be classified as white.

Finally, the report noted that there was no governmentwide guidance on which groups to include in the "All Other Minority Groups" category. Most federal agencies included Polynesians, Aleuts, Eskimos, and Creoles. There was confusion about whether the category also included European national origin groups—such as Italians, Poles, Slavs, and Portuguese—that had lower-than-average socioeconomic status.

Grouping all whites together, the report contended, obscured the special needs of insular ethnic groups such as French Canadians and Portuguese in New England. Such groups may need bilingual education and medical programs that include bilingual staff, among other federal assistance.

When the federal government created uniform racial and ethnic classifications a few years later, it ignored almost all the commission's concerns.

A 1973 report from the Subcommittee on Minority Education, a division of the Federal Interagency Committee on Education (FICE) identified a lack of useful data about Chicanos, Puerto Ricans, and American Indians. When a group of educators from those groups was gathered to discuss the draft report, they wound up storming out due to what they saw as ethnic misidentification in the report. The report remained unpublished, but it was forwarded to Secretary of Health, Education, and

Welfare (HEW) Caspar Weinberger. Weinberger asked FICE to "coordi-
nate development of common definitions for racial and ethnic groups."[30]

FICE responded by creating an Ad Hoc Committee on Racial and
Ethnic Definitions. The committee decided to make recommendations
for uniform federal racial and ethnic classifications of all Americans.
And it did, recommending the following categories: American Indian
or Alaskan Native, Asian or Pacific Islander, Black/Negro, Caucasian/
White, and Hispanic. How FICE decided to adopt these classifications
and not others, such as All Other Minorities, has been lost to history.

The categories were defined as races, except for Hispanic. Hispanics
was defined as an ethnicity "because there was no conceivable justification
for calling Hispanics a race" given that a Hispanic American could be any
combination of African, European, indigenous, or Asian by ancestry.[31]

FICE's report discussed several issues that had caused controversy
within the Ad Hoc Committee.

First, the committee had debated the proper category in which to
place Asian Indians. It ultimately recommended classifying them as White.

Second, the committee rejected "Afro-American" as an alternative
name for the Black/Negro category.

Third, the committee rejected a proposal from committee members
who were civil rights professionals to rename the White category,
"Persons not included in the other four categories."

Finally, some committee members wanted the American Indian
category to instead be "Original Peoples of the Western Hemisphere."
This alternative category would have included Latinos of indigenous
origin. Instead, the final proposed category was defined to include only
"federal Indians," those North American Indians recognized as such by
the federal government.

The federal Office of Management and Budget, the General
Accounting Office, HEW's Office for Civil Rights, and the EEOC
adopted these categories for a one-year trial period. FICE then made
minor revisions to its definitions based on feedback and circulated a final
draft. The relevant categories became effective for all racial and ethnic

---

30.   Fears, Darryl. Oct. 15, 2003. "The Roots of 'Hispanic,'" *Washington Post.*
31.   Wright. "One Drop of Blood."

reporting required by the federal agencies represented on the Ad Hoc Committee.[32]

The Carter Administration: The Categories Harden

In 1977, the Office of Management and Budget issued "Race and Ethnic Standards for Federal Statistics and Administrative Reporting," known as Statistical Policy Directive No. 15.[33] The directive created uniform standards for all federal agencies charged with collecting racial and ethnic data.

OMB cautioned that the "classifications should not be interpreted as being scientific or anthropological in nature." OMB warned that they should not be "viewed as determinants of eligibility for participation in any Federal program," such as affirmative action programs.[34]

Directive 15 followed FICE's recommendations with slightly different nomenclature and with one major exception; as will be discussed in more detail in Chapter Three, in response to lobbying by the Association of Indians in America, Directive 15 moved Americans with origins in the Indian subcontinent from the White category to the Asian or Pacific Islander category.[35]

The Directive 15 categories, with minor modifications, continue to guide government and government-mandated data collection today. The categories also became "the de facto standard for state and local agencies, the private and nonprofit sectors, and the research community."[36] The categories were defined as follows:

32. This part of the history is recounted in Review of Federal Measurements of Race and Ethnicity: Hearings Before the Subcomm. on Census, Statistics and Postal Pers. of the House Comm. on Post Office and Civil Serv., 103d Cong. 218 (1993) (prepared statement of Sally Katzen, Administrator, Office of Information and Regulatory Affairs, Office of Management and Budget).

33. Directive No. 15, Race and Ethnic Standards for Federal Statistics and Administrative Reporting, 43 Fed. Reg. 19,260 (May 4, 1978). They were adopted in 1977, but not published in the Federal Register until 1978.

34. Idler, Jose Enrique. 2007. *Officially Hispanic: Classification Policy and Identity*. (Lanham, MD: Lexington Books), 16; Directive No. 15.

35. As a result, the Equal Employment Opportunity Commission immediately did the same for its purposes, to keep federal statistical categories consistent. Government-Wide Standard Race/Ethnic Categories, 42 Fed. Reg. 17,900 (Apr. 4, 1977).

36. Omi, Michael and Winant, Howard. 2015. *Racial Formation in the United States*. (New York: Routledge/Taylor & Francis Group), 122.

American Indian or Alaskan Native. A person having origins in any of the original peoples of North America and who maintains cultural identification through tribal affiliation or community recognition.

Asian or Pacific Islander. A person having origins in any of the original peoples of the Far East, Southeast Asia, the Indian subcontinent, or the Pacific Islands. This area includes, for example, China, India, Japan, Korea, the Philippine Islands, and Samoa.

Black. A person having origins in any of the black racial groups of Africa.

Hispanic. A person of Mexican, Puerto Rican, Cuban, Central or South American or other Spanish culture or origin, regardless of race.

White. A person having origins in any of the original peoples of Europe, North Africa, or the Middle East.

To provide flexibility, it is preferable to collect data on race and ethnicity separately. If separate race and ethnic categories are used, the minimum designations are:

Race:

— American Indian or Alaskan Native

— Asian or Pacific Islander

— Black

— White

Ethnicity:

— Hispanic origin

— Not of Hispanic origin

When race and ethnicity are collected separately, the number of White and Black persons who are Hispanic must be identifiable and capable of being reported in that category.

If a combined format is used to collect racial and ethnic data, the minimum acceptable categories are:

— American Indian or Alaskan Native

— Asian or Pacific Islander

— Black, not of Hispanic origin

— Hispanic

— White, not of Hispanic origin

The category which most closely reflects the individual's recognition in his community should be used for purposes of reporting on persons who are of mixed racial and/or ethnic origins.

While all the categories alluded to "origins," there is no symmetry in how the categories are defined. People qualify as "American Indian" only if they maintain an (undefined) "cultural identification." But someone who has origins in a "black racial group of Africa" qualifies as "Black" regardless of cultural identification.

"Black" is defined racially; people of Asian or European descent who were born and raised in Africa do not count, nor do the Arab and Berber populations of northern Africa. By contrast, Directive 15 does not define "White" with reference to the white racial groups of Europe or elsewhere, but only by geographic origin.

"Asian" is defined solely by the geographic region of one's distant ancestors, the "original peoples" of the region. A person of Latin American heritage whose family spent many generations living in Japan would not count as Asian. However, a person whose ancestors immigrated to South America from Japan in the late nineteenth century would count as Hispanic.

Nor are the categories coherent sociologically or anthropologically. The Asian or Pacific Islander category included people descended from wildly disparate national groups. These groups do not have similar physical features, practice different religions, have distinct ancestral languages, vary dramatically in culture, and sometimes have long histories of conflict with one another. One critic asks how Samoans can "be said to be ethnically 'like' Chinese? Or Vietnamese 'related to' Pakistanis? These groups come from vastly different cultures and look almost nothing alike. How then do we justify grouping them together?"[37]

Asian American groups also have extremely varied levels of socioeconomic success in the United States—Indian Americans, for example, have the highest median income of any ethnic group in the United States, while the average incomes of Burmese and Nepalese Americans are well below the American mean. Korean Americans have the highest rate of business formation of any ethnic group in the United States, while Laotians have the lowest.

The Asian category meanwhile excludes people from the western part of Asia, such as Arabs and Iranians. For reasons never publicly expressed, the dividing line between "Asians" and "Whites" lies at the western border of Pakistan, and further north, China.

The government defines "Hispanic" as someone of "Spanish culture or origin, regardless of race." This classification established a novel ethnic category based on a common descent from a Spanish-speaking country. The Hispanic category includes everyone from immigrants from Spain—including people whose first language is Basque or Catalan, not Spanish—and their descendants to Argentine Americans of mixed European extraction to Puerto Ricans of mixed African, European, and indigenous heritage to individuals fully descended from indigenous Mexicans.

The government's White category, meanwhile, combines all of Europe, Asia west of Pakistan, the Asian parts of the former Soviet Union, and North Africa into one ancestry group. There is a tremendous amount of ethnic, cultural, linguistic, and religious diversity among people the government classifies as White. The category includes, among many others, Arabs, Chaldeans, Georgians, Germans, Greeks, Hungarians, Icelanders, Kurds, North African Berbers, Norwegians, Poles, and Scots, classified together arbitrarily.

The National Academy of Sciences has pointed out several additional bugs in the American race classification system: "There is no race category that includes persons native to Central and South America. There is no race category for blacks who come from areas in the world other than Africa, and there is uncertainty about many persons from northern parts of Africa." There is also no category for indigenous peoples like Australian Aborigines and New Zealand's Māori, and an "ambiguous or confused" status for people from countries such as Brazil, Madagascar, and Cape Verde.[38]

Directive 15 recommended that self-identification replace visual identification by third parties for determining an individual's classification. Americans of multiracial heritage were to select only one category, the one that most closely reflects the individual's "recognition in his community."[39]

The Public Works Employment Act of 1977 marked the first time Congress, rather than bureaucrats from the executive branch, specified which minority groups were eligible for affirmative action programs. The act set aside 10 percent of certain government contracts for minori-

---

38.   National Research Council. 1995. *Spotlight on Heterogeneity: The Federal Standards for Racial and Ethnic Classification* (Washington, DC: The National Academies Press), 25, 37-38.
39.   Robbin, Alice. 2000. "Classifying Racial and Ethnic Group Data in the United States: The Politics of Negotiation and Accommodation," *Journal of Government Information* 27: 134.

ty-owned businesses, defined as business owned by "citizens of the United States who are Negroes, Spanish-speaking, Orientals, Indians, Eskimos, and Aleuts." [40]

As Justice John Paul Stevens pointed out, Congress did not explain why it chose these minority categories. "No economic, social, geographical, or historical criteria are relevant for exclusion or inclusion. There is not one word in the remainder of the Act or in the legislative history that explains why any Congressman or Senator favored this particular definition over any other or that identifies the common characteristics that every member of the preferred class was believed to share."[41]

Congress passed the Small Business Investment Act in 1978, belatedly authorizing the SBA's Section 8(a) DBE program. After rejecting proposals that the program should be race-neutral, Congress specified that the program applied to businesses owned by "Black Americans, Hispanic Americans, Native Americans, and other minorities."[42]

In contrast to the earlier SBA rule, a "Hispanic" category replaced "Spanish-speaking" and "Spanish-Americans," and Asian Americans were not specifically included in the law. Representative Parren Mitchell, the leading congressional policymaker for minority business enterprise (MBE) programs, likely excluded them intentionally.[43] Mitchell, however, claimed the omission of was an "oversight."[44]

Following an outcry from Asian American groups and their Congressional allies, the SBA published an interim rule one year

---

40. Act of May 13, 1977, Pub. L. No. 95-28, 91 Stat. 116 (codified in significant part at 42 U.S.C. §§ 6705(e)-6707(j) (1982)).
41. Fullilove v. Klutznick, 448 U.S. 448, 535 (1980) (Stevens, J., dissenting).
42. Act of Oct. 24, 1978, Pub. L. No. 95-507, 92 Stat. 1757; Letter from Rep. Parren J. Mitchell to "Brainstormers," Sept. 19, 1978.
43. Graham, Hugh Davis. 2001. "Affirmative Action for Immigrants? The Unintended Consequences of Reform," in *Color Lines: Affirmative Action, Immigration, and Civil Rights Options for America,* ed. Skrentny, John David (Chicago: University of Chicago Press); La Noue and Sullivan, "Deconstructing Affirmative Action Categories," 122-25; News from Congressman Parren J. Mitchell: President Carter Signs Major Legislation Affecting Minority Business Enterprise, Oct. 26, 1978; press release. "The legislation, at the outset, was designed to positively assist Blacks, Hispanics and other notable racial groups," quoting Rep. Parren J. Mitchell.
44. 125 Cong. Rec. 12083 (1979).

later stating that "other minorities" included Asian Pacific Americans. Congress later amended the act to explicitly include Asian Americans.[45]

Previous administrative practice had limited the category of "Orientals" to the major pre-1924 Asian immigrant groups—Filipinos, Chinese, and Japanese. The new SBA Asian American category also included people with roots in Vietnam, Korea, Samoa, Guam, US territories in the Pacific, the Northern Mariana Islands, Laos, Cambodia, and Taiwan.[46] Over the next decades, and as detailed in Chapters Three and Four, the SBA rejected petitions for inclusion as presumptively disadvantaged minorities from Hasidic Jews, Iranians, and Afghans, but added Asian Indians to the Asian category.

In the 1990s, plaintiffs challenging SBA minority preferences deposed a former associate director for the SBA's Minority Enterprise Program and a former associate administrator of the SBA's Office of Minority Enterprise Development.[47] Neither could explain why certain ethnic groups were included or excluded in the Section 8(a) program. They also could not explain how membership in the groups was defined, nor why descendants of Spanish immigrants were included in the Hispanic category.

Documents that surfaced during the lawsuit also showed that the SBA had no guidelines for reviewing whether a group should retain socially disadvantaged status. The SBA also had no procedures for determining how a multiracial person should be classified. Despite these issues, the SBA classifications became the template for a host of other preferences and set-asides ordered by Congress for businesses in everything from agriculture to space exploration.[48]

---

45. Act of July 2, 1980, Pub. L. No. 96-302, § 118, 94 Stat. 833, 840; Minority Group Consideration, 44 Fed. Reg. 31,055 (May 30, 1979); Designation of Eligibility Asian Pacific Americans Under Section 8(a) and 8(d) of the Small Business Act, 44 Fed. Reg. 42,832 (July 20, 1979); Wong, Diane. June 30, 1979. "Exciting and Frustrating: Consultation on Asian Problems," *International Examiner* (Seattle); "Minorities Push for Contracts at White House Caucus." Jan. 23, 1980. *The Skanner* (Portland).
46. Designation of Eligibility Asian Pacific Americans Under Section 8(a) and 8(d) of the Small Business Act, 44 Fed. Reg. at 42,832 (July 20, 1979).
47. La Noue and Sullivan, "Deconstructing Affirmative Action Categories," 119.
48. Congressional Research Service, *Compilation and Overview of Federal Laws and Regulations Establishing Affirmative Action Goal. or Other Preference Based on Race, Gender, or Ethnicity* (Feb. 17, 1995), 4.

The Reagan Administration and Beyond

America's official racial and ethnic categories have only been modified slightly since the Reagan administration. In the 1980s, the SBA added individuals with origins in Tonga, Indonesia, Nauru, and Tuvalu to its Asian Pacific Americans and Subcontinent Asian Americans categories.[49] The SBA now has formal regulations dictating how a group can become eligible for presumptive disadvantaged status.[50] The rules do not provide a mechanism for decertifying a group whose members have already received presumptively disadvantaged status but whose socio-economic status has improved.

In 1997, the Office of Management and Budget, still in charge of federal data collection policies, separated "Native Hawaiian or Other Pacific Islander" from the "Asian" category. Native Hawaiians had found that when applying to colleges on the mainland, being placed in the same category as Asians sometimes resulted in discrimination for being part of an "overrepresented" group. Being put in the Native American category, by contrast, would make them eligible for affirmative action preferences.

The government, however, did not want to classify Native Hawaiians with Native Americans for fear of stirring sovereignty claims from Hawaiians akin to those from Native American tribes. Native American groups, meanwhile, did not want Hawaiians to be eligible for federal programs designated for American Indians. In the end, a new compromise category for Native Hawaiians and Pacific Islanders was created.[51]

OMB also decreed that it was not just preferable for race and Hispanic ethnicity to be asked separately, but that individuals should first be asked whether they are of Hispanic origin and then asked for

---

49. 54 Fed. Reg. 34,717 (Aug. 21, 1989); Designation of Minority Group Eligibility of Asian Indian Americans, 47 Fed. Reg. 36,743 (1982); La Noue and Sullivan, "Deconstructing Affirmative Action Categories," 126.
50. "Who Is Socially Disadvantaged?" Code of Federal Regulations, ecfr.gov. 13 C.F.R. § 124.103 (2016).
51. Revisions to the Standards for the Classification of Federal Data on Race and Ethnicity, 62 Fed. Reg. 58,782 (Oct. 30, 1997); "Counting in the Dark: Michael Omi Shows that the Census Has Become a Critical Racial Battleground." Apr. 30, 2001. *Colorlines*, 12.

their race. Meanwhile, the name of the Hispanic category was changed to "Hispanic or Latino."

As discussed in more detail in Chapter Four, under pressure from multiracial activists OMB announced that individuals may now check more than one racial category on demographic forms. Americans were still not, however, allowed to define themselves as multiracial.

Meanwhile, the most far-reaching federal status-based contracting program is the US Department of Transportation's (DOT) Disadvantaged Business Enterprise program. Congress established the federal DBE program in the early 1980s. It set a goal that at least 10 percent of transportation funds be allocated to "small business concerns [that are] owned and controlled by socially and economically disadvantaged individuals." Congress reiterated this goal in 2012 and 2015.[52]

Under DOT regulations, individuals are presumed to be socially and economically disadvantaged if they belong to one of the nonwhite Directive 15 groups.[53] The main difference between the DOT rules and OMB's Directive 15 guidelines is that DOT's Hispanic category includes Brazilian and Portuguese-descended Americans.

To prove minority status for federal affirmative action programs, a petitioner need only check the appropriate box and present a signed affidavit attesting that they have been subjected to discrimination based on their identity.[54] The SBA has also required applicants to demonstrate if requested that "he or she has held himself or herself out, and is currently identified by other, as a member of a designated group."

In 2016, the SBA provided guidance for administrators when someone's minority identity is called into question. For example, "individuals who claim disadvantaged status as Hispanic Americans may establish their membership in that designated group by providing a

52. Surface Transportation Assistance Act, Pub. L. No. 97-424, 96 Stat. 2097 (1983); Fixing America's Surface Transportation Act, Pub. L. No. 114-94, § 1101, 129 Stat. 1312, 1322-25 (2015); Moving Ahead for Progress in the 21st Century Act, Pub. L. No. 112-141, § 1101(b), 126 Stat. 405, 414-16 (2012); History of the DOT DBE Program, Dep't of Transp., http://perma.cc/N83h-6Mzp.
53. Code of Federal Regulations, ecfr.gov. 49 C.F.R. § 26.5(2) (2010); 49 C.F.R. § 26.67(a)(1) (2015).
54. Code of Federal Regulations, ecfr.gov. 49 C.F.R. § 26.63 (2020).

birth certificate showing race, membership cards to exclusive Hispanic groups, or other evidence."[55]

State Categories and Rules

State regulations defining racial and ethnic classifications generally follow the Directive 15 guidelines. Some states, however, define the scope of the Asian American, Hispanic, or Native American categories more broadly or narrowly than the federal government does.[56] A few states add Portuguese Americans as a separate ethnic category eligible for affirmative action.

Unlike federal agencies, most states require proof of the owner's ethnicity as part of an application for MBE status. One oddity of state rules is that many use the race listed on one's birth certificate as an important criterion. Birth certificates, however, no longer list an individual's race and have not for decades.

In Alabama, Arkansas, California, Florida, Iowa, Maryland, Minnesota, New Jersey, North Carolina, Ohio, Oregon, Rhode Island, Texas, Virginia, and Wisconsin, minority status can be proven by the race or ethnicity listed on one's passport, birth certificate, naturalization papers, green card, or tribal card. Alabama, Iowa, Maryland, New Jersey, Oregon, and Virginia allow an applicant to rely on the race listed on their driver's license—though Virginia licenses, at least, no longer list one's race. Indiana requires a birth certificate, driver's license, and a membership letter or certificate of an ethnic organization, tribal certificate, Bureau of Indian Affairs card, passport, armed services discharge papers, or any other document that provides evidence of ethnicity.

California, Delaware, and Ohio allow applicants to rely on their parents' birth certificates. Mississippi requires an affidavit of ethnicity, while North Carolina requires this only if one's passport, green card, and birth certificate do not prove minority ethnicity. For those not certified by the NMSDC, Florida requires a personal statement of

55. Office of Business Development US Small Business Administration, Standard Operating Procedure for the Office of Business Development SOP 80 05 5 (2016), 81.
56. For citations to the relevant statutes and regulations, see Bernstein, David E. 2021. "The Modern American Law of Race," *Southern California Law Review* 94, No. 2: 171-250.

ethnic designation. The Delaware Office of Supplier Diversity (OSD) instructs applicants not to offer any documentation of ethnicity unless specifically requested to do so.

In addition to its other rules, California requires three declarations from "recognized minority or ethnic community organizations" that the applicant is a member of their community. California also allows Native American applicants to submit letters from tribal chairmen or from the Bureau of Indian Affairs attesting to their status as Native Americans.

Kentucky's program requires "proof of racial/ethnic minority… status" but provides no definition as to what that entails. South Dakota allows contractors to rely on written representations by subcontractors regarding their status as MBEs in lieu of independent investigation.

Arkansas, Florida, and Pennsylvania allow an applicant to rely on copies of certifying documents from the National Minority Supplier Development Council. Under NMSDC rules, minority group membership is established by "a combination of screenings, interviews and site visits." Applicants are permitted to submit letters of appeal if their applications are denied.

The NMSDC considers minority group members to be individuals with at least one-quarter Asian, Black, Hispanic, or Native American ancestry. How this works in practice is unclear. For example, if an applicant has a grandfather who was half-Mexican and half-Irish but was known as Mexican American in his community, does this make the applicant one-quarter Hispanic or one-eighth Hispanic?

The NMSDC requires applicants for minority status to be US citizens; the DOT, by contrast, allows permanent residents to claim DBE status. The NMSDC's definitions for each minority group are also generally narrower than DBE definitions. Asian Indian excludes those with origins from Bhutan, the Maldives Islands, Nepal, and Sri Lanka. Asian Pacific excludes those with origins from Burma, Brunei, Macao, Fiji, Tonga, Kiribati, Tuvalu, Nauru, Federated States of Micronesia, and Hong Kong.

In contrast to federal law, NMSDC excludes people of direct Spanish or Portuguese heritage from its definition of Hispanic, and Brazilians, defined as "Afro-Brazilian or indigenous/Indian only," are listed as Hispanic for "review and certification purposes." The NMSDC also limits its definition of Hispanic to those of "true-born Hispanic heritage" without further explanation or elaboration. The NMSDC's definition of Caribbean Hispanics is broader than the federal one; the NMSDC's version includes the entire Caribbean Basin, including English-speaking countries, while the federal definition is limited to Puerto Ricans, Cubans, and Dominicans.

Whatever means federal and state authorities use to ascertain membership in the relevant official racial groups, the groups themselves—and how they are defined—have been remarkably stable and consistent since 1977. This stability and consistency, however, masks the fact that the official classifications have attracted controversy over the years.

This book's next three chapters discuss groups that have been on the borderline of legal whiteness. As our modern racial categories developed, there was no clear precedent that controlled whether these groups would be classified as official minorities or as generically white.

Chapter Two addresses the history of the Hispanic category. Hispanics are unique in that they are classified as an ethnic group whose members can be of any race—but in practice they are often treated like members of a distinct racial minority.

CHAPTER TWO
The Borderlands of Legal Whiteness:
The Anomalous Hispanic Category

A s discussed in Chapter One, the Hispanic category is one of the official racial and ethnic classifications the federal government established in 1977 via Statistical Directive No. 15. At the time, the notion of a pan-ethnic identity for all Americans of Spanish-speaking ancestry was relatively novel.

Unlike the other minority classifications, Directive 15 defined Hispanic as an ethnicity, not a race. Nevertheless, for many Americans Hispanic identity implies something akin to racial traits. Geoffrey Fox, author of *Hispanic Nation*, points out that Americans often say someone "looks Hispanic." They usually mean "someone who is too dark to be white, too light to be black, and has no easily identifiable Asian traits."[1]

The legal definition of Hispanic, however, does not address appearance. Rather, Hispanic is defined as a person of "Spanish origin or culture." Most Hispanics in the United States are primarily of mixed European and indigenous ancestry, but Hispanics may be of any combination of African, Asian, European, and indigenous descent. It follows that a Hispanic person need not have a certain "look."

For example, Texas's fair-skinned Senator Ted Cruz's father's Canary Islander family immigrated to the US by way of Cuba. His mother is of non-Hispanic European descent. Cruz meets the government's defini-

---

1. Fox, Geoffrey. 1997. *Hispanic Nation: Culture, Politics, and the Construction of Identity* (Tucson: University of Arizona Press), 33.

tion of Hispanic just as much as a brown-skinned Guatemalan American immigrant of multiracial ancestry does.

The Hispanic category also includes people whose ancestors' first language was not Spanish and who may have never spoken Spanish. This includes immigrants from Spain and their descendants whose ancestral language is Basque or Catalan. It also includes indigenous immigrants from Latin America whose first language is not Spanish, whose surnames are not Spanish, and whose ethnic and cultural backgrounds are not Spanish.[2]

Americans of Portuguese or Brazilian ancestry are sometimes defined as Hispanic by government fiat. Notably, only 2 percent of Portuguese and Brazilian Americans consider themselves Hispanic.[3]

The Hispanic classification is an American construct; residents of Spanish-speaking countries do not use it to refer to individuals' ethnicity. Critics of the category contend that the differences among those Americans classified as Hispanics "are greater than their imputed commonalities." The Hispanic label, Professor Martha Gimenez argues, "fulfills primarily ideological and political functions...it identifies neither an ethnic group nor a minority group."[4]

Another label, "Latino," eventually became a government-endorsed official alternative to Hispanic. In other words, the official federal clas-

2.   North American Association of Central Cancer Registries; Uniform Data Standards Committee; Subcommittee on Methodological Issues of Measuring Cancer Among Hispanics. 1996 *Final Report of Atlanta Symposium*, 9 (calling Hispanic "an artificial rubric for a set of diverse populations that resulted from the mixture of indigenous American peoples, African slaves, and Europeans"); Forbes, Jack D. 1992. "The Hispanic Spin: Party Politics and Government Manipulation of Ethnic Identity," *Latin American Perspectives* 19, No. 4: 64 ("The concept of Hispanic...is especially absurd as applied to Maya, Mixtec, Zapotec, or other American peoples who often do not even speak Spanish (except perhaps as a second, foreign language), whose surnames are often not of Spanish origin, and whose racial and cultural backgrounds are First American....").
3.   Pew Research Center, "Who Is Hispanic?" https://www.pewresearch.org/fact-tank/2019/11/11/who-is-hispanic.
4.   Gimenez, Martha E. 1989. "'Latino'/'Hispanic'-Who Needs a Name? The Case Against a Standardized Terminology," *International Journal of Health Services* 19, No. 3: 568. "To see the absurdity" of placing all people with Spanish-speaking ancestry into one category, another critic writes, "one has only to assert in parallel the non-existing Anglo linguistic cultural ethnicity 'common' to the native English-speaking Irishman, the Australian, the Indian from India, the Jamaican, the Belizean, the Aruban, the Englishman, and the US citizen who also speak 'the same language.'" Labaro, Salvatore. 2016. "The Declining Significance of Ethnicity: The Impact of Race Amongst Hispanics," PhD diss., (SUNY Albany Press), 97.

sification is now "Hispanic or Latino." The definition of the category—of Spanish-speaking origin or culture—has remained the same.

The term Latino attracts similar criticism as Hispanic. The Latino category is "artificial" and "preposterous," argues Michael Lind of the New America Foundation. It "include[s] blond, blue-eyed South Americans of German descent as well as Mexican-American mestizos and Puerto Ricans of predominantly African descent."[5]

Meanwhile, many American Hispanics do not consider themselves to be part of a minority group, much less a racial minority group.[6] Slightly more than half of Americans of Spanish-speaking descent identify as white. Among Latinos, this ranges from 82 percent among Cubans to 22 percent among Dominicans.[7] Some "Hispanos"—southwestern descendants of Spanish colonists who became Americans when the US seized territory from Mexico in the nineteenth century—insist that they are the original European (and thus white) population of the area.[8]

Many Hispanic or Latino demographic subgroups are more culturally connected to the general white population than to people from other Spanish-speaking national origin groups. Hispanic subgroups can differ from each other in political outlook as much or more than they differ from the general non-Hispanic white population.[9]

Hispanic subgroups also have varying levels of socioeconomic and educational attainment.[10] For example, a 2012 study found that while 32 percent of Colombian Americans had a college degree, only 7 percent of Salvadoran Americans did.

In short, the Hispanic population is heterogeneous on a variety of metrics. That said, the Hispanic and Latino labels caught on quickly. Spanish-language media executives who were eager to create a national

5.   Lind, Michael. May 29, 2012. "The Future of Whiteness," *Salon*.
6.   Skerry, Peter. 1993. *Mexican Americans: The Ambivalent Minority* (Cambridge: Harvard University Press), 16–18.
7.   Rumbaut, Ruben. April 27, 2011. "Pigments of Our Imagination: The Racialization of the Hispanic-Latino Category," *Migration Policy Institute*, https://www.migrationpolicy.org/article/pigments-our-imagination-racialization-hispanic-latino-category.
8.   Skerry, *Mexican Americans* 26.
9.   McGowan, Miranda Oshige. Summer 1996. "Diversity of What?" *Representations*, 133; Coughlin, E.K. "Political Survey Notes Difference Among Latinos," *Chronicle of Higher Education*, Sept. 11, 1991, 12.
10. Gimenez, "Who Needs a Name?" 562.

media market for Spanish content encouraged Hispanic pan-ethnic identity.[11] Political activists found that these pan-national categories create the sense of a large, homogenous, politically powerful group.[12] Spanish-speaking immigrants and their descendants, meanwhile, sometimes adopted one of these identities as a means of asserting their Americanness, because these labels are used only in the United States.[13]

Nevertheless, Americans of Spanish-speaking ancestry still overwhelmingly prefer to be labeled by their country of origin or "just American" rather than as Hispanic or Latino. Most accept Hispanic or Latino as a secondary identity, though Americans with only partial Hispanic ancestry often reject those labels.[14] Almost no one prefers Latinx, the gender-neutral alternative recently promoted by left-leaning activists.

Meanwhile, the scope of the Hispanic category remains contested. Some Chicano activists of mixed-race ancestry, for example, argue that fair-skinned immigrants from Mexico's European-descended elite should not be eligible for affirmative preferences for Hispanics. These preferences are intended, in their view, for nonwhite minorities, not for Hispanics who were considered white in their home countries.[15]

Other Hispanic activists resent that Cuban Americans, who overwhelmingly identify as white and on average are more politically conservative than other Hispanic groups, share their minority classification. And many Latinos think that immigrants of Spain and their descendants should be classified with other white Americans of European descent, not as Hispanic/Latino.

Political and cultural elites, however, often behave as if Hispanics are a homogenous population. For example, the producers of the recent *West Side Story* movie committed to ensuring that the movie is culturally sensitive in depicting the members of the Puerto Rican gang "The Sharks" and their families. The producers proudly announced that "Hispanic actress Rachel Zegler" would play the role of Maria.

11. Mora, G. Cristina. 2014. *Making Hispanics: How Activists, Bureaucrats & Media Constructed a New American Identity* (Chicago: University of Chicago Press), 159.
12. Francis-Fallon, Benjamin. 2019. *The Rise of the Latino Vote: A History* (Cambridge: Harvard University Press).
13. Fox, *Hispanic Nation*, 243.
14. Mora, *Making Hispanics*, 7–8.
15. Gimenez, "Who Needs a Name?" 567.

Zegler grew up in New Jersey and has one parent of Colombian descent, one of European descent, and (obviously) none of Puerto Rican descent.[16] Exactly how casting a half-Colombian, half-European actress to play a Puerto Rican character is culturally sensitive was left unexplained.

A Google search for Supreme Court Justice Sonia Sotomayor brings up around eighteen thousand results for "first Hispanic Justice" and around six thousand results for "first Latina [or first Latino] Justice." The more precise "first Puerto Rican Justice" brings up a paltry twenty-nine hits.

Controversy continues over whether Hispanic/Latino should be deemed a racial category or an ethnicity. Even though most Hispanics identify as white on the census and in surveys, they are often referred to as "people of color," that is, nonwhites.

In the 1960s, the Ford Foundation funded various individuals and organizations with the goal of having Mexican Americans emulate African American success in achieving political goals as a racial minority. Decades later, some Mexican American civil rights organizations still treat Hispanic is a racial category.[17]

As noted previously, when the Office of Management and Budget created the official Directive 15 categories in 1977 (see Chapter One), it dictated that Hispanic was an ethnic classification, not a racial one. Government agencies that collected racial and ethnic statistics mostly responded by placing a two-part race/ethnicity question on demographic forms. These forms asked individuals if they were Hispanic and what race they belonged to.

The Department of Education, however, demurred. Its Office of Civil Rights (OCR) requires almost all schools in the United States, from elementary to graduate school, to gather demographic statistics on matriculants. OCR left it up to the schools and universities gathering those statistics to decide whether to use a two-part question or a

16. Bernstein, David. June 26, 2020. "Identitarianism Comes to Hollywood," The Volokh Conspiracy, https://reason.com/2020/06/26/identitarianism-comes-to-hollywood.
17. Gonzalez, Mike. 2020. The Plot to Change America (New York: Encounter Books), 28, 40-45, 166-67; Mora, Making Hispanics, 53-58; Skerry, Mexican Americans 323-24, 369-70.

one-part question. A one-part question asks individuals whether they are Black, White, Hispanic, Native American, or Asian.

Universities overwhelmingly chose the one-question route. This made Hispanic status the equivalent of a racial status—for example, one could not be both Hispanic and White on these universities' admissions forms.

The Department of Education did not change its rules to require a two-question ethnicity classification until 2007. By then, the notion that Hispanic affirmative action preferences in university admissions amounted to a "racial" preference was entrenched.

Similarly, for two decades the Equal Employment Opportunity Commission's EEO-1 form filled out by all big companies listed five races, including Hispanics. The EEOC finally changed to a two-question format with Hispanic listed as an ethnicity and not a race in 2007.

The notion that Hispanic/Latino is a racial category has found its way into Supreme Court opinions. Justice Sotomayor, for example, has argued that affirmative action for African Americans and Hispanics is necessary because "race matters."[18] This implies that Hispanics are a racial minority. Supreme Court decisions more generally treat affirmative action preferences for Hispanics as racial preferences.

Other parts of the federal government also describe Hispanics as members of a racial minority. For example, the SBA's guidance on disadvantaged business enterprises still depicts Hispanic as a racial category.

Notwithstanding the frequent racialization of Hispanicness, the federal government's statistical rules, including those used by the Census Bureau, define Hispanic as an ethnic, not racial, classification. In the late 1970s and early 1980s, the Census Bureau proposed making "Hispanic" a racial category akin to "Black" or "White." Most major Latino organizations aggressively opposed the change.[19]

Census Bureau employees specializing in racial demography also strongly opposed categorizing Hispanic as a racial identity. Their opposition reflected deference to civil rights and ethnic identity organizations. These groups worried that creating a Hispanic racial category

18. Schutte v. BAMN, 572 U.S. 291 (2014).
19. "Census Advisors Finally Meet," *Hispanic Link Weekly Report*, May 26, 1986, 1.

would reduce their groups' reported populations and therefore their political clout.

African American groups feared that Afro-Latinos would identify as Hispanic, not Black; American Indian organizations were concerned that some individuals of indigenous heritage would identify as Hispanic, not Native American; and Asian American activists worried that some Filipinos would identify as Hispanic and not Asian.[20] The bureau ultimately shelved the proposal.

In 1997, the OMB rejected a request from the National Council of La Raza, a Latino advocacy group, to combine the race and Hispanic origin questions into a single Race/Ethnicity category.[21] In 2018, the Census Bureau recommended that "Hispanic or Latino" be changed from an ethnicity to a race category. The Trump administration, however, declined to adopt this recommendation.[22]

All of this raises the question of how Hispanics—unlike many other relatively dark-complexioned groups—came to be classified as members of an ethnic minority group distinct from non-Hispanic whites. Historically, the US government classified Hispanics as white. The Census Bureau presumptively classified Hispanics as white except in 1930, when the Census included a racial category for Mexicans.

From 1940 until 1970, census takers were instructed to either rely on Mexican Americans' racial self-identification or to classify them as white unless they obviously appeared to belong to another race.[23] In five southwestern states, the bureau used Spanish surnames to estimate the Mexican American population, but this was a national origin category, not a racial one.[24]

Americans of European descent also generally accepted Hispanics as fellow whites, at least if their complexions were relatively light. White Hispanic Hollywood stars of the pre-Civil Rights era included Desi

---

20.   Gómez, Laura E. 2020. *Inventing Latinos: A New Story of American Racism* (New York: The New Press), 157–58.
21.   Rodriguez, Clara E. 2000. *Changing Race: Latinos, the Census, and the History of Ethnicity in the United States* (New York: NYU Press).
22.   Gómez, *Inventing Latinos*, 160–61.
23.   Hattam, Victoria. 2007. *In the Shadow of Race: Jews, Latinos, and Immigrant Politics in the United States* (Chicago: University of Chicago Press), 113.
24.   Ibid., 19, 105–06.

Arnaz, José Ferrer, Rita Hayworth, and Anthony Quinn. White Hispanic baseball stars included Lefty Gomez, Adolfo Luque, and Miguel Angel González. (Ted Williams, however, hid his maternal Mexican heritage.) Latino players who appeared to have African ancestry and could not "pass" as white were relegated to the Negro Leagues.

Despite generally being considered white by the federal government, Hispanics sometimes experienced harsh treatment and discrimination. This included mass deportations of Mexican aliens (along with their children, who were often American citizens) in the 1930s and 1950s. It also included more localized discrimination, such as public school segregation and other forms of government discrimination in parts of the Southwest.

The Texas legislature passed a resolution in 1943 guaranteeing all Caucasians—that is, including Mexican Americans but excluding African Americans—equal accommodations. Local Texas governments nevertheless continued to discriminate against and segregate people of Mexican descent.

In 1954, the Supreme Court reviewed the case of Pete Hernandez, a Mexican American who was convicted of murder in Jackson County, Texas.[25] Hernandez argued that prosecutors in Jackson County illegally engaged in race discrimination by excluding people of Mexican descent from juries, including his own. Texas courts rejected his argument. Because Mexicans were white, the courts argued, excluding them from the jury in favor of other whites could not be racial discrimination.

The Supreme Court disagreed. Whether Mexican Americans could be subjected to race discrimination by whites, the court explained, depended on whether local custom and law treated them like nonwhites. For many years, children of Mexican descent in Jackson County had been enrolled in an elementary school segregated from Anglos through fourth grade. At least one restaurant in town openly refused to serve Mexicans. The county courthouse had segregated toilets, one unmarked and the other marked "Colored Men" and "Hombres Aqui." The court

---

25.   Hernandez v. Texas, 347 U.S. 475 (1954).

concluded that the way Jackson County residents distinguished between "Whites" and "Mexicans" amounted to race discrimination.

Overall, Mexican Americans teetered on the edge of the white category, especially if they had darker skin and Spanish-sounding names. Before World War II, nonwhite legal status presented only disadvantages. The most influential Mexican American group, the League of United Latin American Citizens (LULAC), lobbied to have Mexican Americans classified as whites in government data collection, especially by the Census Bureau.[26] Other Mexican American leaders insisted that their constituents were white, just like Italians, Irish, and other Catholic ethnic groups.[27]

By the 1950s, however, LULAC and other Mexican American lobbying groups changed course. They worked with Mexican American legislators to urge that a Mexican American category be listed on forms filled out by government contracting firms to show that they met anti-discrimination requirements.

The lobbying groups asserted that Mexican Americans had brown skin and mixed-race heritage. They therefore experienced a level of racial discrimination akin to what African Americans faced. In response, the government added a "Spanish-Americans" category to the main form but as an ethnic rather than a racial category.[28]

Three developments in the 1960s influenced the ultimate creation of "Hispanic" as a legal category. First, Mexican American activists established a militant "Chicano" movement seeking redress of Mexican American grievances. Second, Puerto Rican activists, including those based on the US mainland, developed an equally militant and sometimes violent Puerto Rican independence movement. Finally, tens of thousands of Cuban refugees fled Castro's Cuba and established a political and cultural base in Miami.

These groups were quite "distinct in terms of geography, political agenda, and cultural understanding of race" and therefore were rarely

---

26.   Hattam, *In the Shadow of Race*, 105.
27.   Skerry, "Mexican Americans," 17.
28.   Ibid.

thought of as sharing an ethnic identity.[29] Through the late 1960s, government civil rights forms generally listed the Mexican American and Puerto Rican categories separately. Cubans, generally considered by themselves and others to be white,[30] were rarely listed at all.

Mexican American activists in the late 1960s pressured US census officials to create a category for Spanish speakers and their descendants. The officials declined to do so. Some found the category too diverse to be useful; others thought of Hispanics as a white ethnic group that would eventually assimilate into the broader white population. The Census Bureau classified Hispanics as generically white in the 1970 census.

This decision met with strong criticism from Latino civil rights organizations. Their leaders believed that better data collection on the Spanish-origin population was crucial to persuading the civil rights bureaucracy to pay more attention to discrimination against Hispanics. The Nixon administration responded by adding a question about "Mexican, Puerto Rican, Cuban, Central or South American, [or] Other Spanish" origin or descent to the detailed census questionnaire sent to 5 percent of American households.[31]

In a post-1970 census report, the Census Bureau defined the "Spanish Heritage population" as including three groups: people living in five southwestern states who had a Spanish surname or whose first language was Spanish; those who had a Puerto Rican birth or parentage in three middle Atlantic states; and Spanish-language speakers in the rest of the country.[32]

President Nixon sought to reward the Cuban community for voting Republican. He ordered federal agencies to include Cuban Americans when researching, discussing, or providing benefits and services to Mexican Americans and Puerto Ricans.[33]

29. Mora, *Making Hispanics*, 5; see also Pager, Sean A. 2007. "Antisubordination of Whom? What India's Answer Tells Us About the Meaning of Equality in Affirmative Action," *University of California Davis Law Review* 41, No. 1: 303–08.
30. Mora, *Making Hispanics*, 106; Rodolfo de la Garza et al., 1992. *Latino Voices: Mexican, Puerto Rican, and Cuban Perspectives on American Politics* (Boulder: Westview Press), 23.
31. Perlmann, Joel. 2018. *America Classifies the Immigrants: From Ellis Island to the 2020 Census* (Cambridge: Harvard University Press), 353.
32. Siegel, S. 1979. *Coverage of the Hispanic Population of the United States* 34.
33. La Noue and Sullivan. "Deconstructing Affirmative Action Categories," 83.

Nixon, "the Dark Father of Hispanicity,"[34] also pushed for the government to develop a pan-ethnic category for people with Spanish-speaking ancestors. If people came to identify with such a category, Nixon thought, the influence of radical Mexican American and Puerto Rican activists would wane.[35] Nixon insisted that Cuban Americans be included in this new classification.

The original justification for singling out Mexican and Puerto Rican Americans for government attention was the sense that this would primarily benefit people with significant, visible nonwhite heritage. Given that most Cubans identified as white, adding them to the mix made it almost inevitable that any future official Hispanic category would eventually include all or almost all Americans of Spanish-speaking heritage.

Some Mexican American activists objected to the notion of a new pan-ethnic classification for descendants of Spanish-speakers. Most activists, however, decided it would be politically beneficial to recast the Mexican-specific Chicano movement as a pan-ethnic movement that included all Latinos. This would allow activists to expand their political base from the Southwest to Florida and the Northeast.

Once the government began to recognize a pan-ethnic category for Americans with Spanish-speaking ancestry, the question of how to identify members of that category naturally arose. Most government agencies initially defined members of the category as those with a "Spanish surname."

"Spanish surname" was chosen because it allowed employers and others to identify Hispanic employees via a more objective means than visual identification. And it did not require reliance on self-identification, which was still out of favor. Moreover, while mixed-race, dark-complexioned Hispanics attracted much more discrimination than white Hispanics, an employer or other decisionmaker who saw a Spanish surname on a job application might reject that individual based on general racial prejudice against Hispanics.

---

34. Rodriguez, Richard. 2004. *Brown: The Last Discovery of America* (New York: Viking), preface.
35. Mora, *Making Hispanics*, 49; *Forbes*, "The Hispanic Spin," 67.

Nevertheless, relying on Spanish surnames to identify people of Hispanic heritage caused predictable problems. A Spanish-sounding surname is not a reliable indicator that someone is Hispanic. Many Filipinos have Spanish surnames; many Italian and Portuguese surnames—such as Hernandez[s]—overlap with Spanish surnames; and non-Hispanic women can "marry in" to their husbands' Spanish surname.

Spanish surnames may have worked well enough for compiling discrimination statistics. However, once affirmative action programs commenced, relying on Spanish surnames to identify an eligible cohort risked including a large percentage of people who were not the intended beneficiaries.

The Spanish surname category was also manipulable. In the late 1970s Robert Earl Lee, a Montgomery County, Maryland, employee, changed his legal name to Roberto Eduardo Leon.[36] He hoped minority status as a Spanish surnamed employee would help him get promoted.

"My job with the county environmental protection agency is spotting loopholes and I spotted one," Leon told the *New York Times*. Leon added, "Fortunately, I still have the same initials. So the monogrammed towels—if I had them—wouldn't have to be changed."

"He has a knack for figuring out loopholes in things," agreed Eric Mendelsohn, Leon's boss. "Bob, I mean Roberto, is a highly regarded professional, a little eccentric in some ways. It's nice to have a Hispanic on our staff."

"This is an insult to Hispanics," an angry Carlos Anzoategui, head of the governor's commission on Hispanic affairs, responded. "You don't become Hispanic by liking enchiladas and tortillas."

"This isn't funny, it's absurd," added Raul Yzaguirre, president of the National Council of La Raza, a Mexican American organization.

---

36. This discussion draws on "A Bored and Unpromoted Robert E. Lee Takes Affirmative Action: Meet Roberto E. Leon," *People*, April 16, 1979; Lyons, Richard D. March 17, 1979. "Job Seeker's Ploy: 'Bob,'" *New York Times*; Mansfield, Stephanie. March 16, 1979. "Roberto Leon is Now Called Other Names," *Washington Post*; Mansfield, Stephanie. March 11, 1979. "Roberto Leon, Instant Hispanic; New Name Qualifies County Employee for Job Preference," *Washington Post*, March 11, 1979; and "Gilchrist Ruling Costs Leon-Lee Minority Status," *Washington Post*, April 27, 1979.

Leon denied that his new Hispanic identity was contrived. He claimed that he grew up surrounded by Mexican American classmates in San Diego, that he was fluent in Spanish, that his mother told him that her father was Spanish. (His maternal grandfather actually seems to have been a man named James Herman Fuhrmeister of San Antonio, whose father immigrated to the US from Prussia.) Peter Chen, Montgomery County's director of employee relations, reclassified Leon as requested.

Leon and his coworkers apparently took his new Hispanic identity less than fully seriously, however. "One of my compatriots called me a Spic," he told *People Magazine*, "and we had a big laugh over it." Cesar Morinigo, a colleague of Leon's from Paraguay, chimed in, "Bob may have changed his name but he's still a gringo to me."

Meanwhile, the federal Equal Employment Opportunity Commission was not amused. It informed Montgomery County Executive Charles W. Gilchrist that it would be "an abuse of federal law and regulations to accept mere conversion...to a Spanish surname" as a basis for granting minority status. The EEOC explained that this status would allow Leon illegally to gain preference in employment over other non-Hispanic whites.

Chen responded that he "never would have granted him the Hispanic designation based on the name change alone. The real reason was because he claimed Hispanic ancestry." Chen's claim is confusing. While federal law required the county to keep track of its Hispanic employees, for county affirmative action purposes "Spanish surnamed" was the only relevant category.

Anzoategui was not appeased. "To me, the man is a conniver. He can call himself anything he wants. My beef is with the county which has become a partner in the sham. We'll sue if we have to." Leon, for his part, did not object to those who called him an opportunist. He volunteered that "there's nothing wrong with being an opportunist."

Gilchrist eventually decreed that Leon did not qualify for minority status. Gilchrist acted on the advice of the county attorney and recommendations from the county employees' Affirmative Action Council.

Leon objected to the ruling. "It appears there are no objective methods for making a decision," he told the *Washington Post*. "This is subjective, and I thought government was to run by objective means… the hard evidence is that I have a Spanish grandfather…. All I want is equal opportunity."

While some non-Hispanics have Spanish-sounding surnames, real or contrived, the converse, Hispanics who do not have Spanish surnames, is also common. Leon's antagonists, Anzoategui and Yzaguirre, were Hispanic but had Basque surnames.

Many other Hispanics, including Hispanic women married to non-Hispanic men and individuals with Hispanic mothers but not fathers, do not have Spanish surnames. Hispanics may also have ancestry from parts of Europe other than Spain, or from Africa or Asia.

The Federal Communications Commission was among the federal agencies that adopted the "Spanish surnamed" category in the 1970s. The FCC granted broadcasting licensing preferences to members of designated minority groups to diversify the demographics of media ownership. The agency soon confronted petitions for minority preferences by two broadcast companies whose owners sought minority preferences as Hispanics but did not have Spanish surnames.[37]

The first claim involved the Liberman family. The patriarch of the family, Adolfo Liberman, was a Polish-born Jew. Liberman claimed (dubiously) that his ancestors were Sephardic Jews expelled from Spain in 1492 and that he spoke "Castilian Spanish" while growing up in Poland.

Liberman had immigrated from Poland to Mexico, and then to Guatemala and Costa Rica. In each country, he and his wife had a son. Eventually, the Liberman family moved to the US and became citizens. The family continued to use Spanish in everyday conversation.

The second case involved the sale of a radio station to Oscar Luis Kramer, a Cuban-born American citizen. Kramer averred that he identified as Hispanic, worked as the general manager of a Hispanic-oriented radio station, and served as president of the Hispanic division of

---

37.   In re Application of Storer Broad. Co., 87 F.C.C.2d 190 (1981).

the local chamber of commerce. In 1979, Kramer was honored as the Seventh Day Adventist Church's Hispanic Citizen of the Year.

As FCC bureaucrats struggled with how to classify Kramer and the Libermans, the agency announced that it was changing the "Spanish Surnamed" category to "Hispanic."[38] In light of that change, the FCC gave minority preferences to the companies owned by the Libermans and Kramer.

This raises the question of how "Hispanic" became the official classification for those of Spanish-speaking heritage. In 1976, President Ford signed legislation requiring the federal Office of Management and Budget (OMB) to "develop a government-wide program for the collection of data with respect to Americans of Spanish origin or descent."[39] The legislation had been sponsored by Congressman Ed Roybal, a strong advocate for Mexican American interests.

A year later, OMB adopted "Hispanic" as the official category for government record-keeping in 1977 as part of its Statistical Directive No. 15 (see Chapter One). A task force of three federal employees with Spanish-speaking ancestry—a Mexican American, a Puerto Rican, and a Cuban American—had met for six months to hammer out the Hispanic category and its scope.[40] The task force had considered several terms for identifying the relevant population, including Spanish surname, Spanish language, Hispano, and Latino.[41]

One member of the subcommittee, Grace Flores, a Mexican American, later attributed the choice of Hispanic to her insistence on the term. "Hispanic" had started to gain currency to refer to Americans of Spanish-speaking descent in the early 1970s.[42] By 1975 the Department of Education was using the term on equal opportunity forms sent to institutions of higher education.[43]

---

38. Policy Regarding the Advancement of Minority Ownership in Broadcasting, 92 F.C.C.2d 849 n.1 (1982).
39. Francis-Fallon, *Rise of the Latino Vote*, 306-07.
40. Flores-Hughes, Grace. Sept. 2013. "Is it Latino or Hispanic? Here's Why it Matters," *Voxxi*, https://www.voxxi.com/2013/09/19/latino-or-hispanic.
41. Fears, "Roots of 'Hispanic.'"
42. Boak, Jonathan et al. March 2004. "Who Is Hispanic? Implications for Epidemiologic Research in the United States," *Epidemiology* 15, No. 2: 241.
43. 40 Fed. Reg. 25,195 (1975).

Flores recounted that she preferred Hispanic "because it was better than anything I had been called as a kid…. It was hard eliminating all those terms…I felt alone. But I was determined to stick to Hispanic. We kept going back to Spain. We couldn't get away from it."[44]

Latino was problematic, in Flores's view, because it could be construed to include people with Latin but not Spanish origins such as Italians. Using a Spanish surname as a category had the problems noted above. Flores's fellow panelist Abdin Noboa-Rios, a native of Puerto Rico, preferred the term Latino, while the Cuban member of the panel preferred Hispano. The committee ultimately, but grudgingly, agreed on Hispanic. According to Noboa-Rios, "There was never any consensus in that group to the very end."[45]

The Ad Hoc Committee on Racial and Ethnic Definitions of the Federal Interagency Committee on Education was charged with developing the racial and ethnic categories for Directive 15. Its final report endorsed establishing a Hispanic category, defined as a person of Mexican, Puerto Rican, Cuban, Central or South American, or other Spanish culture or origin, regardless of race. The report explained:

> Once members agreed that it would be inappropriate to refer to Spanish language or surname for purposes of identifying people to be counted in this category, they decided not to use the term "Spanish" in the heading at all. The term "Hispanic" was selected because it was thought to be descriptive of and generally acceptable to the groups to which it is intended to apply. Representatives of one agency, however, still prefer "Spanish" to "Hispanic."

Some Latino activists objected to "Hispanic," arguing that the term was tied to Spanish imperialism. Others, especially Chicano activists, were unhappy with the category's definition. The activists believed that the purpose of the underlying classification should be to combat racial discrimination against people with noticeable indigenous or African

44. Fears, "Roots of 'Hispanic.'"
45. Ibid.

heritage; the broad Directive 15 "Hispanic" category, however, encompassed many people who identified, and were identified by others, as white. Combined with the new norm of self-identification, this meant that the category would include many people with light complexions and predominately or entirely European ancestry.

Meanwhile, the Spanish American Heritage Association, representing Spanish immigrants and their descendants, protested that "Hispanic" should only be used to describe "a Caucasian of Spanish ancestry. The Mexican-American and Puerto Rican people are not Caucasians of Spanish ancestry and therefore are not Hispanic." According to the (apparently openly racist) association, "This misuse causes confusion and embarrassment to Americans who truly are of Spanish ancestry."[46]

Despite these various objections, the Hispanic category soon dominated government nomenclature for people of Spanish-speaking descent. By 1993, for example, every state used this category when reporting the race and ethnicity of newborns.[47] In 1997, the Office of Management and Budget changed the official federal government statistical category from "Hispanic" to "Hispanic or Latino."

Part of the reason that Hispanic became the dominant term to describe people of Spanish-speaking heritage is that the US Census adopted it as an ethnic category in 1980.[48] The adoption was the product of a vigorous lobbying campaign by Latino organizations.

Professional demographers denounced the addition of the Hispanic category as a product of political interference with the Census Bureau. But Vilma S. Martinez, head of the Mexican American Legal Defense and Educational Fund and chairman of a special census advisory committee on Spanish population, was unapologetic about lobbying for a Hispanic census category. She told the *New York Times*, "We are trying to get our just share of political influence and Federal funds. There's nothing sinister about it."[49]

---

46. Quoted in Roger Langley, "It's All a Matter of Classification," *Arizona Republic*, Sept. 26, 1980.
47. Mora, *Making Hispanics*.
48. Ibid.
49. Reinhold, Robert. May 14, 1978. "Census Questions on Race Assailed as Political by Population Experts," *New York Times*.

Meanwhile, controversy erupted over whether the Hispanic category should be limited to Latinos or extend to Spanish immigrants to the United States and their descendants. By including "or other Spanish origin or culture" in its definition, the category seemed to include Spanish immigrants and their progeny.

The Department of Transportation took a different approach. It defined Hispanics for its disadvantaged business enterprise programs to include Brazilians but excluded people of direct Iberian origin—that is, Spanish and Portuguese immigrants and their descendants.[50]

The Hispanic American Contractors Association of McLean, Virginia, petitioned for this rule to be replaced with the Directive 15 language.[51] The DOT noted that the "most important rationale for such a change was that discrimination against Hispanics occurs regardless of their place of origin."[52]

According to Robert Ashby, a DOT official at the time, the comments received on the proposed change were overwhelmingly favorable. The limited "opposition wasn't particularly strong or strident, so we then decided to go along with that change." To avoid excluding Brazilians, the DOT changed the Directive 15 language to "or other Spanish or Portuguese origin or culture."[53] This also made Portuguese immigrants and their descendants eligible for preferences.

In 1983, Congress passed a law creating uniform definitions of minorities for federal minority business enterprise programs. The law required all departments and agencies to follow the definition used by the Small Business Administration. This definition did not include Portuguese, so the DOT excluded them from its MBE program for several years.[54] In 1986, however, the SBA determined that Portuguese were Hispanics under prevailing law, so the DOT reinstated them.[55]

---

50.   45 Fed. Reg. 21,172 (1980).
51.   Request for Comment on Petition to Amend 49 C.F.R. Part 23, 46 Fed. Reg. 969 (Jan. 5, 1981) (requesting comments in response to the petition); Definition of "Hispanic" in Department of Transportation Minority Business Enterprise Regulation, 46 Fed. Reg. 60458 (1981) (issuing a final rule amending the definition of Hispanic).
52.   Ibid.
53.   Brone, Tom. "Minority Status Not So Simple—Politics, Agency Quirks Often Shape Definition," *Seattle Times*, Oct. 5, 1998.
54.   Ibid.
55.   Ibid.

Some states and localities also included Portuguese Americans in their definition of Hispanic. A minor scandal erupted when the *Washington Post* reported that from 1986 to 1990 companies owned by the Rodriguez brothers, immigrants from Portugal, won 80 percent of the District of Columbia's contracts set aside for minorities.[56] At the time, most of DC's population was African American.

In 1997, DOT reaffirmed its policy of including Iberians in the Hispanic category. The department acknowledged "that the inclusion of persons of European Spanish and Portuguese origin is controversial.... Absent legislative direction to the contrary," however, "we believe it is necessary to leave the definition unchanged."[57]

* * * *

The question of who counts as Hispanic has vexed courts and administrative agencies ever since the category was adopted.

Marinelli Construction Corp. v. State involved a company that applied for minority business enterprise certification in New York State as a Hispanic-owned business.[58] The owner's father was born in Argentina and spoke Spanish, but his paternal grandparents were born in Italy and immigrated to Argentina. New York's MBE certification program officer found that the underlying law required that the owner be of Hispanic "origin." Because the owner's Argentine ancestry was via Italy and not Spain, the officer found he was not of Hispanic origin. Marinelli unsuccessfully appealed in New York state court.

In *Major Concrete Construction v. Erie*,[59] the company's owner appealed an administrative ruling that his company did not qualify as a Hispanic business. The county government had found that the owner was not "of Spanish culture" as the law required. The county noted that the owner was only 25 percent Mexican; he kept no contact with the Hispanic community or its culture; and neither he nor members

56. Schneider, Howard and Ragland, James. June 1, 1992. "Ford Dominated DC Minority Contracting," *Washington Post*.
57. Participation by Disadvantaged Business Enterprise in Department of Transportation Programs, 62 Fed. Reg. 29548, 29550 (1997).
58. Marinelli Constr. Corp. v. State, 613 N.Y.S.2d 1000 (N.Y. App. Div. 1994).
59. 521 N.Y.S.2d 959 (NY. App. Div. 1987).

of his family identified as Hispanic. A trial court reversed the ruling, but an appellate court reinstated the denial of Hispanic status. The latter court found that the decision was supported by a rational basis, all the law required.

The federal SBA Section 8(a) program provides set-aside and sole-source contracts to "disadvantaged" businesses. Hispanic-owned small businesses are presumed to be disadvantaged. Perhaps more than any other government agency, it has publicly struggled with the definition of Hispanic.

In one case the SBA found that Hispanic status depends on one's looks, self-identification and identification by others as Hispanic, and evidence that one has suffered discrimination because of being Hispanic. In two other cases, however, the SBA concluded that simply being of Hispanic origin is sufficient to claim Hispanic status.

The SBA's finding that Christine Combs was not Hispanic despite being bilingual and having Spanish grandparents was discussed in the Introduction. So was the SBA's conclusion that Steve Lynn qualified as Hispanic based solely on his Sephardic Jewish origins. Beyond those cases, in *Garza Telecommunications*,[60] an SBA official determined that two siblings whose mother was Hispanic were legally non-Hispanic whites because their birth certificates identified their color or race as white. On appeal, an administrative law judge reversed. The judge chided the SBA for suggesting being white and being Hispanic were mutually exclusive. The judge concluded that "whether an individual is white, black, or any other race bears no relationship to his or her ethnicity."[61] Once the SBA had found that the siblings' mother was Hispanic, it should necessarily have found that the siblings were also Hispanic.

The Federal Communications Commission also struggled with the question of who counted as Hispanic for minority preferences. One case raised the question of whether a radio station should get minority credit for hiring a general manager, W. Carlos O. Fox, whose paternal grandfather was born in Cuba.[62] Initially, an administrative law judge

60.   In re Application of Kist Corp., No. 620 MSBE-98-05-11-10, 1998 WL 847993.
61.   Ibid.
62.   99 F.C.C.2d 201, 1983 WL 183032 (1983).

denied minority credit, finding that Fox was not presumptively Hispanic because he:

- did not have a Spanish surname, nor did his Cuban grandfather;
- was not fluent in Spanish;
- only heard Spanish spoken occasionally in his home growing up;
- had no connection to the local Hispanic community;
- had a non-Hispanic mother;
- was born in the United States, as were his parents;
- had no immediate relatives living outside this country; and
- did not belong to any Hispanic organizations.

On appeal, a review panel split the baby. The panel concluded that Fox was Hispanic enough for the radio station to get a partial minority credit, but not Hispanic enough to get a full credit.

In another FCC case,[63] Highlands Broadcasting Company sought recognition as a minority-owned broadcaster. It claimed that its owner, Gilbert F. Wisdom, qualified as Hispanic because he had one Mexican great-grandparent; some knowledge of Spanish short of fluency; co-owned a vacation home in Tijuana with his ex-wife; and contributed to Mexican American civic activities.

An administrative law judge held that Wisdom did not qualify as Hispanic. The judge noted that Wisdom's surname was not Spanish; his Hispanic heritage was not evident from his appearance; he had no affiliation with any Hispanic group or activity; and, he did not read Hispanic periodicals.

On appeal, Highlands noted that Wisdom's claim that he was "Hispanic by blood and culture" was uncontested by the FCC. This, the

---

63.   In re Applications of Lone Cypress Radio Associates, Inc., 7 F.C.C. Rcd. 4403, 1992 WL 690184.

company argued, was enough for the FCC to recognize that Wisdom was Hispanic. The FCC's review board disagreed.

The board concluded that distant Hispanic ancestry and marginal ties to Mexico and the Spanish language were insufficient to support a Hispanic classification. The board added that while it "has credited proposals based on one-quarter Hispanic ancestry" it was not willing "to extend this precedent to a much remoter one-eighth relation claim."

The FCC also rejected a claim that a company, Capital City Community Interests, was entitled to a minority preference based on the Portuguese ancestry of one of the company's principals.[64] "Portuguese descent is not the same as Hispanic," the FCC ruled, "and persons of Portuguese descent are not entitled to any minority enhancement credit." The agency noted that EEOC employment rules exclude Portuguese Americans from their definition of Hispanic.

Controversy has also erupted over who qualifies as Hispanic for affirmative action in government employment. Following a notorious case in which two Boston firefighters lost their jobs for falsely claiming to be African American (see Chapter One), Boston launched a city-wide investigation of ethnic identity fraud in city agencies. Assertions of Hispanic status received particular scrutiny.

The city's fire department was bound by a 1976 legal settlement that required it to define Hispanic as people born in a Spanish-speaking country or raised in a Spanish-speaking household.[65] The city penalized several self-identified Hispanic firefighters who did not meet this definition.[66]

The Boston public school system threatened to fire two teachers from Spain who self-identified as Hispanic. According to a spokesperson, the school system followed EEOC guidelines for Hispanic status, which does not include Spain.[67] In common with other agencies bound by Directive 15, the EEOC's definition of Hispanic was "persons

---

64. In re Applications Capital City Community Interests, Inc., 1986 WL 292051.
65. Marantz, Steven and Hernandez, Peggy. , Oct. 23, 1988. "Defining Race a Sensitive, Elusive Task: Boston Hiring Probe Brings System Under Fire," *Boston Globe*.
66. Squires, Catherin R. 2007. *Dispatches from the Color Line: The Press and Multiracial America* (Albany: SUNY Press), 83-84.
67. Wen, Patricia. Oct. 19, 1988. "Schools on Lookout for Affirmative Action Abuses," *Boston Globe*.

of Mexican, Puerto Rican, Cuban, Central or South American origin, or other Spanish culture or origin." How the school system concluded that people from Spain were not of Spanish culture or origin was not explained.

The San Francisco Fire Department, meanwhile, faced a long and bitter controversy over the scope of its Hispanic classification.[68] In 1975, Thomas Santoro changed his ethnic designation with the fire department from white to Hispanic. Fifteen years later, a Mexican American colleague, Peter Roybal, learned that Santoro was on a list of Hispanics taking a promotion test. Roybal thought to himself, "Bull, this man has been a proud, loud Genoese Italian with no connection to the Hispanic community. I had to do something."[69]

Roybal filed a complaint. Santoro told fire department officials that his mother was born in Mexico. He produced a baptismal certificate stating that his mother, Josephine Ann Colla, had been born in Mexico and baptized a few days later in Hayward. The persistent Roybal, however, located a birth certificate stating that Santoro's mother was born in Hayward.

At a civil service commission hearing, Santoro claimed that the California birth certificate was not his mother's. He failed to persuade the commission, which ordered his classification be changed from Hispanic to white. The commission also launched a fraud investigation, but no punitive action was taken. Some of Santoro's colleagues started mockingly referring to him as Tom Sancholo, "cholo being Spanish slang for a stereotypical lowrider Latin street dude."[70]

Roybal also filed a complaint about another firefighter, Lieutenant Lawrence Giovacchini. After seventeen years in the department, Giovacchini petitioned to change his classification from white to Hispanic. Giovacchini's petition was granted because he proved that his mother's parents were born in Spain and that his family retained ties to Spanish culture.[71]

---

68. McCoy, Charles. "The Race to Get Ahead: Minority Impostors Take Advantage of Affirmative-Action Programs," *Albany Times Union*, Feb. 17, 1991.
69. Ibid.
70. Ibid.
71. Ibid.

Roybal, however, believed that only Latinos should receive Hispanic preferences. As for others of Spanish culture, Roybal commented, "I don't know what [Spanish] culture is, other than what I read in National Geographic. They live a totally white life."[72]

According to Roybal, "Larry Giovacchini, many times, to my face, has called me a 'beaner'" (a slur for "Mexican"). Another Mexican American firefighter added, "All his life he calls himself a proud Italian, he calls us beaners, and suddenly he decides he wants to be a beaner himself."[73]

"For someone to be an Italian for forty years and then become a Latino in the forty-first year is blatant opportunism," added Roybal.[74]

Giovacchini denied using the beaner slur but was otherwise unapologetic. "If the city wants to give me an advantage for being Hispanic, fine."[75] The city ultimately concluded that descent from Spanish immigrants qualified employees to be classified as Hispanic.

Another controversy in the San Francisco Fire Department involved Captain Alberto Da Cunha. De Cunha's parents were Portuguese residents of the colony of Macao in Asia, where he was raised. San Francisco did not recognize people of Portuguese descent as Hispanic, so the city classified Da Cunha as white. In 1988, he applied to have his ethnic status changed to Asian.

His bosses accepted the application, but the civil service commission rejected it. According to Da Cunha, "At the time, there were a few minorities at the top.... I figured I'd let somebody else decide if I was a minority or not." He claimed that his peers and bosses encouraged him to claim minority status to "make the ethnic balance of the captains look better."[76]

New York City has had similar employment controversies. Some police officers who had checked the white box when hired sought to change their status to Hispanic to improve their prospects for promotion. A police spokesperson responded that applicants for a change in ethnic classification must present proof of ethnicity that meets federal

---

72.   Kirp, David L. Dec. 12, 1990. "Ethnic Purity," *Baltimore Sun.*
73.   McCoy, "The Race to Get Ahead."
74.   "Ethnic Fraud at S.F. Fire Department," *San Francisco Examiner,* Dec. 2, 1990.
75.   McCoy, "The Race to Get Ahead."
76.   Ibid.

EEOC standards—which is odd because no such standards existed. The police department stated it would consider, among other things, birth certificates and parents' birth records.[77]

One NYPD officer, John Lagrua, wound up in court after trying to change his status from white to Hispanic based on his Gibraltarian ancestry.[78] To substantiate his claim of Hispanic identity, Lagrua asserted that his mother was born in Gibraltar and that her parents' grandparents were of Spanish origin.

The department ultimately refused to reclassify Lagrua. A state court upheld this decision. The court concluded that Gibraltarians, even if they have distant Spanish ancestry, are not Hispanic. The court reasoned that "Gibraltar is and has been under British rule since 1718; the culture there is mixed, the official language is English, and the law is based on English Common law. Although Spanish is widely spoken, the Gibraltarian way of life is predominantly British."[79] An appellate court affirmed the ruling and the reasoning.

Another NYPD case, *Blake v. Sanchez*,[80] involved a police officer, George Sanchez, who had classified himself as Hispanic when hired by the police department. His parents were Jamaicans of African descent who had moved to Costa Rica before his birth. He spoke fluent Spanish and was a member of both the Hispanic and black police officer organizations. He took a promotion test, scoring high enough to be promoted if he were classified as black but not as Hispanic. Sanchez therefore asked the police department to reclassify him as Black. The Deputy Police Commissioner for Equal Opportunity denied this request because "no mistake in his current (self) classification" had been found. Sanchez appealed. The court ruled against him, noting that Sanchez originally classified himself as Hispanic as an outgrowth of a settlement of a class-action lawsuit regarding cutoff scores, "part of the very process whose result he now seeks to avoid...." In these circumstances, the court concluded, the police department's "refusal to grant reclassification was necessary to protect the integrity of the administrative process."

77.   Kolbert, Elizabeth. Dec. 6, 1985. "White Officers Seek Minority Status," *New York Times*, Dec. 6, 1985.
78.   Lagrua v. Ward, 136 Misc.2d 655 (N.Y. Sup. Ct. 1987).
79.   Ibid.
80.   155 A.D.2d 364 (App. Div. 1989).

United States v. Brennan involved a settlement of a class-action discrimination claim against the New York City Board of Education. As part of the settlement, the defendants agreed to give preferential benefits to members of certain minority groups, including Hispanics.[81] This raised the question of who counted as Hispanic. A federal judge held that anyone with "an ancestral place of origin" in a Spanish-speaking country could assert Hispanic status. The Second Circuit Court of Appeals agreed.

In *Peightal v. Metropolitan Dade County,*[82] Peightal claimed that Dade County, Florida's affirmative action preferences for Hispanic applicants for firefighter positions were both over- and underinclusive. Peightal argued that the program was overinclusive because it favored white European Spaniards with no significant cultural, linguistic, or physical differences from non-Hispanic white people.

Peightal's brief alleged that the county's plan allowed persons to qualify for a "Hispanic" preference by tracing a single grandparent to a "Spanish culture." Indeed, the plan allowed people to self-classify as Hispanic if they "culturally and linguistically identified" with Spanish-speaking countries.

Peightal also argued that the program was underinclusive. Once the program included Spaniards, he argued, it was arbitrary to exclude other Caucasian groups at least as susceptible to ethnic and cultural discrimination, such as Greeks, Italians, Portuguese, Jews, Israelis, and Iranians.

The Eleventh Circuit Court of Appeals rejected the plaintiffs' arguments. The court acknowledged that granting employment preferences "to a light-skinned descendant of Spanish grandparents who speaks no Spanish and has no individual cultural ties to an American Spanish community or to Spain" would be problematic. The Dade County program, however, required that a claim of Hispanic status be accompanied by "strong visible indication that the person culturally and linguistically identify" with the Hispanic community. What this means in practice is unclear, but it was enough to satisfy the court.

---

81.   United States v. New York City Bd. of Educ., 448 F. Supp. 2d 397, 423 (E.D.N.Y. 2006), *aff'd*, United States v. Brennan, 650 F.3d. 65, 70 (2d Cir. 2011).
82.   940 F.2d 1394 (11th Cir. 1991).

Beyond that, the court rejected the contention that strict judicial scrutiny applies to the scope of government affirmative action categories. The court instead applied the weakest constitutional test, the rational basis test. The Dade County program passed the test because the county "rationally" limited it "to those minority groups in the local workforce that are most in need of remedial efforts."[83]

Jana–Rock Constr., Inc. v. New York State Dep't of Econ. Dev.,[84] raised the issue of whether a state may use different definitions of minority groups for affirmative action purposes than the federal government uses. In 1987, the New York State Department of Economic Development certified Jana–Rock Construction as a Hispanic-owned company eligible for minority business enterprise status and recertified it thereafter.[85] Rocco Luiere Jr., a Spanish American, owned 75 percent of the company.

In 2003, however, state officials notified Jana–Rock that it was revoking this status. Luiere, being of direct Iberian lineage, did not come within the state's definition of "Hispanic." A state administrative law judge recommended that Jana–Rock's state certification be renewed and that the state waive its definition of Hispanic. The judge relied in part on the federal government's certification of the company as a minority contractor.

State officials rejected the ALJ's recommendation. They argued that the state tailored its MBE program to benefit those groups that had faced significant discrimination in New York's construction market. The officials asserted that they had no reason to believe that Spanish Americans had suffered such discrimination.[86]

Jana–Rock sued in federal court, alleging that people of Spanish descent were a "suspect class." The company argued that this meant that New York could only exclude people of Spanish descent from its MBE program if the state showed a "compelling interest" in doing so. Like the Eleventh Circuit, however, the court held that the weak rational basis test applied to the scope of affirmative action categories. New

83.   Ibid., 1409-10.
84.   438 F.3d 195 (2d Cir. 2006).
85.   Ibid., 199, 201-02.
86.   Ibid.

York's distinction between people directly descended from residents of Spain and Hispanics from the Americas passed that test.[87]

The court opined that Spanish Americans are less likely than Latinos to have "visibly discernible 'Hispanic' characteristics" such as "skin color, language or a Spanish surname." (The court did not explain why it had the counterintuitive belief that people from Spain are less likely than Latinos to have a Spanish surname.) Spanish Americans, the court added, ordinarily do not have "strong visible indications of cultural and linguistic identification with the Hispanic community that leads to stereotyping." Luiere presented no evidence that he was dark-skinned, spoke Spanish, or had a Spanish surname. In the absence of Luiere having "discernable Hispanic characteristics" it was "obviously" rational for New York to deny him Hispanic status, the court ruled.[88]

The decision was upheld on appeal.[89] The Second Circuit concluded that the law passed the rational basis test and therefore was constitutional. The court speculated that the federal government could have concluded that on a national level all Hispanics faced discrimination, while New York found that Spanish Americans did not face significant discrimination in that state.

In *Builders Association of Greater Chicago v. County of Cook*,[90] the Seventh Circuit Court of Appeals held that the government must treat Americans of Spanish and Portuguese descent the same as non-Hispanic whites. The court held that Cook County, Illinois' MBE program was unconstitutional because it defined Hispanic to include Portuguese and Spanish immigrants and their descendants.

According to the court, "The concern with discrimination on the basis of Hispanic ethnicity is limited to discrimination against people of South or Central American origin." Such individuals "often are racially distinct from persons of direct European origin because their ancestors include blacks or Indians or both." By contrast, "there is nothing to differentiate immigrants from Spain or Portugal from immigrants from Italy, Greece, or other southern European countries so far as a history of discrimination in the United States is concerned."

---

87. Jana-Rock Const., Inc. v. New York State Dept. of Econ. Dev., 2004 WL 5550699 (N.D.N.Y.).
88. Ibid, 19.
89. 438 F.3d at 205-06.
90. 256 F.3d 642 (7th Cir. 2001).

*   *   *   *

The "Hispanic or Latino" category is an anomaly in the modern American law of race. It's the only category in which someone can be both white and have legal nonwhiteness. It's officially an ethnic, not a racial, designation. In practice, however, Hispanic/Latino is often treated as a race. And but for the opposition of the Trump administration, Hispanic/Latino would now be listed as a racial category on the census.[91]

Hispanic status generally rests on self-reporting. However, when such status is challenged, an agency or court must rule on the petitioner's Hispanic status. The boundaries of the Hispanic/Latino classification have proven especially porous and ill-defined, with decision makers arbitrarily including or excluding individuals with Spanish-speaking ancestry.

The Hispanic category developed out of categories created to monitor racial discrimination against Americans of Spanish-speaking descent who were perceived to be nonwhite, especially dark-skinned Mexican Americans and Puerto Ricans. If Hispanic people are often subject to discrimination because people perceive them to be nonwhite, collecting general statistics to help identify such discrimination makes sense. This is true even if a minority of Hispanics will typically be perceived as white and not be subject to that discrimination, or at least subject to much less of it.

Some scholars and activists have suggested that the Hispanic/Latino category should be replaced with a narrower category, such as Indigenous Latino/Mestizo. This adjustment would allow dark-skinned Latinos of primarily indigenous background to self-identify as members of a racial minority. Other people with Spanish-speaking ancestry would identify themselves as white, black, or occasionally Asian.

There seems, however, to be little appetite for such change in the government. Hispanic groups that have built their political power based on their diverse, multiracial constituents being perceived as having a common Hispanic identity are even less likely to pursue such a reform.

---

91. Gomez, *Inventing Latinos*, 162–63.

CHAPTER THREE
The Borderlands of Legal Whiteness:
Italian, Polish, Jewish, Armenian, and Cajun Americans

mmigrants from Eastern and Southern Europe began arriving in the United States in large numbers toward the end of the nineteenth century. Most were Catholic, while some were Eastern Orthodox Christians or Jews. They faced substantial discrimination because of their non-Protestant religions, their ethnicity, and, in some cases their dark complexions. Responding to popular sentiment, in 1924 Congress enacted a law that drastically reduced immigration from those parts of Europe.

Americans of Southern and Eastern European origin continued to face substantial ethnoreligious discrimination from white Protestants for several more decades. Today, few Americans even notice that we have a Catholic president who defeated two prominent Jewish candidates in the Democratic primaries. We also have six Catholics and two Jews out of the nine justices on the Supreme Court, a Jewish senate majority leader, and a Catholic speaker of the House of Representatives.

It's easy to forget that in 1937, only 46 percent of Americans surveyed said they would be willing to vote for a Jew for president. When John F. Kennedy ran for president as a Democrat in 1960, millions of Protestants who were otherwise staunch Democrats refused to vote for him because he was Catholic—and millions of Catholics who had voted for Republican Dwight Eisenhower in 1956 voted for JFK for the same reason.

Despite the discrimination and hostility faced by some European immigrant groups, government at all levels classified individuals of European descent as white. Americans of full European ancestry were identified as white on the US census; were placed in whites-only units in the armed forces; attended whites-only schools and used other whites-only facilities in the Jim Crow South; and in states that banned interracial marriage, were permitted to marry white people and could not marry members of nonwhite groups.

The 1964 Civil Rights Act banned religious and national origin discrimination in employment. Representatives of white ethnic groups hoped that the government would use the act to combat discrimination against their constituents. These representatives were quickly disappointed; government agencies focused almost all their enforcement energy on combatting discrimination against African Americans. These agencies did not gather statistics on religious and national origin discrimination to identify possible violations of the '64 act and other antidiscrimination laws.

When affirmative action programs commenced, minority groups of European origin were not included. Catholics of Eastern and Southern European descent often resented that other Catholic ethnic groups, notably Mexican Americans and later Cuban Americans (see Chapter Two), received attention from civil rights agencies, but Italians, Poles, and others did not.

Some ethnic organizations tried to have their constituents classified as official ethnic minority groups akin to Hispanics. Complaints of government indifference to discrimination against white ethnics were amplified by politicians with large white ethnic constituencies.

In a 1969 speech on the House floor, Rep. Roman Pucinski of Illinois argued that the government should expand its record keeping to keep track of possible discrimination against "Americans of Italian descent, of Polish descent, or any of the other Slavic groups, of Irish descent, of English descent, of German descent, or of any other ethnic origin."[1] During a 1970 committee hearing, Pucinski interrogated

---

1.   *Congressional Record* 115, Dec. 12, 1969, 39,062-63.

Equal Employment Opportunity Commission (EEOC) Director Irving Kantor about the agency's failure to maintain statistics on employment of white ethnics.[2]

At the time, the federal government was promoting racial integration in fields traditionally dominated by white ethnics, such as unionized construction jobs in the Northeast. This led to political pressure to increase employment opportunities for white ethnics elsewhere.[3] The Department of Labor issued proposed regulations in December 1971 that would have required federal contractors to remedy the "underutilization" of Catholics, Jews, and others in executive and management positions.[4]

The proposed regulations faced significant resistance. Critics within the Nixon administration argued that white ethnics were successfully assimilating into American life and therefore were not in need of special government attention. The proposed regulations, opponents argued, would distract agencies from combatting discrimination against racial minorities more isolated from the mainstream, especially African Americans. Critics also argued that if implemented, the proposed rules would result in invasions of privacy as employers sought to determine their employees' religion.

Nixon officials also worried that the proposed rule invited vexatious litigation and would encourage ethnic and religious organizations to unduly pressure big companies to hire their constituents.[5] Employers objected for the same reasons, adding corporate lobbying heft to internal Nixon administration opposition.

By the time the proposed regulations became law in revised form in 1973, administration officials had deleted the language about underutilization of members of white ethnic groups. The final regulations also did not require government contractors to collect and

---

2.   See Equal Employment Opportunity Enforcement Procedures: Hearings Before the Gen. Subcomm. on Labor of the H. Comm. on Education & Labor, 91st Cong. (1970), 205-15.
3.   Skrentny, John D. "Policy-Elite Perceptions and Social Movement Success: Understanding Variations in Group Inclusion in Affirmative Action," *American Journal of Sociology* 111, No. 6 (May 2006): 1782.
4.   36 Fed. Reg. 25165 (Dec. 29, 1971).
5.   Skrentny, "Policy-Elite Perceptions," 1782-84.

report ethnic and religious data about their employees. Contractors were left to police themselves.[6]

Advocates for white ethnics, however, refused to drop the issue. At a House of Representatives subcommittee hearing in 1974, two Congressmen, Democrat Mario Biaggi and Republican Jack Kemp, grilled EEOC chairman John Powell about the commission's approach to combatting discrimination against white ethnics:

> Mr. Biaggi: I keep hearing Mr. Powell saying Spanish surnamed [as examples of victims of discrimination needing redress]. The thought that comes to my mind is why Spanish surnames and not Italian surnames?

> Mr. Kemp: Polish surnames. What ethnic groups are included in this heterogeneous society?...

> Mr. Biaggi: Under the law, form EEO-6 [regarding staff at institutions of higher education] requires the administrator to break down statistics and it goes down to "(a) black, (b) white, including Pakistanians and East Indians," and you come to (c) Spanish surnamed, and why was that distinction made?

Powell responded that African Americans and the Spanish surnamed complained the most of discrimination. Biaggi retorted that whites facing discrimination based on ethnicity believed that the government did not care about them, so they did not bother reporting discrimination to authorities. Powell rejoined by highlighting the special problems African Americans faced with employment discrimination. He did not address the Spanish surnames versus Italian surnames query.[7]

---

6. 38 Fed. Reg. 1932 (Jan. 19, 1973); 41 CFR § 60-50.2 (1997).
7. Federal Higher Education Programs Institutional Eligibility (Part 2A): Hearings before the Special Subcommittee on Education of the H. Comm. on Education & Labor, 93rd Cong., 1974, 25–29.

Advocates for white ethnic interests pressed on. In April 1979, a convention of the National Federation of American Ethnic Groups adopted a resolution requesting that additional (white) groups be eligible for affirmative action.[8] A few months later, Congress directed the US Commission on Civil Rights to prepare a report to Congress about "denials of equal protection...involving Americans who are members of eastern- and southern-European ethnic groups."[9]

The commission produced the report in December 1979.[10] The report documented past and present discrimination against white ethnics. It suggested that the government collect data about which groups were being negatively affected by discrimination and to what extent. The relevant government agencies ignored these recommendations.

Meanwhile, Italian and Polish American leaders complained to the Labor Department that their constituents remained unofficially barred from high-level corporate jobs. Their pleas for assistance were resisted by the department.[11]

Italian and Polish groups also joined forces to lobby the Office of Federal Contract Compliance (OFCC) to address discrimination against white ethnics. The OFCC director rejected their request. He commented, "I don't think [discrimination against such groups] is as much a problem as is discrimination against black people...Hispanics, and...women in this country."[12]

Organizations representing Italian and Polish Americans also made specific pleas for their constituents to be considered separately from other whites in antidiscrimination and affirmative action policy.

---

8.   US Commission on Civil Rights, "Civil Rights Issues of Euro-ethnic Americans in the United States: Opportunities and Challenges" (1979), 493 note 2.
9.   Pub. L. No. 96-81, 93 Stat. 642 (1979).
10. "Civil Rights Issues of Euro-ethnic Americans."
11. Skrentny, "Policy-Elite Perceptions," 1785.
12. Skrentny, John D. 2002. The Minority Rights Revolution (Cambridge: Harvard University Press), 292.

Italian Americans

Despite some sloppy claims to the contrary, Italian Americans have always been considered white by law.[13] They have, however, historically faced significant anti-Catholic discrimination. Many also faced prejudice because of their relatively dark complexions, a product of the fact that most Italian Americans are of southern Italian and especially Sicilian ancestry.[14] Italian immigrants sometimes faced organized violence, most infamously when a mob in New Orleans lynched eleven men in 1891.

President Benjamin Harrison declared a national Columbus Day holiday the following year. The idea was to help Italian immigrants integrate into American society by officially recognizing a figure associated with Italy as a national hero. The development of Columbus Day as a national holiday thereafter was a product of efforts by Italian immigrants and their descendants to be recognized as full-fledged Americans.

By the early 1920s, anti-Italian stereotypes had proliferated and become entrenched in American society. Italian Americans were associated with organized crime. The Sacco and Vanzetti trial of 1921 associated Italian immigrants with violent anarchism. Anti-Italian sentiment was sufficiently high that the 1924 immigration law almost entirely barred immigration from Italy.

Italy's participation in World War II as an enemy of the United States fed negative perceptions of Italian Americans. Many Italian Americans born in Italy, including naturalized American citizens, faced restrictions such as curfews during the war.[15] Not even being the parent of a national hero protected immigrants from such restrictions. Along

13.   For rebuttal of a sloppy claim, see Bernstein, David. *The Weakness of the "Whiteness" Literature*, Reason: The Volokh Conspiracy, May 31, 2019. https://reason.com/2019/05/31/the-weakness-of-the-whiteness-literature. Guglielmo argues that contrary to the whiteness literature, Italian immigrants enjoyed white status in areas such as citizenship, housing, jobs, the military, schools, and politics. Guglielmo, Thomas A. 2003. *White on Arrival: Italians, Race, Color, and Power in Chicago, 1890-1945* (New York: Oxford University Press); Fox, Cybelle and Guglielmo, Thomas A. September 2012. "Defining America's Racial Boundaries: Blacks, Mexicans, and European Immigrants, 1890-1945," *American Journal of Sociology* 118, No. 2: 327-379.

14.   Cornnell, William J. and Gardaphe, Fred, eds. 2011. *Anti-Italianism: Essays on a Prejudice* (New York: Palgrave MacMillan); LaGumina, Salvatore J. 1973. *WOP!--A Documentary History of Anti-Italian Discrimination in the United States* (New York: Straight Arrow Books).

15.   Taylor, David A. Feb. 2, 2017. "During World War II, the U.S. Saw Italian-Americans as a Threat to Homeland Security," https://www.smithsonianmag.com/history/italian-americans-were-considered-enemy-aliens-world-war-ii-180962021.

with other Italian immigrants who had never naturalized, baseball star Joe DiMaggio's father was deemed to be an enemy alien. The government seized his fishing boat, and authorities banned him from going to Fisherman's Wharf in San Francisco, where he had worked for decades.

When the 1964 Civil Rights Act was enacted, Italian American activists hoped the government would combat persistent discrimination against Italian Americans in elite Protestant strongholds like elite law firms, banks, insurance companies, and universities. A Census Bureau study published in 1969 showed that Italian Americans were near the bottom of the American ethnic hierarchy by almost every socioeconomic measure.[16] Significant discrimination against Italians in white-collar executive positions continued into the late 1970s.[17]

The Italian American population of approximately nine million people was concentrated in the New York City metropolitan area. The massive City University of New York system was notorious for discriminating in faculty hiring. For example, in 1960 the New York State Human Rights Commission found extensive anti-Italian and anti-Catholic discrimination by the predominately Protestant faculty at Queens College.[18]

In April 1967, Vincent Trapani, president of the New York Federation of Italian-American Democratic Organizations, requested that the EEOC collect statistics from employers on all minority groups. These groups would include Italian Americans, Polish Americans, German Americans, Irish Americans, and Jewish Americans. He pointed out that the 1964 Civil Rights Act prohibited discrimination based on national origin. The EEOC would be unable to enforce that prohibition if the agency failed to collect relevant data.[19]

In a 1977 editorial, Chairman of the National Italian American Foundation Jeno F. Paulucci argued that Italians should be eligible for affirmative action.[20] But with no one collecting data on Italian Amer-

---

16. Skrentny, *Minority Rights*, 309.
17. US Commission on Civil Rights, "Civil Rights Issues of Euro-ethnic Americans in the United States: Opportunities and Challenges" 1979, 492-99.
18. Barbaro, Fred. Autumn 1974. "Ethnic Affirmation, Affirmative Action, and the Italian-American," *Italian Americana* 1: 51-52; Calandra, John D. 1978. "A Report: A History of Italian-American Discrimination at City University of New York" (New York Senate), 3.
19. Skrentny, *Minority Rights*, 282.
20. "For Affirmative Action for Some Whites," *New York Times*, Nov. 26, 1977.

ican employment, there was no way to show the sort of "underrepresentation" that would facilitate recognition of Italian Americans as an official minority group.

One Italian American took his effort to secure minority status to court. In the mid-1970s, Philip DiLeo sued the University of Colorado Law School, demanding that his application be included with minority applicants in the school's "Special Academic Assistance Program" (SAAP).

DiLeo argued that he was "a product of slum schools" and had been "educationally, socially, and economically disadvantaged" because he grew up in New York's Little Italy to poor, uneducated parents. DiLeo applied for admission to the law school through the SAAP for the entering classes of 1973 and 1974. The law school rejected his applications because it limited SAAP eligibility to African Americans, Native Americans, Mexican Americans, and Puerto Ricans.[21]

DiLeo's lawsuit was novel because he only challenged the government's decisions about which groups it deemed eligible for affirmative action preferences, not the preferences themselves. If the lawsuit had proceeded to trial, the law school would have had to explain why it chose certain groups for preferences and not others. The Colorado Supreme Court, however, dismissed the case. The court asserted that DiLeo could not show that he would have been admitted to the law school if SAAP did not exist. He therefore could not show that he suffered an injury within the power of the court to address.

A dissenting justice would have ruled in DiLeo's favor. The dissent argued that "when the Law School designates a minority group, the members of which it wishes to prefer, it may not designate that group by reference to its racial characteristics." Because the law school excluded DiLeo from consideration due to his race, the SAAP program was unconstitutional as applied to him.[22] A gruesome aside: in 2009, DiLeo, who never did attend law school, shot his wife, son, and himself in a well-publicized murder-suicide.

Italian Americans have officially qualified for affirmative action in one venue, the City University of New York. As noted previously,

---

21.   DiLeo v. Bd. of Regents of Univ. of Colorado, 196 Colo. 216, 218-19 (1978).
22.   Ibid., 224 (Erickson, J., dissenting).

for decades CUNY discriminated against Catholic faculty in general and Italian Americans in particular. In the 1960s, several Italian American faculty members won discrimination complaints against CUNY's Queens College. These professors later organized an Italian American faculty association that lobbied for the hiring of additional Italian Americans.

Increasing the number of Italian American faculty faced two major obstacles. First, CUNY had launched an aggressive affirmative action program to recruit African American and Hispanic professors. This left fewer available slots for Italian Americans. Second, New York City experienced a budget crisis in 1975, forcing it to lay off CUNY faculty by seniority. Italian American faculty absorbed a disproportionate share of the layoffs because they tended to be recent hires. And unlike recent African American and Latino hires, Italian Americans were not shielded from layoffs to help the CUNY meet its affirmative action goals.

Seeing this dynamic, Italian American faculty argued that Italian Americans should be recognized as an official minority eligible for affirmative action at CUNY. They had a plausible case; in addition to strong evidence of longstanding discrimination at CUNY, advocates noted that Italian Americans were significantly underrepresented on the faculty relative to the percentage of PhDs awarded in New York City to Italian Americans. Moreover, the percentage of Italian American faculty at CUNY lagged that of private university faculties in the city.

Italian American politicians supported the faculty's demands. CUNY's chancellor Robert Kibbe could not ignore the politicians; in the wake of New York City's financial crisis in 1975, he needed all the political support he could get. Kibbe announced in December 1976 that CUNY would recognize Italian American as an affirmative action category. This ensured that the university system would keep track of Italian American faculty and student numbers.[23]

This concession does not imply to have been entirely sincere. Former CUNY general counsel Robert E. Diaz explained that "[Kibbe]

---

23. Letter from Robert J. Kibbee, Chancellor, City College of New York, to CUNY Council of Presidents (Dec. 9, 1976), in Kirillova, Liana. 2017. "The Ironies of Whiteness: Italian Americans Pursue Affirmative Action in the City University of New York, 1976–2015," *Essays in History* 50. http://www.essaysin2history.com/the-ironies-of-whiteness-italian-americans-pursue-affirmative-action-in-the-city-university-of-new-york-1976-2015.

buckled to community pressure. He figured that by keeping records, he could demonstrate that there is no discrimination against Italian Americans at CUNY."

Kibbe later claimed that his directive on affirmative action "was not a recognition that discrimination existed in CUNY. It was a means by which the University could legitimately and systematically collect data regarding Italian Americans to determine whether or not discrimination existed."[24]

Italian American faculty and their supporters resolved to continue pressuring CUNY. They sought to ensure that the new Italian American affirmative action category was more than symbolic.

The result was a series of studies and legislative hearings on discrimination against Italian Americans at CUNY. These in turn resulted in the formation of special academic programs focusing on Italian American heritage and the reaffirmation of the Italian American affirmative action category by subsequent CUNY chancellors. Over time, though, CUNY's commitment to assisting Italian Americans did become primarily symbolic.

Meanwhile, on another civil rights front, a series of puzzling court decisions held that Italian Americans are not a "cognizable racial group" under a legal doctrine known as the *Batson* rule. In most jurisdictions, attorneys in criminal trials can exclude some potential jurors from the jury without stating a reason. Prosecutors would sometimes exclude all African American jurors from a case with a black defendant. *Batson*, decided by the Supreme Court in 1985, forbids prosecutors from excluding jurors based on race.

Some courts have held that *Batson* applies to racial groups but not national origin groups, including Italians. That conclusion is strange. The underlying constitutional provision, the Fourteenth Amendment's equal protection clause, prohibits discrimination based on race and national origin.

---

24. Collison, Michele N-K. Nov. 24, 1993. "A Tangled Tale of Affirmative Action," *Chronicle of Higher Education.*

Most courts that have considered the issue have held that *Batson* does not protect Italian Americans.[25] In other words, Italian American defendants cannot successfully claim discrimination if a prosecutor rejects potential jurors with Italian-sounding surnames.

For example, the Third Circuit of Court Appeals rejected a *Batson* claim by Italian American defendants. The court found that the defendants had not presented adequate evidence that people with Italian surnames "either have been or are currently subjected to discriminatory treatment," including with respect to jury service.[26]

In a subsequent case, the Third Circuit contended it did not know how to define "Italian-American":

> Is an "Italian-American" one who came from Italy and became a United States citizen? Or is it one who is a first—or second—or third generation "Italian-American?" How much "ethnicity" is enough? What of the woman who has no Italian heritage but bears an Italian name because she took the name of her Italian—or "Italian-American"—husband? And, how is one to even begin to know whether a man or woman is "Italian-American" when his or her name is ethnically-neutral or...when an ethnically-neutral name has been changed to an Italian name?[27]

Similar issues arise when defining "Hispanic" in *Batson* litigation. Yet courts treat Hispanics as a cognizable racial group. Indeed, sometimes courts simply assume this without any discussion.[28] A Maryland court was even willing to resort to dubious anthropology in defining "Hispanicness." The court suggested that "visual observations, along with other criteria, such as surnames, language, etc.," make a potential juror Hispanic.[29]

---

25. E.g., United States v. Campione, 942 F.2d 429 (7th Cir. 1991); United States v. Angiulo, 847 F.2d 956 (1st Cir. 1988).
26. United States v. Di Pasquale, 864 F.2d 271, 277 (3d Cir. 1988) (quoting United States v. Bucci, 839 F.2d 825, 833 (1st Cir. 1988)).
27. Rico v. Leftridge-Byrd, 340 F.3d 178, 185 (3d Cir. 2003).
28. E.g., United States v. Alvarez-Ulloa, 784 F.3d 558, 566 (9th Cir. 2015).
29. Mejia v. State, 616 A.2d 356 (Md. 1992).

The salient distinction between Hispanics and Italians for *Batson* purposes seems to be that Hispanics, unlike Italians, are recognized by the government as an official minority group.[30] Official recognition provides courts with an objective indication that Hispanics face significant discrimination.

By contrast, courts in cases involving Italian Americans typically require defendants to prove that Italian Americans are regularly subject to discriminatory treatment. Criminal defendants have mostly been unable to persuade courts that anti-Italian bias meets this standard.[31]

Two courts, however, have held that Italian American defendants come within *Batson*'s protections. A New York State court concluded that *Batson* covers all national origin groups, including Italians.[32] The federal Second Circuit Court of Appeals found that *Batson* applies to "Americans of Italian descent." Italian Americans, the court stated, share a common experience and culture, often share the same religious and culinary practices, often have identifiable surnames, and have been subject to stereotyping, invidious ethnic humor, and discrimination."[33]

Polish Americans

Polish Americans have mostly assimilated into the general white population. This was much less true in the 1960s and '70s, when distinctly Polish neighborhoods in cities like New York and Chicago were still common.

Like other Eastern and Southern European Catholic groups, Poles had faced significant discrimination. The 1924 immigration law strictly capped immigration from Poland. WASP-dominated corporations, law firms, and other elite institutions excluded Poles already in the US from their institutions. As late as 1972, Polish Americans were overwhelmingly concentrated in blue-collar jobs.[34]

---

30.   People v. Trevino, 704 P.2d 719, 726 (Cal. 1985).
31.   E.g., United States v. Marino, 277 F.3d 11 (1st Cir. 2002); United States v. Campione, 942 F.2d 429 (7th Cir. 1991); United States v. Angiulo, 847 F.2d 956 (1st Cir. 1988).
32.   People v. Rambersed, 649 N.Y.S. 2d 640, 642 (2d Cir. 1996).
33.   United States v. Biaggi, 853 F.2d 89 (1988).
34.   Skrentny, *Minority Rights*, 309.

Because of this longstanding history of discrimination, in 1968 a Polish American organization urged the EEOC to add a category of "Polonians" to the EEO-1 form used by government contractors to track minority hiring. The agency refused. If the agency recognized Polish Americans as a minority, one EEOC official asked, "where do we put Italians, Yugoslavs, Greeks, etc., who are sure to want to be separately identified?"[35]

Affirmative action started to become institutionalized in the 1970s. The leading Polish American organization, the Polish American Congress (PAC), advocated that Polish Americans be eligible for minority preferences.

PAC commissioned a 1976 study that found that Poles and Italians were underrepresented in Illinois state government and major Chicago corporations.[36] Among other things, the study found that although individuals of Polish descent comprised 20 percent of Chicago residents, of 106 major corporations headquartered in Chicago, 102 had no Polish directors, and ninety-seven had no Polish officers.

PAC Executive Director Leonard Walentynowicz persuaded the federal Office and Management and Budget to adopt Circular A-46 on May 12, 1977. This authorized the government to collect data on the hiring of various white ethnic groups for federal jobs.[37] This authorization had little practical effect, however.

That same year, Walentynowicz testified before the federal Civil Service Commission.[38] He argued that the commission's affirmative action plan improperly favored some minority groups over others—such as Polish Americans—without justification.

Walentynowicz questioned why the commission favored providing preferences for white Hispanics but not for members other white

35. Ibid., 281–82.
36. Oversight Hearings on Federal Enforcement of Equal Employment Opportunity Laws (Part 3): Hearings Before the Subcomm. on Equal Opportunities of the House Committee on Education & Labor, 94th Cong. 354 (1976).
37. Skrentny, Minority Rights, 294-95.
38. Statement of Leonard F. Walentynowicz, Exec. Dir., Polish American Congress, to the United States Civil Service Commission, Dec. 5, 1977, in United States Commission on Civil Rights, Civil Rights Issues of Euro-ethnic Americans in the United States: Opportunities and Challenges (Washington, D.C.: Government Printing Office, 1979), 390-95.

ethnic groups with below-average socioeconomic standing. He noted that unlike the vast majority of Polish Americans, many Hispanics had recently immigrated to the US and therefore might never have been subject to ethnic discrimination by their fellow Americans.

Also in 1977, Walentynowicz filed a friend-of-the-court brief on PAC's behalf in the *Bakke* affirmative action case pending before the Supreme Court. The brief argued that quotas for nonwhite minority groups in university admissions were unconstitutional.[39]

PAC's brief urged the Supreme Court to consider "whether there is a substantial difference between a Black being called a 'Nigger' and a Polish American being called a 'Pollack'...; whether the lack of recognition of Blacks and Latins in senior levels of corporate management is more serious than the lack of recognition of Polish and Italian Americans." PAC, the brief concluded, "believe[s] that we will never achieve true equality unless we recognize that America is also more than black and white, male and female, Hispanic and non-Hispanic, and part of that 'more' is us."

The brief reflected a broader resentment among many white ethnics against the Protestant-dominated establishment. White ethnics who had themselves faced discrimination and were only starting to integrate fully into the American mainstream thought that they were unfairly being asked to sacrifice their interests to help members of other minority groups. The brief asked rhetorically, "Why are 'Whites' who never practiced discrimination, but fought for and championed equality, and who themselves suffered discrimination obliged to continue to suffer simply because other Whites practiced racial discrimination?" (Despite the brief's protestations, the notion that white ethnics had never practiced discrimination against blacks is absurd.)

Justice Lewis Powell, who wrote the controlling opinion in *Bakke*, found quotas to be unconstitutional but allowed the use of race and ethnicity in university admissions to enhance "diversity." Powell quoted Justice William O. Douglas as objecting to quotas for "selected minority groups" as "fraught with...dangers, for one must immediately deter-

---

39.   See Brief of the Polish American Congress et al. as *Amici Curiae*, Regents of Univ. of California v. Bakke, 438 U.S. 265 (1978) (No. 76-811), 1977 WL 187975.

mine which groups are to receive such favored treatment." If a university included only certain minority groups, "then Norwegians and Swedes, Poles and Italians, Puerto Ricans and Hungarians, and all other groups which form this diverse Nation would have just complaints."[40]

Powell concluded, however, that the "just" objections of the non-favored groups would disappear if a school indulged only in preferences based on race and ethnicity but not quotas. Powell apparently assumed that such preferences would only be pursued in the context of a general quest for students with diverse backgrounds, which would include white ethnics.

In 1978, Walentynowicz wrote to EEOC Commissioner Eleanor Norton. He requested that the agency collect data on white ethnics so that discrimination against them could be more easily identified.[41] Walentynowicz also testified before the US Civil Rights Commission in 1979. Representing the PAC, he made essentially the same plea for improved federal data collection on employment of white minority groups.[42]

Walentynowicz noted that while some people dismissed Polish Americans' discrimination claims because they are of European origin, the same is true of people from Spain, who are included in the Hispanic category. Polish Americans had no data available to show discrimination in the corporate world, he added, because the government only collected data regarding official minorities. Walentynowicz suggested that the government could collect employment data for Polish Americans without making them eligible for affirmative action.

Walentynowicz objected that the SBA's Section 8(a) program provided presumptive disadvantaged status for members of designated minority groups but required members of European subgroups to provide evidence that their group suffered discrimination. "How," he asked rhetorically, "can a small businessman, such as an Italian, Ukrainian or what have you, spend money he doesn't have to collect the

---

40.   Bakke, 438 U.S. 265, 297 n.37 (1978).
41.   United States Commission on Civil Rights. 1979. *Civil Rights Issues of Euro-ethnic Americans in the United States: Opportunities and Challenges* 444-47 (Washington, DC: Government Printing Office).
42.   Ibid., 379-86 (statement of Leonard F. Walentynowicz, Exec. Dir., Polish American Congress).

data to provide it? So it's a Catch-22. It's an absurdity, an illusion.... It becomes even more absurd when one considers that the government concentrates its data collection on the two groups that automatically qualify for Section 8 benefits."

Walentynowicz suggested that if the government gathered data about European ethnic groups and found they were doing poorly, it could try to find ways to assist them. And if the data showed otherwise, "don't you think that that perception would help secure the kind of consensus we need to help those groups that are not doing too good?"

Finally, Walentynowicz complained that the government permits people "to identify themselves as Puerto Ricans, Mexican Americans, Cuban Americans and so forth, but deny me the same right." Instead, Polish Americans are placed into the "White, Non-Hispanic" category.

He asked, "Is this really an improvement or just another insult? I mean, how do I get my identity by reference to someone else's identity?" Walentynowicz agreed that "blacks have a unique situation here." But he argued that the government should give "anyone else that qualifies, extra help like we did veterans, a point system."

In 1981, Walentynowicz again testified before the Commission on Civil Rights, where he argued for the inclusion of white ethnics in affirmative action programs.[43] Walentynowicz's testimony led to a tense exchange with commission vice-chair Mary Frances Berry. Berry accused Walentynowicz of undermining efforts to assist African Americans. She asserted that Poles, unlike groups already eligible for affirmative action, "needed to rebut the presumption that they have 'white skin privileges.'"[44]

In the end, Walentynowicz's efforts went nowhere.

Jewish Americans

While Jews have immigrated to the United States from all over the world, around 90 percent of Jewish immigrants have been Ashkenazim

---

43. *Consultations on the Affirmative Action Statement of the U.S. Commission on Civil Rights.* 1981. vol. 2: 161-71.
44. Skrentny, "Policy-Elite Perceptions," 1786.

from Europe. Ashkenazic Jews have always been legally classified as white in the United States.

This designation was seriously questioned only once, at the height of Jewish immigration to the United States from Eastern Europe around 1910. The Census Bureau held hearings to discuss whether Jews should be counted as a separate race from other European whites. The underlying issue was that the bureau wanted to distinguish, for example, ethnic Hungarians from Hungarian Jews for statistical purposes.

Faced with strong opposition from Jewish organizations, the bureau instead distinguished immigrants from Europe by "mother tongue," rather than race. Most Jewish immigrants could be distinguished from their Gentile neighbors on this basis because Yiddish was most Jewish immigrants' first language.[45]

In the twentieth century, Jewish organizations helped develop the idea of "ethnic groups." Previously, the accepted notion was that immigrants either assimilated into white Protestant culture or were relegated to being a minority that could never be "real Americans." Instead, Jewish organizations promoted the notion that people of different heritages could retain "ethnic" ties to their ancestral cultures while still integrating into American society.[46]

Jews in the Western world suffered from both religious and racial hostility, the latter culminating in the Holocaust. American Jewish organizations have therefore consistently been opposed to singling out Jews in government statistics, whether as a religious or as a racial group.[47]

American Jewish organizations believed that any official classification of Jews by the government carried more risk than reward. After World War II, Jewish organizations were especially fearful that if a question about religion was added to the census, cross-tabulations with other data would reveal that Jews' incomes were higher than average. This revelation might stoke antisemitism.[48] These organizations also

---

45. Hattam, Victoria. 2007. *In the Shadow of Race: Jews, Latinos, and Immigrant Politics in the United States* (Chicago: University of Chicago Press).
46. Ibid.
47. Ibid., 81; Perlmann, Joel. 2018. *America Classifies the Immigrants: From Ellis Island to the 2020 Census* (Cambridge: Harvard University Press), 366-67.
48. Perlmann, *America Classifies*.

thought that government classification by religion would undermine their increasingly successful support for government neutrality regarding religion.

American Jews remain extremely sensitive to any hint that they should be classified by the government separately from other Americans. The *New York Times* incorrectly reported in 2019 that the Trump administration was about to issue an executive order "interpreting Judaism as a race or nationality." Much of the American Jewish world was briefly up in arms, until it became clear that the *Times* report was wrong.[49]

American Jews are among the most economically successful American ethnic and religious groups. Nevertheless, for much of the country's history institutionalized antisemitism meant that Jews were essentially barred from working in many industries, especially at high levels, including finance and insurance.

As late as 1966, of 173 officers in the nine largest commercial banks in New York City, only one was Jewish. This is a remarkable statistic for a city that had a well-educated Jewish population amounting to almost a quarter of city residents.[50]

Jews were also barred from many private clubs where executives made connections and closed business deals. Through the 1950s, elite universities enforced quotas on Jewish enrollment and discriminated against Jews in faculty hiring. If Jews managed to get admitted to medical school despite antisemitic quotas, they were often unofficially barred from residencies in hospitals, leading Jewish philanthropies to open "Jewish hospitals" in many large cities to accommodate Jewish physicians.

When the civil rights movement started to gather momentum after World War II, Jews were disproportionately active participants in the movement. Jews were also some of the movement's intended beneficiaries, given the significant ethnic and religious discrimination Jews faced at the time.

---

49.   Bernstein, David. "The New York Times Misreported Trump's Executive Order on Antisemitism," *Volokh Conspiracy*, Dec. 11, 2019. https://reason.com/volokh/2019/12/11/the-new-york-times-misreported-trumps-executive-order-on-antisemitsm.

50.   Skrentny, *Minority Rights*, 284.

As noted in Chapter One, President Dwight Eisenhower's Committee on Government Contracts (PCGC) encouraged employers with a substantial number of Jewish employees to provide the government with statistics on such employees to facilitate enforcement of anti-discrimination rules.[51] In its efforts to counter discrimination against Jews, the PCGC collaborated with the American Jewish Congress, American Jewish Committee, Anti-Defamation League of B'nai B'rith, Bureau of Jewish Employment Problems, Jewish Labor Committee, and the National Conference of Christians and Jews.[52]

During the Kennedy administration, African American groups objected to the inclusion of Jews in federal civil rights efforts. These groups argued that Jews had not suffered economic deprivation as a group and that including them distracted from the task of tackling discrimination against black people. Jewish organizations were quiescent in the face of this opposition—in part because they recognized that discrimination against African Americans was a more pressing priority, and in part because the organizations wanted to maintain good relationships with their African American counterparts.

Jewish organizations also remained uncomfortable with the government collecting statistics about Jews. They feared any such data could be used to limit rather than enhance Jews' employment opportunities.

The result was that Jews were no longer counted in federal contractor surveys and forms monitoring contractor compliance.[53] Nor were Jews included in the groups that the EEOC prioritized for antidiscrimination enforcement following passage of the 1964 Civil Rights Act. When the Office of Management and Budget issued Statistical Directive 15 in 1977 designating official minority groups, the document made no mention of Jews.[54]

A few prominent activists thought that Jews should receive more explicit attention from the civil rights bureaucracy. Some Jewish activ-

51. Hattam, *In the Shadow of Race*.
52. President's Committee on Government Contracts. 1958. "Five Years of Progress, 1953–1958: A Report to President Eisenhower," 23, 35.
53. Orlans, Harold. May 1989. "The Politics of Minority Statistics," *Society*, 24; Skrentny, *Minority Rights*, 101–102.
54. Office of Management and Budget, Statistical Directive No. 15 (May 12, 1977).

ists, such as Emanuel Muravchik, executive director of the Jewish Labor Committee, advocated including Jews on the EEO-1 form government contractors used to report their employment statistics to the government.[55] Such efforts were ultimately unsuccessful.

Occasionally, Jewish leaders even expressed support for including Jews in affirmative action programs. For example, at a 1972 meeting of the National Jewish Community Relations Advisory Council, Rabbi Samson Weiss proposed that the council endorse affirmative action and support Jews gaining status as an official minority so that they could "get in on preferential hiring."[56] The council rejected Weiss's proposal.

Jews gained minority status for affirmative action purposes at least once. In 1975, the Englewood, New Jersey, city council designated Jews as a minority eligible for preferences in municipal employment.[57] Local congregational Rabbi Isaac Swift and others claimed that designating Jews as an official minority was a cynical political move calculated to blunt opposition to quotas required by Englewood's affirmative action program, which had been approved the previous year.[58] Swift commented that adding Jews to Englewood's vigorous affirmative action program involved a "ridiculous policy carried out to an absurd conclusion."

Rather than lobby for recognition as a disadvantaged minority, most Jewish organizations initially opposed affirmative action preferences altogether, fearing that Jews would be targeted for being "overrepresented" at elite universities.[59] Jews found themselves uncomfortably in the center of the debate over affirmative action in higher education when Marco DeFunis, a Sephardic Jew, sued the University of Washington Law School over its preferential admissions policies for other minority groups. Ironically, DeFunis, whose immigrant grandparents only spoke Ladino (Judeo-Spanish), would qualify for affirmative action preferences in admission today if he chose to assert a Hispanic identity.

---

55. Skrentny, *Minority Rights*, 283.
56. Deslippe, Dennis. 2012. *Protesting Affirmative Action: The Struggle over Equality after the Civil Rights Revolution* (Baltimore: Johns Hopkins University Press), 93.
57. Deslippe, *Protesting Affirmative Action*, 94.
58. Sullivan, Ronald. "Englewood Names Jews Official Minority Group," *New York Times*, Oct. 27, 1975.
59. See Skrentny, *Minority Rights*, 284–85.

Reflecting on the *DeFunis* case, Larry M. Lavinsky, Chairman of the National Law Committee of the Anti-Defamation League of B'nai B'rith, wrote that affirmative action preferences "[discriminated] against all people who are white." The implication of this discrimination was that "the white majority is monolithic and so politically powerful as not to require the constitutional safeguards afforded minority racial groups." However, Lavinsky continued, "Groups within the white majority, such as Jews…are vulnerable to prejudice and to this day suffer the effects of past discrimination. Such groups have only recently begun to enjoy benefits of a free society and should not be exposed to new discriminatory bars."[60]

The Supreme Court eventually evaded ruling on DeFunis's lawsuit. Once the Supreme Court took quotas off the legal table in *Bakke*, Jewish organizations largely made peace with, and indeed became proponents of, affirmative action preferences for other minority groups, so long as the preferences did not amount to explicit quotas.[61]

Jews today are classified as non-Hispanic whites unless they are also members of one of the official minority categories. There are a few additional exceptions to Jews' legal whiteness.

First, the 1866 Civil Rights Act's prohibition of racial discrimination in contracting covers discrimination against Jews. The Supreme Court has explained that Jews, like many other ethnic groups, were considered a separate racial group at the time Congress enacted the law.[62]

Similarly, Jews are protected from racial discrimination in education if the perpetrator is motivated by racist beliefs, believing Jews to be a racial group, even though federal law does not classify Jews as a racial minority.

Finally, the Supreme Court has held that Jews, like Hispanics but unlike other predominately white ethnic groups, are a "cognizable racial group" and are therefore protected from discrimination in jury selection under the *Batson* rule.[63]

---

60. Lavinsky, Larry M. April 1975. "Defunis vs. Odegaard: The 'Non-Decision' with a message," *Columbia Law Review* 75, No. 3: 533.
61. Urofsky, Melvin I. 2020. *The Affirmative Action Puzzle: A Living History from Reconstruction to Today* (New York: Random House), ch. 9.
62. Shaare Tefila Congregation v. Cobb, 481 U.S. 615 (1987).
63. Murchu v. United States, 926 F.2d 50 (1st Cir.1991); United States v. Somerstein, 959 F. Supp. 592 (E.D.N.Y. 1997).

One subgroup of American Jews, Hasidic Jews, has tried, with limited success, to receive designation as an official minority group. Hasidic Jews trace their religious lineage to an eighteenth-century populist religious movement led by a mystic rabbi known as the Ba'al Shem Tov or "Besht." The Besht emphasized spirituality available to the common man over advanced Talmud study available only to an elite. Hasidim became known for wearing traditional clothing and the men wearing long beards, living in tight-knit communities led by a charismatic rabbi, and strictly following Jewish law and tradition.

Relatively few Hasidim immigrated to the United States before World War II. Many of those who did find their way to the US assimilated into the broader and much more secular American Jewish public. After World War II, however, a few Hasidic sects attracted Holocaust survivors and established communities in Brooklyn, New York.

From small beginnings, thanks to a very high birthrate and minimal assimilation Hasidim became a large established presence in the New York metro area, with smaller offshoots in other cities. They also became a political force, as they often vote as a bloc according to their rabbis' instructions or in deference to strong communal sentiment.

Hasidim got a hard lesson in the consequences of not being deemed an official minority group in the early 1970s. Federal civil rights officials determined that New York's 1970 apportionment of state legislative districts violated the Voting Rights Act by diluting the voting power of African American residents of Brooklyn. The officials ordered a redistricting that concentrated African American voting strength.

The same redistricting plan, however, divided the Hasidim of Williamsburg, Brooklyn, who had previously been concentrated in one district, into two different districts. A Hasidic organization sued. The lawsuit alleged that the Hasidim were being disadvantaged and their voting strength diluted to create a "quota," that is, to ensure that an African American legislator represent a particular district.

The case reached the Supreme Court, which ruled in favor of the government by a seven-to-one margin.[64] The court treated the Hasidim

---

64.   United Jewish Organizations v. Carey, 430 U.S. 144 (1977).

as part of an undifferentiated mass of white voters, rather than as a minority group protected from dilution of their voting strength by the Constitution and the Voting Rights Act.

Justice William Brennan, in a concurring opinion, gave a nod, but only a nod, to the Hasidim's concerns. Brennan noted that evidence was presented to the court that the same level of African American voting strength could have been "attained through redistricting strategies that did not slice the Hasidic community in half." But state authorities "chose to localize the burdens of race reassignment upon" the Hasidim. The "impression of unfairness," Brennan concluded, "is magnified when a coherent group like the Hasidim disproportionately bears the adverse consequences of a race assignment policy."

Only Chief Justice Warren Burger objected to the court's failure to recognize Hasidim as a distinct subgroup with unique interests. Burger wrote, "The assumption that 'whites' and 'nonwhites'…form homogeneous entities for voting purposes is entirely without foundation. The 'whites' category consists of a veritable galaxy of national origins, ethnic backgrounds, and religious denominations." He argued that the Hasidim have a "constitutional right not to be carved up so as to create a voting bloc composed of some other ethnic or racial group through… racial gerrymandering."

Meanwhile, organizations representing Hasidic Jews petitioned for the inclusion of their constituents as an affirmative action category eligible for preferences for minority owned-businesses. Lobbyists for the Hasidim pointed out that unlike other American Jews, Hasidim wear distinctive attire that makes them targets for discrimination. Moreover, Hasidim have high rates of poverty and receive little secular education, as their schools emphasize study of Jewish religious texts. The strict tenets of their faith, such as avoiding contact with the opposite sex, make it difficult for them to enter the secular business world. Finally, many Hasidim, especially members of the large and prolific Satmar sect—one elderly Satmar woman who lived in Brooklyn had approximately two thousand (!) descendants when she died—use Yiddish as their everyday language and speak English only as a second language.

In the early 1970s, the US Department of Housing Development included companies owned by "Hasidic Jewish Americans" as a minority business enterprise category under the 1968 Housing and Urban Development Act.[65] The US Department of Commerce placed Hasidim on the list of groups qualified as socially or economically disadvantaged for commerce's Minority Business Development Agency assistance. And the SBA deemed Hasidim eligible for the Minority Enterprise Small Business Investment Company program.[66]

Emboldened by these victories, Hasidim and their political allies in 1979 sought recognition by the SBA as a presumptively disadvantaged group under the SBA's Section 8(a) program. SBA General Counsel Ed Norton concluded that Hasidim met the program's requirements. The Carter administration tentatively planned to have the SBA draft a very narrow opinion accepting the Hasidim that would exclude other groups that might try to claim minority status.

The SBA invited public comments on the Hasidim's application. The agency received strongly negative feedback, primarily from African Americans. Congressman Parren Mitchell, the leading congressional advocate for the Section 8(a) program, sent a letter to numerous African American entrepreneurs and politicians warning that "inclusion of Hasidic Jews would 'dilute…existing resources earmarked for…other minorities.'"[67] (As discussed in Chapter Four, this concern did not prevent Mitchell from lobbying for Indian Americans to be included in the Section 8(a) program.)

Norton, meanwhile, had a change of heart. He reasoned that the Hasidim were primarily disadvantaged because of their religious traditions, and that it would be unconstitutional to provide special benefits to a group defined by religion because of their religion. The

65.   Procurement Handbook for Public Housing Agencies, 7460.8 REV 2, Feb. 2007. https://www.hud.gov/sites/documents/DOC_10725.PDF.

66.   La Noue, George R. and Sullivan, John. 1994. "Presumptions for Preferences: The Small Business Administration's Decisions on Group Eligibility," *Journal of Policy History* 6, No. 3: 445; Betts, Roy and Giles, Jr., Lewis. 1985. "Kestenbaum Discusses the Opportunity Development Association's Assistance to the Hasidic Community," *Minority Business Today* 4: 13-16.

67.   La Noue and Sullivan, "Presumptions for Preferences," 447-48.

SBA therefore denied the Hasidim's petition, and the Hasidim apparently did not appeal.[68]

Hasidim as a group remain unrecognized as presumptively disadvantaged by the SBA. Several individual Hasidim, however, have proven their individual disadvantaged status and been deemed eligible for the Section 8(a) program.[69] Hasidic Jews are still an affirmative action category for several Department of Housing and Urban Development and Department of Commerce programs.

Cajuns

The first Cajuns, descendants of French settlers of Canada, arrived in the United States in the mid-1750s after the British expelled the French from Nova Scotia. Reduced to poverty, many sold themselves as indentured servants in the American colonies. Eventually, most settled in the swampy areas of Louisiana where they subsisted by farming and fishing.[70]

Cajuns began to assimilate into broader white Louisiana society in the 1930s, as new roads reduced their isolation and public education became available. Cajun schoolchildren were punished if they spoke French, however. "Several generations of Cajun children wet their pants because they didn't know how to ask to go to the bathroom in English," explains Professor Barry Ancelet, of the University of Southwestern Louisiana. "Does that qualify as minority misery? I think it does."

Memories of such discriminatory treatment convinced many Cajuns that they deserve the advantages that come with minority status. In 1988, Louisiana Rep. Raymond "La La" Lalonde introduced a bill to make state residents of Cajun descent eligible for state affirmative action policies.[71] Many of his colleagues dismissed it as a joke, calling it La La's Ha Ha bill.

68. Ibid., 447–50; 45 Fed. Reg. 42,832.
69. Myers, Laura. "SBA Opens Door to Hasidic Jew in Disadvantaged Business Program," *Associated Press*, Sept. 21, 1995; In the Matter of Tenco Enterprises, Inc., SBA No. 425, 1993 WL 566035 at 8.
70. Note. 1986. "Native-Born Acadians and the Equality Ideal," *Louisiana Law Review* 45, No. 5: 1151.
71. For background on the bill, see Belkin, Lisa. "A Legislator's Bayou Boyhood Is at Root of a Bill to Aid Cajuns," *New York Times*, June 14, 1988; Schmich, Mary T. "Minority Status for Louisiana's Cajuns?" *Washington Post*, May 31, 1988.

Things got serious when the state House of Representatives passed the bill overwhelmingly, resulting in a brouhaha. Black politicians angrily denounced the bill.

State Senator Jon Johnson, for example, exclaimed that the bill was "a very shrewd, diplomatic, vicious way of trying to water down affirmative action in this state. How can they say they are discriminated against when the most popular Governor in 50 years, Edwin Edwards, is a Cajun?" he asked. "When some of the state's most successful businessmen are Cajun? One of our U.S. Senators, John Breaux, is Cajun. The present Lieutenant Governor is Cajun. The previous Lieutenant Governor. The president of the Senate."[72]

Lalonde denied ill intent. "I just want to do something for my people," he told a reporter. "I don't want to take anything away from the blacks. I simply want to give the Acadians the same opportunities."[73]

Lalonde grew up speaking French in a small town in Louisiana where French was still the primary language. He recounted being mocked in school for his Cajun accent and receiving no accommodations for the fact that he spoke no English when he started public school at age six. Later, he was slurred as a "coon-ass" (a derogatory term for Cajuns) in bars, schools, and military camps.

A supporter of Lalonde's explained, "Cajuns were very, very poor many years ago down by the bayous, after we got chased out of Canada. When we got to Louisiana, the Anglos and the French Creoles down by New Orleans really didn't care for us. My mama used to say, don't tell people you eat crawfish and turtle, 'cause the girls aren't gonna want to dance with you."

"And they didn't want us to go out with their daughters because we were Catholic," Lalonde interjected. The bill "was never a joke with me," Mr. Lalonde said. "It may have been taken lightly by others, but it's a very serious thing with me."[74]

State Rep. Alvin Alexander, an African American civil rights veteran, retorted, "If you follow their concept to its logical conclusion,

72.   Schmich, "Minority Status."
73.   Ibid.
74.   Ibid.

then everyone is a minority."[75] Alexander tried to sabotage Lalonde's bill by introducing an amendment making Irish American an official minority too. The amendment failed.

Despite this opposition, the state Senate, like the House, approved Lalonde's bill. The governor, however, vetoed it. There does not seem to have been any further effort to classify Cajuns as an official minority.

Armenian Americans

Like Arabs and Iranians (see Chapter Four), Armenians had to persuade authorities in the early twentieth century that they should be considered whites eligible for immigration and naturalization and not Asians. They won that fight at the Supreme Court and have been considered white for legal purposes ever since—except in the City of Pasadena, California.

In the early 1980s Pasadena became an Armenian American hub. The city's Armenian population was divided between established Americans and new immigrants. The former were descendants of immigrants who arrived in the United States between 1895 and 1925. The latter were recent refugee arrivals from the Middle East, mostly Beirut. In the early 1980s, observers estimated that about 10 percent of Pasadena's population was of Armenian descent. A 1989 study commissioned by the city suggested it was closer to 5 percent.

In 1980, Pasadena adopted an affirmative action program for city contracts and employment that benefited the usual minority groups and therefore did not include Armenians. Armenian activists, however, perceived that they were still facing both overt discrimination in hiring for city employment and an "old boy" network for government contracts that excluded them.

Activists raised questions about the city's award of a lucrative contract for towing illegally parked cars from city streets. A city councilman alleged that the police department failed to use a competitive bidding process for this contract. Instead, the department awarded it

---

75. Ibid.

routinely to S. N. Ward & Son, a company owned by a well-connected, non-Armenian white businessman.

Under political pressure, the police department opened the contract for bidding in 1985. Two companies owned by Armenians bid for the contract. One of these companies, Johnnie's Tow Service, already had towing contracts with the state highway patrol and a local sheriff's office. Johnnie's submitted the lowest bid. The police department nevertheless awarded the contract to S. N. Ward & Son. The department claimed that Johnnie's would not be able to handle the extra towing volume.

Bill Paparian, an Armenian member of the city's Human Rights Commission, responded by pushing for Armenians to be added to the city's affirmative action program. He won the support of a major local Armenian organization and of Rick Cole, a liberal member of the city council. Cole believed that expanding affirmative action to Armenians would broaden support for the program, help undermine the city's old-boy network, and encourage recent Armenian immigrants to join a governing coalition of white liberals and minorities.[76]

Some Armenians who took pride in Armenians' economic success and assimilation did not want to be treated as a disadvantaged minority group. African American activists also opposed the move, worrying that it would dilute the benefits they were starting to receive after decades of exclusion from city contracts.

John Kennedy, president of the local chapter of the NAACP, argued that affirmative action should be limited to those who had suffered centuries of discrimination in the US, not "to right the wrongs of atrocities that occurred in Turkey." Nevertheless, the city Human Rights Commission endorsed adding Armenians to Pasadena's list of official minorities. Two weeks later, the city council approved the addition.

---

76.   For details, see Kennedy School of Government, Case Program, C15-88-833 0.

CHAPTER FOUR
The Borderlands of Legal Whiteness:
South Asian, Arab, Iranian, and Multiracial Americans

Most official racial classifications are closely tied to public perceptions, but there are exceptions. South Asians have been classified as Asian Americans for decades. Nevertheless, only 46 and 37 percent of Americans consider Asian Indian and Pakistani Americans, respectively, to be Asian or Asian Americans.[1] By contrast, approximately 80 percent of respondents consider Chinese, Japanese, and Korean American to be Asian or Asian American.

Meanwhile, even though the federal government has classified Arab Americans as white for over a century, many Americans consider Arab Americans to be something other than white. One study found that 31 percent of Americans consider Arab Americans to be Asian or Asian American.[2]

Similarly, while the government classifies Iranian Americans as white, many Iranians believe their fellow citizens treat them as nonwhites, especially if they have dark complexions.[3] How these groups came to be classified as they are and what the future may hold for these classifications is our next topic.

1. Lee, Jennifer and Ramakrishnan, Karthick. 2020. "Who Counts as Asian," *Ethnic and Racial Studies* 43, No. 10: 1733–56.
2. Shachter, Ariela and Flores, René D. and Maghbouleh, Neda. March 2021. "Ancestry, Color, or Culture? How Whites Racially Classify Others in the U.S.," *American Journal of Sociology* 126, No. 5: 1220–63.
3. Maghbouleh, Neda. 2020. "From White to What? MENA and Iranian American Non-White Reflected Race," *Ethnic and Racial Studies*, 43, No. 4: 613–631.

South Asians

Large-scale South Asian immigration to the US began in the 1960s. The existing racial taxonomy recognized only whites, blacks, Native Americans, and Orientals. "Orientals" referred to what we now call "East Asians"—people with ancestry from countries like China, Japan, South Korea, and Vietnam.

Indian immigrants literally found themselves on the border of the Asian and white classifications—the government classified people from India's neighbor to the east, China, as Asian/Oriental while classifying people from Afghanistan to the west as White. South Asians' place in this taxonomy was unclear. The federal government classified Indians as Asian Americans but, as we shall see, almost put them in the white category.

Several thousand Indians immigrated to the United States beginning around the turn of the twentieth century. US law excluded "Asians" from citizenship at the time. Indian applicants for citizenship therefore argued that Indians, or at least North Indians who tend to have relatively fair skin and light eyes, were Caucasian and therefore white, not Asian.

The Supreme Court disagreed.[4] The relevant law, the court concluded, made "white persons," not "Caucasians," eligible for citizenship. The words "white persons…are words of common speech and not of scientific origin," the court explained. Indians, though recognized by anthropologists as Caucasian, were not white because in common speech Americans did not consider even light-skinned, high-caste Indians to be white.

Local federal officers sometimes defied the court's ruling and naturalized Indian immigrants. Officially, however, Indians were nonwhite Asians and ineligible for citizenship. Congress changed the law in 1946 to allow people from "all the races of India" to be naturalized.

Only sixteen thousand or so Indians immigrated to the US before 1965. Thanks to immigration reform, however, by 1970 every year over ten thousand Indian immigrants were arriving in the US.[5] In the 1960s,

---

4.   United States v. Thind, 261 U.S. 204 (1923).
5.   Fisher, Maxine P. 1980. *The Indians of New York City: A Study of Immigrants from India* (New Delhi: Heritage Publishers), 11-12.

a group of Indian Americans established the Association of Indians in America (AIA).

The influx of South Asian arrivals led Indian American leaders to consider how American law should categorize Indian Americans' racial status. The AIA discovered that the government had been classifying Asian Indians as "White/Caucasian."[6] For example, a February 1975 Office of Federal Contract Compliance memo explained that Pakistanis and Indians "are regarded as white."[7] A Department of Education form likewise defined persons with ancestry in the Indian subcontinent as white.[8] AIA officials were distressed to discover that because Indians were classified as white, Indian organizations were not invited to conferences organized by federal agencies focused on challenges facing Asian Americans.

The AIA learned that official minority status could depend on whether a group is large enough to justify record keeping. The organization therefore asked the Census Bureau how many Indians lived in the US. The bureau could not answer; the 1970 census form gave Indians the opportunity check either the "White" or "Other" box. The bureau then classified those who checked Other as White.[9] The bureau was unable to disaggregate Indians from the rest of the white population.

After toying with the notion of lobbying for a new nonwhite classification, "Asian Indian," AIA leaders decided that Indians should be included in the Asian and Pacific Islander category.[10] This would give Indian Americans the advantages of being classified within a larger and more influential group. AIA's constituents would gain minority status, making them eligible for affirmative action preferences.

The AIA's priority was to change the Federal Interagency Committee on Education's (FICE) pending federal rule requiring all government agencies to classify Indians as white (see Chapter One). FICE had proposed the Asian American category be limited "to peoples with

6.   Ibid.
7.   Ibid., 119.
8.   40 Fed. Reg. 25,195 (1975).
9.   Fisher, Maxine P. Fall 1978. "Creating Ethnic Identity: Asian Indians in the New York City Area," *Urban Anthropology* 7, No. 3: 271-285.
10.   Ibid.

origins formerly called 'Oriental' and to natives of the Pacific Islands."[11] This excluded Indian Americans, who were instead to be placed in the white category.

FICE explained, "The question at issue was whether to include them in the minority category 'Asian' because they come from Asia and some are victims of discrimination in this country, or to include them in this category because they are Caucasians, though frequently of darker skin than other Caucasians. The final decision favored the latter. While evidence of discrimination against Asian Indians exists, it appears to be concentrated in specific geographical and occupational areas."

In January 1976, AIA officials lobbied FICE representatives for Indians to be reclassified as Asian. Civil rights agencies were unaware of discrimination against Indians, the AIA contended, because these agencies classified Indians as white. Indians were entitled to a minority classification because they "are equally dark-skinned as other nonwhite individuals and are, therefore, subject to the same prejudices."[12]

Some Indians are not Caucasian, AIA representatives explained. Moreover, even Indians who thought of themselves as Caucasian considered themselves to be brown-skinned, not white. The only label applicable to all Indians, the representatives contended, "is Asian by virtue of geographic origin."

The AIA also noted that in the early twentieth century the Supreme Court had allowed Indians excluded from citizenship because they were "Asian." FICE, the AIA argued, should consider this precedent when reconsidering scope of the Asian category.[13]

Most Indian Americans were educated professionals, which weakened their claim to disadvantaged minority status. As AIA noted, however, Korean and Japanese Americans had similar economic and educational profiles to Indians. FICE nevertheless classified those

---

11. Federal Interagency Committee on Education's Ad Hoc Committee on Racial and Ethnic Classifications, *Report of the Ad Hoc Committee on Racial and Ethnic Definitions of the Federal Interagency Committee on Education* (April 1975).
12. Murarka, Bina. "The Reclassification-Minority Status Issue - An Update," *India-West*, May 1977: 8.
13. Fisher, *The Indians of New York City*, 123-24.

groups as Asian American. Moreover, over time Indian Americans would inevitably bring less educated and poorer relatives to the US.[14]

FICE ultimately relented to the AIA's lobbying campaign. The final federal rules for ethnic and racial classifications published by the Office of Management and Budget classified Indians as members of the Asian American category. This led to Indians being classified as Asians on the 1980 census form as well.[15]

The Chicago-based Indian League of America (ILA), a rival organization to the AIA, had been oblivious to the classification controversy. When the ILA's leaders discovered that the government planned to classify Indians as Asians, they expressed concern that affirmative action dynamics might lead to restrictive quotas for Indian employees and students.[16]

For example, consider a government agency that has a goal of, say, giving 10 percent of its contracts to minority-owned business. If this agency were to award Indian-owned businesses 5 percent of the total contracts, and Indians were considered a minority group, Indians might be accused of crowding out blacks, Hispanics, and other much-more-numerous and politically powerful minority groups. The easiest solution would be to put a restrictive quota on Indian-owned businesses. Instead of affirmative action setting a floor for Indian Americans, it might end up setting a ceiling.[17]

Some individual Indian Americans also worried that minority status for Indians invited a backlash. Whites would resent Indians' eligibility for racial preferences despite their high average economic and educational status, some feared. Members of other minority groups, meanwhile, would resent Indian American newcomers taking advantage of preferences designed primarily to help members of other groups, espe-

---

14. Ibid., 129.
15. Gonzalez, Mike. 2020. *The Plot to Change America* (New York: Encounter Books), 61.
16. Fisher, *The Indians of New York City*, 131.
17. Something like this has happened in elite universities. South Asian students are by far the most successful "Asian American" group in winning admittance relative to their population numbers, and now face discrimination against "overrepresented" Asian American students.

cially African Americans.[18] Despite these concerns, Indians remained classified as Asians.

The reclassification of Indians from the White to the Asian category had an immediate impact on a lawsuit brought by white employees of Alabama State University alleging racial discrimination against whites. The court certified a class of all white employees and applicants. A faculty member of Asian Indian descent, Dr. Satyendra Nath Dutt, sought permission of the court to intervene as a member of the white class. The court denied the request. Indian Americans, the court acknowledged, were classified as white when the alleged discrimination occurred. However, the Equal Employment Opportunity Commission, charged with enforcing employment discrimination law, now classified South Asians as Asian. The court therefore could not classify Dutt as white in the context of an employment discrimination lawsuit.[19]

In 1980, the Small Business Administration added an Asian category to its Section 8(a) racial and ethnic preference program. People from the Indian subcontinent were excluded; instead, the SBA classified them as white. A lobbying campaign for Indian Americans to have their own minority classification soon followed.[20]

In July 1981, the National Association of Americans of Asian Indian Descent (NAAAID), led by Professor Jan Pillai, petitioned the SBA for inclusion in the Section 8(a) program.[21] The SBA rejected the petition. The agency concluded that the evidence NAAAID provided failed to show that Asian Indian-owned businesses were disadvantaged. The SBA also expressed doubts that NAAAID represented the views of Indian Americans, some of whom preferred to remain in the white category.[22]

Pillai filed a new petition the following year. The NAAAID's lobbying campaign received support from Democratic Representative

18. Ibid., 131–32.
19. Craig v. Alabama State Univ., 451 F. Supp. 1207 (M.D. Ala. 1978), aff'd, 614 F.2d 1295 (5th Cir. 1980); Young, W. Michael. 1980. "Racial Classifications in Employment Discrimination Cases: The Fifth Circuit's Refusal to Prescribe Standards," Cumberland Law Review 11, No. 2: 349–50.
20. La Noue and Sullivan, "Presumptions for Preferences," 450–52.
21. Potts, Michel W. "NAAAID Petitions SBA for Minority Status," India-West, July 17, 1981.
22. La Noue and Sullivan, "Presumptions for Preferences," 450–52.

Parren Mitchell, Chairman of the House Small Business Committee, and his colleague Joseph Addabbo. The congressmen told the SBA that Congress had not intended to exclude Indian Americans from the Asian category.[23] The NAAAID also won the support of Republican Representative Joseph McDade, the ranking Republican member of the House Small Business Committee.[24]

Some Indian Americans, however, continued to oppose being deemed part of an official nonwhite minority. *India Abroad* published several letters criticizing Pillai's petition. This opposition, however, generated few negative comments to the SBA. Out of almost two thousand comments the SBA received, only six opposed the petition.[25]

The SBA ultimately granted NAAAID's request to grant Indian Americans the status of a socially disadvantaged group eligible for Section 8(a) preferences. The agency justified this decision by noting that Indian Americans owned fewer—and less lucrative—businesses than certain Asian Pacific American groups already embraced by Section 8(a). The SBA also decreed that the "Indian" subcategory would include Pakistanis and Bangladeshis.[26] Seven years later, the agency changed the name of the category to Subcontinent Asian-Americans and expanded it to include Americans with origins in Sri Lanka, Bhutan, and Nepal.

In 2008, an immigrant from Uzbekistan sought certification from the SBA as an "Asian" under the "Indian subcontinent" subcategory. He pointed out that Uzbekistan is in Subcontinent Asia and shares a common culture and heritage with India and Pakistan. Uzbekistan had been part of the Soviet Union when the SBA last revised its regulations; the central Asian country did not exist at the time. Now, however, Uzbekistan's new independence made it eligible for inclusion in the list of "Subcontinent Asian" countries.[27]

23.   Glazer, Nathan. 1983. *Ethnic Dilemmas, 1964-1982* (Cambridge, MA: Harvard University Press), 10.
24.   Shubow, Robert M. "Minority Status Granted to Asian Indians by SBA," *India-West*, Jul 30, 1982.
25.   Glazer, *Ethnic Dilemmas*, 10.
26.   48 Fed. Reg. 42241 (Sept. 19, 1983); Graham, Hugh Davis. 2002. *Collision Course: The Strange Convergence of Affirmative Action and Immigration Policy in America* (New York: Oxford University Press), 62; Potts, Michel W. "Minority Status Approval Close, SBA Publishes NAAAID Petition," *India-West*, May 21, 1982.
27.   Timely Eng'g Soil Tests, LLC, SBA No. BDP-297, 2008 WL 4296007.

Adding Uzbekistan to the list would have raised some interesting questions. Uzbekistan has a large Russian minority. Would ethnic Russian immigrants from Uzbekistan be eligible for minority status? And what of the substantial population of Jewish immigrants to the United States from Uzbekistan, some of whom lived in the region for centuries, but most of whom were recent transplants from the European parts of the Soviet Union?

These questions were left unanswered because the SBA's hearing officer rejected the petition. On appeal, the SBA agreed to certify the petitioner as socially disadvantaged for other reasons, leaving Uzbekistan off the list of Subcontinent Asian countries.

The classification of Americans with Indian ancestry as "Asian" has gone unchallenged since the early 1980s, with a couple of curious exceptions. In 1989, Chinese American businesspeople persuaded the San Francisco government to exclude Asian Indians from a city bid-preference program for designated minorities. The Chinese argued that Indian Americans were recent immigrants who had no history of discrimination in the United States. Courts therefore might find the inclusion of Indians was arbitrary, rendering the entire program unconstitutional.

This reasoning was a stretch; by 1989 most Chinese Americans were also post-1965 immigrants and their descendants. But this argument allowed the Chinese American lobbyists to disguise their self-interest in limiting competition from Indian Americans as concern for the viability of the entire minority business program.[28]

Indian businesspeople in San Francisco and elsewhere, especially those whose businesses depended on government contracts, were horrified. "It is very discomforting to have this happen in San Francisco. If Indians and South Asians get excluded here, we will get excluded everywhere else," worried Rajendra Sahai, founder of a San Francisco-based engineering firm. Hersh Saluja, president of E2 Consulting Engineers, complained, "They're saying Indians aren't Asians and that's ridiculous." He suggested that city officials be given a geography lesson.[29]

28.   Sohrabji, Sunita. "City Excludes Indians from Minority Contracts," *India-West*, July 28, 1989.
29.   Ibid.

Sahai, who was a leader of the Asian Indian Association of America, led the effort to put Indians back into the set-aside program. City Traffic Commissioner Darshan Singh helped organize the San Francisco Indian American community to lobby the city government. In July 1991, San Francisco's mayor signed legislation restoring Indian Americans' eligibility for bidding preferences as members of the Asian category.[30]

Another controversy over the racial status of Indian Americans arose in Ohio. In 1979, the state adopted a minority business enterprise program. The program reserved a percentage of government contracts for companies owned by members of minority groups, including "Orientals."[31] Administrators of the program defined "Oriental" as "all persons having origins in any of the original people of the Far East, including China, Japan, and Southeast Asia."[32]

In 1984, Indian American businesspeople proposed a new regulation adding people of Asian Indian origin to the law's definition of "Orientals." One of the sponsors of the original legislation, Rep. C. J. McLin, told regulators that the sponsors excluded Indian Americans after determining they had not been the victims of discrimination in state contracting. State officials relied on McLin's testimony in rejecting the proposal.[33]

In the late 1980s, several Indian American businessmen became active in the Ohio Republican Party. In 1991, they persuaded Republican Governor George Voinovich to add "Asian Indians" to the Oriental classification. Sixty-three Indian-owned businesses soon acquired minority business enterprise status.

Black Elected Democrats (BED), a group of African American Ohio legislators, opposed adding the newcomers to the state's MBE program. Voinovich added Indians to the Oriental category, BED alleged, as a payoff for the $278,000 in campaign contributions he received from the Indian American community. Ohio Inspector General David Sturtz investigated but found no connection.[34]

---

30.   Ibid.
31.   1979-1980 Ohio Laws, Part II 3062 (Am.Sub.H.B.584, eff. Dec. 17, 1980).
32.   Ohio Administrative Code, Vol. 1, Section 123:2-15-01(A)(9).
33.   1993 Ohio Op. Atty. Gen. No. 93-014, 1993 WL 666607 (July 27, 1993).
34.   Springer, Richard. "Indians in Ohio Could Lose Minority Preference," India-West, Dec. 17, 1993, 33.

The state auditor, however, requested input from the Ohio attorney general as to whether the term "Oriental" in state affirmative action law included Indian Americans. The attorney general concluded it did not. Ohio therefore again excluded Indian American-owned business from the state set-aside program.[35] The businesses filed an administrative appeal. When that failed, they sued in Ohio state court. The court reversed the denial of minority status.[36]

Governor Voinovich asked Attorney General Lee Fisher not to appeal this decision, but Fisher ignored him. The case proceeded to the Ohio Court of Appeals. The court concluded that classifying Indian Americans as Oriental was lawful. The judges cited several dictionaries that defined "Oriental" as including the Indian subcontinent.[37]

Ohio later amended its affirmative action statute to change "Oriental" to "Asian." The new Asian category explicitly included Indian Americans. Since then, there have been no legal controversies over Indians' (and other South Asians') Asian status.

Nevertheless, many South Asians are dissatisfied with being lumped into the Asian American category. First, South Asians are a small minority within the Asian category. They therefore lack influence within Asian American organizations founded and dominated by East Asians.

Second, some Sikhs and Muslim South Asians find more common ground with Middle Easterners than with East Asians. Sikhs are often mistaken for Arabs because of the turbans Sikh men wear; Muslim South Asians share their religion with many Arabs but few East Asians.

Third, increased immigration from South Asia has increased the diversity of the South Asian population in the United States. South Asians have found it difficult to create and maintain common South Asian identity, much less find sufficient commonalities with East Asians to create a common Asian American identity.

Universities relying on Directive 15 categories continue to classify Indians as Asian Americans. Meanwhile, however, just about every university in the United States with a large South Asian population has

---

35.   1993 Ohio Op. Atty. Gen. No. 93-014, 1993 WL 666607 (July 27, 1993).
36.   DLZ Corp. v. Ohio Dept. Admin. Serv's, 658 N.E.2d 28 (Ohio Ct. App. 1995).
37.   Ibid; "Fisher's Courageous Decision," *Call & Post* (Columbus, Ohio), Aug. 25, 1994.

at least one South Asian student organization. Many universities have one organization dedicated to American "South Asians," and one or more for foreign students based on nationality—Indian, Pakistani, and so on. Indians and Pakistanis studying in the US, coming from enemy countries, are generally not enthusiastic about adopting a common South Asian identity.

The South Asian student organizations are incubating future South Asian American leaders. It would not be surprising if, in the future, they were to lobby for a separate classification for South Asian Americans. Such a category could also include Americans with origins in nearby countries, such as Persian, Armenian, Afghani, Uzbekistani, and Kazakh Americans.

Iranians

Speaking of Persians, American law has always classified Iranian Americans as white. Some Iranian American activists, however, reject being placed in the white category. They note that many Iranians have dark skin, which can make them targets for harassment and discrimination. Iranian Americans have also faced hostility following the Iranian seizure of the American embassy in 1979 and as an outgrowth of subsequent tensions between the US and Iran.[38]

In 1987, the National Association of Iranian Americans (NAIA) petitioned the SBA to add Iranians to the list of groups eligible for its Section 8(a) minority preference program. In the wake of tensions between the American and Iranian governments, the NAIA asserted, "Iranian American establishments have been set ablaze. Iranians have been assaulted, verbally abused, and forced from jobs and schools in the fiercest outbreak of prejudice against an ethnic minority since...World War II."[39]

The NAIA petition contended that the average household income of Iranian Americans was "only somewhat above the poverty level." The petition described cultural and racial affinities between Iranians

---

38.   Tehranian, John. 2008. *Whitewashed: America's Invisible Middle Eastern Minority* (New York: NYU Press).
39.   La Noue and Sullivan, "Presumptions for Preferences," 456.

and Asian Indians. The NAIA suggested that since Indian Americans, a wealthier group, were included in the Section 8(a) program, Iranians should be too.[40]

A few months later the SBA denied the petition. The SBA explained that the discrimination "examples dating from the beginning of the 1979 hostage crisis were thought not sufficiently long-standing." The SBA also expressed concern that if it classified Iranians as a disadvantaged minority, other groups would demand the same status. As Hugh Davis Graham explains, "The SBA in effect drew a red line at the border with Afghanistan. This action blocked future claims from Middle Eastern immigrants."[41]

The NAIA revised its petition to address the agency's concerns. However, the SBA again denied the petition. "Discrimination against the Iranians," the SBA explained, "was merely 'politically motivated.'" The SBA then concluded, dubiously, that "animosity toward a group of persons based on political events cannot constitute 'ethnic or racial prejudice or cultural bias' within the meaning of the law."[42]

Around the same time an Iranian American petitioner, Mohammed Farzin, requested socially disadvantaged status under Section 8(a). Farzin argued that he looked South Asian and therefore faced the same discrimination as did South Asians, who were recognized as socially disadvantaged.[43] The SBA disagreed. The agency concluded that its regulations did not permit an applicant to use resemblance to members of a socially disadvantaged group as evidence of prejudice or bias.[44]

In 2005, an Iranian American group announced that it was filing a petition to have Iranian Americans included in the SBA program. The petition attracted bipartisan support from several senators and representatives.[45] The SBA nevertheless denied the petition in 2008.

---

40. Ibid., 457.

41. Graham, *Collision Course*, 149.

42. Quoted in In the Matter of Columbia Gen., Inc., SBA No. 360 (Nov. 14, 1990), 1990 WL 516550, at 8 n.7; La Noue and Sullivan, "Presumptions for Preferences," 458–59.

43. In the Matter of Columbia Gen., Inc., SBA No. MSBE90498, 1990 WL 516550.

44. *Ibid.; see also* In the Matter of: Impaq Computers, Inc., SBA No. MSBE-94-7-15-30, 1995 WL 542358 (upholding denial of DBE status to a business owned by an Iranian American).

45. Press Release, "NIAC Submits Petition to the SBA for Group Inclusion of Iranian Americans to the (8)a Program," March 9, 2005. https://www.niacouncil.org/niac-submits-petition-to-the-sba-for-group-inclusion-of-iranian-americans-to-the-8a-program.

Discrimination against Iranian Americans was not sufficiently "chronic" to justify adding them to the program, the agency concluded.[46]

There are around five hundred thousand Americans of Iranian descent. This includes a majority of Shiite Muslims, a Jewish minority of around seventy-five thousand, and other religious minorities. Many Iranian Americans fled the Iranian theocracy, but others support or are indifferent to it.

The National Iranian American Council (NIAC) represents those more favorably inclined to the incumbent Iranian regime. The NIAC joined with Arab American groups to lobby the federal government to add a Middle East and North Africa (MENA) racial category to the census questionnaire (a controversy discussed in greater detail below). NIAC leaders acknowledged that many Iranian Americans self-identified as white. This made it difficult to drum up grassroots support for the proposed MENA classification.

When the government decided in 2018 not to go forward with the category, the NIAC expressed disappointment. An official MENA category, an NIAC press release suggested, "could lead to the same benefits for Iranian Americans as the 'Hispanic or Latino' category created for Latino Americans," including increased visibility and enhanced data collection.[47]

Arab Americans

Through the late twentieth century, most immigrants to the United States from Arab countries were Christians from Lebanon. A smaller number of Arabic-speaking Jews and Muslims also came to the United States. After some uncertainty, immigrants from Arab countries secured status as white rather than Asian under American immigration and naturalization laws.[48]

46. *NIAC Forges Ahead in SBA Struggle*, Dec. 5, 2008, National Iranian American Council. https://www.niacouncil.org/news/niac-forges-ahead-in-sba-struggle.
47. "MENA Category Rejected by Census Bureau Despite Clear Benefits," Feb. 6, 2018, National Iranian American Council. https://www.niacouncil.org/news/mena-category-rejected-census-bureau-despite-clear-benefits.
48. Dow v. United States, 226 F. 145 (4th Cir. 1915). There were occasional exceptions, as in 1942, when a federal court held that a dark-skinned Yemeni Muslim petitioner was not white and thus not eligible for naturalization. In re Hassan, 48 F. Supp. 843 (E.D. Mich. 1942).

American culture, too, accepted Arab Americans as white. African Americans who sought to "pass" as whites often claimed they were of Arab descent to join white society. Actors and entertainers such as Danny Thomas played "white" roles and co-starred with white leading ladies.

Bolstered by a rise in ethnic consciousness fueled by the civil rights movement, organizations representing Arab Americans began to flower in the 1960s and '70s.[49] Increased racism against Arab Americans in the 1970s, sparked by tensions over terrorism emanating from the Middle East and skyrocketing oil prices, led to a greater desire for communal representation. Perceived unfair American favoritism to Israel at the expense of its Arab rivals also played a role.

Nevertheless, OMB Statistical Directive 15's categorization of people from the Middle East and North Africa as white/Caucasian did not arouse controversy. Most Arab Americans were content to be classified as white.

In 1987 the Supreme Court deemed "Arab" a race for purposes of the 1866 Civil Rights Act, which bans discrimination based on race.[50] The defendant in a discrimination case brought by an Iraqi immigrant had argued that the plaintiff's claim must fail because the plaintiff was Caucasian. Therefore, he could not claim race discrimination by other whites. The Supreme Court, however, cited nineteenth-century sources describing Arabs and other ethnic groups as "races." The law's legislative history, the court added, indicated Congress' intent to protect all identifiable classes of people who face discrimination because of their ancestry or ethnicity.

The only other modern case addressing the racial status of Arabs involved Ritchey Produce Company, Inc., a company owned by a naturalized American citizen from Lebanon.[51] Nadim Ritchey immigrated from Lebanon to Zanesville, Ohio, in 1974. He spoke no English and intended to work in a market owned by relatives. He soon started his own delivery route, learned English at a vocational school, and opened

49.   Rojas, Leslie Berestein. "Are We White?: SoCal's Arab-Americans Debate Which Box to Check on the Census," *L.A. Times*, Feb. 25, 2019.
50.   St. Francis Coll. v. Al-Khazraji, 481 U.S. 604 (1987).
51.   Ritchey Produce Co. v. State of Ohio Dep't of Administrative Services.1997 WL 629965 (Ohio Ct. App. 1997), *rev'd*, 707 N.E.2d 871 (Ohio 1999).

a summer corn and fruit stand.[52] He saved enough money to establish Ritchey Produce. The produce company distributed wholesale fruit, processed fruits and vegetables, and prepared salads.

Ohio's minority business enterprise program reserved a percentage of government contracts for "Blacks, American Indians, Hispanics, and Orientals." Ritchey applied for minority business enterprise certification as an "Oriental"-owned company. In his application, he listed his birthplace as Lebanon and wrote that he was Lebanese. The state granted Ritchey Produce MBE certification as an Oriental-owned company and then recertified the company for an additional three years.

In October 1995, a competitor was upset that Ritchey Produce won a two-year, $10 million contract to provide produce to Ohio's prisons.[53] The rival told a newspaper reporter that Ritchey received an improper affirmative action preference. The reporter grilled Ritchey on whether his produce company qualified as an Oriental-owned business.

Once controversy over Ritchey Produce's MBE status made the news, the state rejected further recertification. A company owned by a Lebanese immigrant, the state reasoned, did not qualify as "Oriental owned."[54] The state then moved to revoke Ritchey Produce's prison contract.[55]

Ritchey requested an administrative hearing. The hearing officer found that Mr. Ritchey was not Oriental. The director of the state Department of Administrative Services adopted the hearing examiner's report and recommendation and refused to recertify the company.[56]

Ritchey Produce then challenged the departments' ruling in court. The court found that Nadim Ritchey qualified as Oriental. If Ritchey did not qualify, the court added, then the law was unconstitutional because it arbitrarily distinguished among people with Asian heritage. The judge commented:

---

52. "Fruits of Their Labor," *Times Recorder*, Jan. 28, 1996, D1.
53. Jackson, Patrick. "Ritchey Lawyers Say Issue Was Settled by State Supreme Court, U.S. Supreme Court," *Times Recorder*, Nov. 28, 1997, 1; Matthews, Peggy. "Ritchey Contract Spurs Expansion," *Times Recorder* (Zanesville, OH), July 7, 1995, 1.
54. 1997 WL 629965, 5 (Ohio Ct. App. 1997), *rev'd*, 707 N.E.2d 871 (Ohio 1999).
55. Editorial, "Common Sense: Ritchey in the Right in Lawsuits," *Times-Recorder* (Zanesville, OH), April 4, 1997, 4.
56. Appellee's Memorandum Contra to Appellant's Memorandum in Support of Jurisdiction, Ritchey Produce Company, Inc. v. Ohio, 1997 WL 33760449, 12.

Working our way north and west from India we first come to Pakistan, then Iran, then Iraq, then Syria, and finally Lebanon. If Asian Indians are "Oriental," shall we exclude Pakistanis separated from India only by the Great Indian Desert? And if Pakistanis are "Oriental," shall we exclude Iranians who share a common border with Pakistan? And if Iran is "Oriental," shall we exclude Iraq separated from Iran only by the Zagros Mountains? And if Iraq is "Oriental," shall we exclude Syria for the Euphrates River flows through both countries? And finally if Syria is "Oriental," how can its contiguous neighbor Lebanon be anything but "Oriental"?

This Court can think of few things more repugnant to our constitutional system of government than the construction of a statute that would exclude a group of United States' [sic] citizens and residents of Ohio from a State program, the sole criteria for exclusion being the side of a river, a mountain range, or a desert their ancestor decided to settle.[57]

On appeal, the Ohio Court of Appeals court found that Ohio's law unconstitutionally excluded Ritchey Produce from qualifying as a disadvantaged business. A set-aside program, the court concluded, may not use a business owner's race as the sole criterion for participation. A concurring judge argued that Mr. Ritchey qualified as Oriental within the meaning of the law.

Ritchey expressed satisfaction with the decision. "Should the president of Honda qualify for set-aside because he is Oriental? Should an athlete making $25 million a year qualify because he is a minority? This is supposed to help small companies or otherwise economically disadvantaged."[58]

---

57. Quoted in Ritchey, 707 N.E.2d at 877-78.
58. *Times Recorder* (Zanesville, OH), April 3, 1997, 3.

Larry Merry, a local government official, commented, "When Nadim came to this country 20 years ago he didn't speak a word of English and has worked hard to build that business. If he doesn't qualify as a minority I don't know what does."[59]

The state appealed to the Ohio Supreme Court, which reversed the lower court's ruling. The court acknowledged that the state's minority contracting law did not define the term Oriental. However, the court added, the general Ohio administrative code defined Orientals as people with family origins in the Far East, including China, Japan, and Southeast Asia. Lebanon is not in the "Far East," and Ritchey was not Oriental, so his produce company was not Oriental-owned.

It would have been preferable, the court agreed, if the law targeted all disadvantaged businesses for assistance. The court, however, was bound to enforce the law as written.

Less than two months later, an Ohio federal court overturned the state contracting preferences law at issue in *Ritchey*. The law arbitrarily distinguished among various demographic groups, the court concluded. For example, "[Ritchey Produce] could have kept that contract if [Ritchey] had been born in India instead of Lebanon."[60]

In the 1980s, Arab American organizations began to lobby for the US census to recognize a new Arab or Middle Eastern racial category. They hoped enumerating the Arab American population would increase its visibility and political clout, and perhaps plant the seeds for eligibility for affirmative action. Around this time, more Muslims from Arab countries began immigrating to the US. Many of them had darker complexions than their Lebanese Christian predecessors. Some wore Muslim garb, making them more identifiable as outsiders.

The Gulf War of 1991, which sparked expressions of anti-Arab racism, heightened sentiment among some Arab Americans that their fellow citizens did not consider them to be white. Arab American organizations settled on advocating a Middle Eastern rather than Arab census category. "Most Arabs don't consider themselves white," said Samer

59. Ibid.
60. Associated Gen. Contractors of Ohio, Inc. v. Drabik, 50 F. Supp. 2d 741 (S.D. Ohio 1999), aff'd, 214 F.3d 730, 737 (6th Cir. 2000).

Khalaf, national president of the American-Arab Anti-Discrimination Committee. "It's a little arrogant for the government to dictate to any citizens what you should be identified as. The MENA category was a bit of a compromise for us. In a perfect world we'd have an Arab category."[61]

When OMB set out to revise its Directive 15 categories in the early 1990s, Arab American organizations lobbied for a new Middle Eastern classification. They were unsuccessful, in part because of an unresolved debate over whether Israeli Americans would be included in the category.[62] The OMB's rejection of the Middle Eastern category ensured that the 2000 census also would not include such a category.

After 9/11, some Arab Americans felt targeted, profiled, and harassed by law enforcement, as if they were a disfavored, nonwhite minority.[63] On the other hand, 9/11 created fear that if the government classified Arab Americans as a race, it would misuse the resulting data. This concern increased when the *New York Times* revealed that the Census Bureau gave the Department of Homeland Security data listing the cities and zip codes in which Arab Americans lived.[64] The push for a separate Arab American category became less vocal.

In the meantime, a new generation of Muslim Arab American progressive political activists began to identify as "people of color."[65] The media and activists from other minority groups have generally accepted this designation. For example, Congresswoman Rashida Tlaib and activist Linda Sarsour, both Muslims of Palestinian Arab descent, have been widely described, and describe themselves, as "women of color."

This is a triumph of political metaphor over phenotypical literalism. Sarsour's complexion falls on the paler side of Caucasian skin tones. She has acknowledged that without her hijab, she looks like "some ordinary white girl from New York City."

61. Cohen, Debra Nussbaum. "New US Census Category to Include 'Israeli' Option: What Racial Category Do Jews Belong in, Anyway?" *Ha'aretz*, June 18, 2015.
62. Yanow, Dvora. 2003. *Constructing "Race" and "Ethnicity" in America* (Philadelphia: Rutledge), 40.
63. Wang, Hansi Lo. "No Middle Eastern or North African Category on 2020 Census, Bureau Says," *NPR.org*, Jan. 28, 2018. https://www.npr.org/2018/01/29/581541111/no-middle-eastern-or-north-la noafrican-category-on-2020-census-bureau-says.
64. Clemetson, Lynette. "Homeland Security Given Data on Arab-Americans," *New York Times*, July 30, 2004.
65. Wang, "No Middle Eastern or North African Category."

Meanwhile, Christians of Lebanese, Palestinian, and Syrian descent are typically categorized as white. For example, a *New York Times* story on minorities in positions of power in America listed Tlaib as a person of color. Christians of Arab descent were listed as white. The latter included the Trump administration's Secretary of Defense Mark Esper and Secretary of Health and Human Services Alex Azar, Congressman Justin Amash, and New Hampshire governor Chris Sununu.[66]

In 2010, a coalition of Arab American groups sponsored an ad campaign urging their constituents to write in Arab on the census form, rather than checking the White box. The goal was to pressure the Census Bureau to add a MENA category on the next census. The tag line for the campaign was, "Check it Right! You Ain't White." Well over 80 percent of Arab Americans nevertheless checked the White box.[67]

In the early 2010s, the Census Bureau again began studying whether it should add a MENA category to the 2020 census.[68] Focus groups run by the bureau during the 2010 census process found that most participants did not identify with any of the existing categories. In July 2013, the Arab American Institute and twenty-five other organizations sent the Census Bureau and OMB a formal letter requesting inclusion of a MENA category on the 2020 Census form.

The bureau began conducting research and extensive outreach with community groups to determine the scope of a potential future MENA classification. At a 2015 Forum on Ethnic Groups from the Middle East and North Africa, participants questioned whether the proposed category was coherent. In particular, they suggested that it may not make sense for non-Arab Middle Easterners and Arabs to be classified the same way.

Some participants saw the category as a way for Arab Americans to assert their identity. Assyrians, Chaldeans, Jews with MENA ancestry,

66. "Faces of Power: 80% Are White, even as U.S. Becomes More Diverse," *New York Times*, Sept. 9, 2020.
67. "Are Arabs and Iranians White? Census Says Yes, But Many Disagree," *Los Angeles Times*, March 28, 2019. https://www.latimes.com/projects/la-me-census-middle-east-north-africa-race.
68. Krogstad, Jens Manuel. March 24, 2014. "Census Bureau Explores New Middle East/North Africa Ethnic Category," Pew Research Center.https://www.pewresearch.org/fact-tank/2014/03/24/census-bureau-explores-new-middle-eastnorth-africa-ethnic-category.

Kurds, and others might therefore decline to list themselves in the MENA category. On the other hand, if non-Arab groups adopted a MENA identity, this combined population would comprise a large percentage of MENA Americans. This might discourage Arab Americans from identifying with the category.

Meanwhile, many Arab Americans preferred to remain classified as white. Lobbyists for the MENA category persisted in their efforts despite grassroots ambivalence. Arab American leaders and intellectuals saw long-term political benefits from official adoption of the category, even if their constituents were divided on the issue.[69]

Khalaf acknowledged a "split" among Arab Americans as to whether they wanted to reject a white identity in favor of a MENA one.[70] Law professor Khaled Beydoun agreed but argued that if the nonwhite MENA classification became an affirmative action category, "there's going to be buy in."[71] Maya Berry, executive director of the Arab American Institute, added, "The whole point of all of this is that it is about arriving at better data.... And I think that's the point.... It allows us to identify the way we want to identify."[72]

Census Bureau staff discussed the proposed MENA category with OMB's Federal Interagency Working Group for Research on Race and Ethnicity. The staff consulted federal statistical agencies, professional demographic and sociological associations, race and ethnicity experts, and individuals with roots in the Middle East and North Africa. In a February 2017 report, Census Bureau researchers proposed adoption of a MENA category.[73]

---

69. Ibid., 82.
70. El-Zobaidi, Dunia. "How Significant is Rejection of MENA Category from the 2020 US Census?," *Arab Weekly*, April 3, 2018.
71. Gonzalez, Mike. 2020. *The Plot to Change America: How Identity Politics is Dividing the Land of the Free* (New York: Encounter Books), 81.
72. Chow, Kat. "For Some Americans of MENA Descent, Checking a Census Box is Complicated," NRP.org, March 11, 2017. https://www.npr.org/sections/codeswitch/2017/03/11/519548276/for-some-arab-americans-checking-a-census-box-is-complicated.
73. US Census Bureau, "2015 National Content Test Race and Ethnicity analysis Report: A New Design for the 21st Century" (Feb. 28, 2017), xiii. https://www2.census.gov/programssurveys/decennial/2020/program-management/final-analysis-reports/2015nct-race-ethnicityanalysis.pdf).

At the same time, OMB's working group recommended that a MENA classification be added to Directive 15. The proposed MENA classification would apply to "a person having origins in any of the original peoples of the Middle East and North Africa. This includes, for example, Lebanese, Iranian, Egyptian, Syrian, Moroccan, Israeli, Iraqi, Algerian, and Kurdish."[74]

Among the issues the working group considered was which non-Arab MENA minorities the category should include. Experts told the working group that Americans who identify as Assyrian, Chaldean, Coptic, or Druze wanted to be included in the MENA category. According to Israeli American and Jewish organizations, however, American Jews did not want to be included in the MENA category because they identify their ethnicity as Jewish, not Middle Eastern.[75]

The latter response, however, is beside the point, because there is no "Jewish" category on census and other forms; most Jews would have the choice between identifying themselves as white or as MENA. Many Mizrahi Jews (Jews of recent Middle Eastern and North African descent) would check the MENA box, as would many Israeli immigrants.[76]

At least some Ashkenazim—Jews whose ancestors lived in Central and Eastern Europe before immigration to the US—also consider themselves to be descendants of a group indigenous to the Middle East. This notion has been reinforced by DNA evidence showing Ashkenazim to have more in common genetically with Middle Eastern populations than with European ones. And if the MENA classification developed into an affirmative action category, Jews would have an incentive to identify themselves as MENA.

In January 2018, the Census Bureau announced that its new form for 2020 would not include a MENA category. This decision upset activists. Congresswoman Tlaib complained to the bureau director, "The community did it right—they went through the process," she

---

74. Proposals from the Federal Interagency Working Group for Revision of the Standards for Maintaining, Collecting, and Presenting Federal Data on Race and Ethnicity 82 Fed. Reg. 12,242 (March 1, 2017).
75. Ibid.
76. For example, Sigal Samuel, "I'm a Mizrahi Jew. Do I Count as a Person of Color?" *Forward*, Aug. 10, 2015. https://forward.com/opinion/318667/im-a-mizrahi-jew-do-i-count-as-a-person-of-color.

said. "You're making us invisible."[77] The executive director of the Arab American Institute complained to the media, "Our communities, like all others, rely on representation through legislative redistricting, civil rights laws, and education and health statistics. A continued undercount will cause harm."[78] The bureau decision also halted progress toward adding a MENA classification to the OMB Directive 15 categories.

The failure to adopt a new MENA category resulted in part from lobbying by conservative political activists opposed to what they saw as further balkanization of the population.[79] Another factor was the relative lack of enthusiasm from the Arab and Iranian American grassroots for a new MENA racial category. Some Middle Eastern Americans were content being categorized as white; others thought any new category should be ethnic, not racial.[80]

The 2020 census form did, however, ask white respondents about their national origins. The answers will inform Census Bureau efforts to estimate the MENA population. But Arab Americans remain classified as white—at least for now.

African and Caribbean Immigrants

Immigrants have formed a significant part of the black American population ever since a wave of immigration from the Caribbean in the early twentieth century. Famous black Americans with at least one parent born in the Caribbean include Harry Belafonte, Shirley Chisholm, Colin Powell, Marcus Garvey, and Malcolm X.

More recently, Caribbean immigration has grown, and there has also been substantial immigration from Africa. Approximately 10 percent of black Americans were born abroad. The most prominent descendant of an African resident of the US is former president Barack Obama. Vice President Kamala Harris is the daughter of a mixed-race Jamaican father and an Indian mother.

77.   Karoub, Jeff and Householder, Mike. "Hard-to-count Arab Americans Urged to Prioritize Census," NBC News, May 3, 2020.
78.   Wang, "No Middle Eastern or North African Category."
79.   Gonzalez, The Plot to Change America.
80.   Wang, "No Middle Eastern or North African Category."

As the black immigrant-derived population has risen, some of the ADOS (American Descendants of Slaves) population have argued that recent immigrants and their descendants should be classified separately; so have some immigrants, who believe that, e.g., being a Nigerian American is quite different from being an "African American" in terms of cultural background and life experience.

When this issue arose in the late 1980s, the Census Bureau clarified that immigrants and their descendants are placed the same Black/African American category as ADOS. This imposed "a collective black identity on members of disparate national-origin groups, who may have chosen to identify otherwise if given an option."[81]

This classification controversy has not been settled. Fueling the debate is the fact that black immigrants and their children make up a highly disproportionate percentage of the black students who attend elite universities.[82]

The issue came to public attention in 2004. The *New York Times* reported that almost two-thirds of the black undergraduate students at Harvard University were West Indian or African immigrants, the children of such immigrants, or, to a lesser extent, children of biracial couples.[83] One Harvard undergraduate told the *Times* that there were so few students like herself, a child of working-class African Americans whose family had been in the US for centuries, that she and her peers of similar background called themselves "The Descendants."

Harvard is one of many elite colleges that has attracted many more immigrant black students than ADOS students relative to their respective percentages of the population.[84] Controversy over whether immigrants and mixed-race students are reaping affirmative action bene-

81.   Lee, Jennifer and Bean, Frank. 2010. *The Diversity Paradox: Immigration and the Color Line in 21st Century America* (New York: Russell Sage Foundation), 40.
82.   Brown, Kevin and Bell, Jeanine. 2008. "Demise of the Talented Tenth: Affirmative Action and the Increasing Under Representation of Ascendant Blacks at Selective Higher Educational Institutions," *Ohio State Law Journal* 69: 1229-1284.
83.   Rimer, Sara and Arenson, Karen W. "Top Colleges Take More Blacks, but Which Ones?" *New York Times*, June 24, 2004.
84.   Massey, Douglas S. et al. 2007. "Black Immigrants and Black Natives Attending Selective Colleges and Universities in the United States," *American Journal of Education* 113, No. 2: 243-271.

fits that were intended for ADOS students continues to occasionally bubble up.

For example, in 2017 ADOS students at Cornell University protested that the "black student population at Cornell disproportionately represents international or first-generation African or Caribbean students." Meanwhile, they added, there was a "lack of investment in black students whose families…have been impacted for generations by white supremacy."[85] The students demanded that the university increase "the presence of underrepresented black students." They defined this as "black Americans who have several generations (more than two) in this country."

People Who Identify as Multiracial

In the late 1980s and early 1990s, a grassroots movement of interracial couples and the children of such couples arose. Activists began to lobby for adding a multiracial category to government forms, including the census.[86] The activists argued that the government should allow Americans to adopt classifications reflecting the full panoply of identity.

Requiring mixed-race children to check only one box, multiracial activists contended, forced them to implicitly reject one of their parents, causing psychological distress. Limiting people to one racial box also reinforced the racist "one-drop" notion that if a person has mixed racial ancestry, only one's minority ancestry "counts." Recognizing a multiracial American category, by contrast, would help counter racial antagonism and separatism.

Multiracial activists publicized the anomalies created by forcing people into one category. For example, social workers often took pains to ensure that black children in need of new homes were placed only with black foster or adoptive parents. The underlying belief was that only black guardians were competent to care for the psychosocial needs of black children.

---

85. Quoted in Jaschik, Scott. "Who Counts as a Black Student?" *Inside Higher Ed*, October 9, 2017.
86. Dacosta, Kimberly McClain. 2007. *Making Multiracials: State, Family, and Market in the Redrawing of the Color Line* (Palo Alto: Stanford University Press).

Multiracial children with one black parent were classified as black. If a child with a black birth father and white birth mother child needed foster care, a white foster mother was considered an inadequate parent for a "black" child, even though the birth mother was white. This was true even if the white foster mother was married to a black man, matching the racial status of the child's birth parents.[87] (Congress has since banned the practice of race-matching in child placement.)

Multiracial activists caught the attention of the media and politicians. Several state governments recognized a new multiracial demographic category. These states adopted rules for translating multiracials into Directive 15 categories for reports to the federal government.[88] Media attention and state-level victories, in turn, caught the attention of the federal bureaucracy.

An Office of Management and Budget study predicted only 2 percent of Americans would check a multiracial box if one were available. Providing this option would noticeably reduce the number of Americans identifying as Asian or Pacific Islander or as Native American. The number of Americans identifying as white or black Americans, meanwhile, would hardly change.

Nevertheless, African American civil rights groups and their allies in the federal government expressed strong and sustained opposition to recognizing a multiracial category. They feared that because many African Americans have known white ancestry, providing a multiracial option might reduce the number of people identifying as black on government forms.[89] This would be make it more difficult to bring voting rights and other legal claims that rely on statistical evidence of discrimination.

---

87. Colker, Ruth. 1996. *Hybrid: Bisexuals, Multiracials and other Misfits under American Law* (New York: NYU Press), 156; see Kennedy, Randall. 2003. *Interracial Intimacies: Sex, Marriage, Identity, and Adoption* (New York: Vintage).
88. Noble, Melissa. 2000. *Shades of Citizenship: Race and the Census in Modern Politics* (Stanford: Stanford University Press), 139.
89. As Henry Louis Gates, Jr., has noted, almost all African Americans not of recent immigrant origin "are genetically mixed, the only question is how much?" Quoted in Prewitt, Kenneth. 2013. *What is Your Race? The Census and Our Flawed Effort to Classify Americans* (Princeton: Princeton University Press), 119.

Asian, Hispanic, and Native American groups also saw official multiracial identity as a "direct threat to their political and legal interests."[90] Minority activists worried that official adoption of a multiracial category would discourage multiracial individuals from identifying with their minority racial heritage. This would, in turn, make them less likely to be involved in racial equity campaigns.[91] Progressive civil rights organizations, meanwhile, saw multiracial activism as aligned with conservative advocacy of a "color-blind" legal system.

Civil rights organizations' allies in the federal bureaucracy lobbied Congress against adopting a multiracial category. They argued that any changes to Directive 15 categories would make comparing future results with past ones difficult. Adding a multiracial category, critics added, would complicate statistics gathering and processing.[92]

Most Republicans in Congress supported creating a multiracial category. Democrats, especially those closely tied to the civil rights establishment, expressed strong opposition.

OMB, beholden to President Bill Clinton, a Democrat, chose a compromise. Instead of recognizing a multiracial classification, OMB ordered federal agencies to allow people to check off more than one race box. That order halted the multiracial movement's momentum, and the movement soon ceased to be a political force.

Meanwhile, civil rights groups and ethnic organizations expressed concern that double-box checkers would reduce minority groups' reported numbers. OMB responded to this concern by ordering agencies to allocate people who identify as white and a minority race "to the minority race." OMB told civil rights enforcement agencies that if someone identified as two minority races, the agencies should allocate the person to whichever ethnicity would be more useful to a discrimination claim.[93] For example, if someone who identified as African American and Native American filed a discrimination complaint, and the evidence

90. Ibid, 137.
91. See, for example, Hernández, Tanya Katerí. 1998. "'Multiracial' Discourse: Racial Classifications in an Era of Color-Blind Jurisprudence," *Maryland. Law Review* 57, No. 1: 97.
92. Prewitt, *What is Your Race?* 141.
93. Office of Mgmt. & Budget, Exec. Office of the President, OMB Bull. No. 00-02, Guidance on Aggregation and Allocation of Data on Race for Use in Civil Rights Monitoring and Enforcement (2000).

showed discrimination against Native Americans but not against African Americans, the complainant would be deemed Native American.

It took the Department of Education Office of Civil Rights and the Equal Employment Opportunity Commission, the two most important civil rights enforcement agencies, a decade to comply with OMB's "check more than one box" policy. Meanwhile, the Census Bureau adopted the policy. As a result, census data files have different variables that calculate findings from its race questions in different ways. One variable counts all the people who checked a single race (for example, "white alone"). A second counts all the people who checked a particular race, regardless of whether they checked another race as well (e.g., "white alone or in combination").

A third census variable counts individuals who checked two or more races. Individuals who, for example, checked Black/African American and White would have their responses detailed in this file. But they would also be included in both "Black/African American alone or in combination" and "White alone or in combination." Using Census Bureau findings now requires a careful and sophisticated use of its data sets. "X Group alone or in combination" will provide higher numbers than "X Group alone."

Allowing people to check two or more boxes on the census form has demonstrated the perils of relying on racial self-identification if one wants coherent, consistent data. Of the respondents who checked off two or more races for the 2000 census, 40 percent gave a different answer to a 2001 Census Bureau survey. And of those who in the 2001 survey identified with more than one race, 45 percent had checked one racial box in 2000.[94]

An emerging issue in the context of multiracial ancestry is whether someone who has identified as white can reclassify himself as a member of a minority group if a DNA test reveals minority ancestry. The first such case to reach the courts involved Ralph Taylor, a business owner from Washington State.

---

94.   Prewitt, *What is Your Race?* 120.

A few years ago, Taylor, who had identified as white his entire life, decided he wanted to be legally classified as black. Taylor's business, Orion Insurance, could then get status as a minority business enterprise (MBE) and hence, an advantage when bidding for state contracts.[95]

Taylor had been told he had a multiracial look. This led him to suspect he had some non-European ancestry. A DNA test seemed to confirm that suspicion. The test found that Taylor was 6 percent Native American and 4 percent Sub-Saharan African.

Taylor could not claim Native American status because he was not a member of a tribe. But relevant federal and state rules defined "Black Americans" broadly as individuals "having origins in any of the black racial groups of Africa." Orion applied for MBE status, claiming that it was owned by a Black American—Taylor.

As Washington law required, Orion submitted Taylor's photograph with its initial paperwork. A state official found that Taylor was not "visibly identifiable" as black. Orion therefore needed to submit more evidence about his minority identity before the state could classify him as black.

Taylor submitted his DNA test results. He also sent along evidence suggesting that he took his new black identity to heart. This evidence included an NAACP membership, a subscription to *Ebony*, and evidence of an interest in social issues of particular concern to African Americans. He submitted affidavits from acquaintances attesting that they thought he was of mixed-race heritage. The state determined that Taylor legally qualified as a Black American, and certified Orion as an MBE.[96]

As Washington law required, Orion submitted a separate application for MBE status for projects that received federal government funding. Despite considering the same evidence, this time the state decided that Taylor could not be classified as black. As a result, according to the state, Taylor was black when Orion applied for state-funded state contracts but white when Orion applied for contracts for federally funded state projects.

95. Appellant's Brief, Orion Insurance Group v. Washington State Office of Minority & Women's Business Enterprises, 2017 WL 6611744, 10.
96. Appellant's Brief, 2017 WL 6611744, 5-6; *Orion Insurance Group*, 2017 WL 3387344, 2.

Orion asked the federal DOT to order Washington to recognize that Orion was a black-owned company.[97] The DOT acknowledged that Taylor's DNA test suggested that, as the law required, he had black African ancestry. But the DOT nevertheless refused Orion's request. MBE status, the DOT explained, is meant for companies owned by people who had encountered discrimination as members of a minority group. Regardless of his DNA test results, this did not describe Taylor's experiences.

Orion and Taylor's next stop was federal district court.[98] The court pointed out that federal law allowed a state to deny a business owner's claim to minority status if the state had "well-founded reasons" to doubt the owner's claim. Taylor's Caucasian looks, the court concluded, combined with his inability to identify a black ancestor, amounted to "well-found reasons." The purpose of the MBE program was to combat discrimination. The state correctly emphasized phenotype (appearance) over genotype (genetics), because the former is typically what provokes discrimination, not the latter.[99]

The Ninth Circuit Court of Appeals, the final stop on Orion and Taylor's litigation journey, agreed. The court ignored the novel issues raised by DNA tests that reveal previously unknown minority ancestry. Instead, in a concise and conclusory opinion, the court found that Washington "did not act in an arbitrary and capricious manner" when it denied minority business enterprise status to Orion.[100]

If Taylor had discovered that his great-grandfather was a former slave who "passed" as a white man, few would question his right to sincerely claim an African American identity based on that discovery. Discovering that one has over 4 percent African ancestry can result in a similar epiphany, and it's not clear why the legal result should be different.

The Taylor case may have been problematic because of perceived insincerity, doubts about the reliability of his DNA test, and skepticism that someone who lived almost his whole life as a white man should get

---

97.   Appellant's Brief, 2017 WL 6611744, 5–6.
98.   Ibid., 11.
99.   Ibid.
100. Orion Insurance Group v. Washington State Office of Minority & Women's Business Enterprises, 754 Fed. Appx. 556, 558 (9th Cir. 2018).

affirmative action benefits. The problem, though, is that no one in the litigation denied that Taylor squarely fit the literal statutory definition of a black American. That definition was initially adopted for record-keeping purposes in a very different era. Agencies and courts may be inclined to either disavow that definition or not allow individuals with the requisite DNA results to claim that identity. However, it's not clear that they have the authority to do anything beyond enforce the law as written until the law is changed.

CHAPTER FIVE
The Borderlands of Legal Whiteness:
American Indians

The Supreme Court considers laws that treat people differently depending on their racial classification to be presumptively unconstitutional. However, the court has held that the legal designation "Indian"—federal law almost always uses that word rather than "Native American"—is political rather than racial.[1] Yet, as we shall see, laws classifying individuals as Indians often do classify by ancestry—and therefore by race.

Like companies owned by members of other minority groups that lack legal whiteness, Native American-owned companies are eligible for minority business enterprise preferences in federal contracting. The DOT and the SBA administer the most significant of these programs.

For decades, both entities were lax in policing whether applicants really qualified as Indian-owned businesses. To combat widespread fraud in claiming Indian identity, the DOT and SBA recently changed their rules to limit Indian status to enrolled members of federally or state-recognized Indian tribes.[2]

Unlike broad affirmative action laws, many federal laws apply only to American Indians. These include laws that provide eligibility for federal benefits for Indians, give employment preferences to Indians, exempt Indians from state civil authority, regulate the distribution of

1.   Morton v. Mancari, 417 U.S. 535 (1974).
2.   Code of Federal Regulations, 13 C.F.R. § 124.103(b)(2).

profits from tribal businesses, and subject individuals accused of crimes
to federal or tribal jurisdiction rather than state jurisdiction.[3]

The leading case on the constitutionality of laws that treat Indians
differently from other Americans is *Morton v. Mancari*, decided by
the Supreme Court in 1974.[4] *Mancari* involved the Indian Reorganization Act (IRA), which provides hiring and promotion preferences to
"qualified Indians" in employment with the federal Bureau of Indian
Affairs (BIA).

The BIA had a long, scandalous history of its white employees cheating
and otherwise taking advantage of Native Americans. By providing an
employment preference for Indians, Congress intended to alleviate that
problem, provide much-needed employment to Indians living on reservations, and make the BIA more culturally sensitive to the Indian population.

The IRA defines Indians as "all persons of Indian descent who are
members of any recognized Indian tribe now under Federal jurisdiction...
[and] all other persons of one-half or more Indian blood." This definition
was vulnerable to a claim of racial discrimination by non-Indians seeking
jobs or promotions at the BIA, because it includes people who are not
tribal members but are of at least 50 percent Indian ancestry.

The BIA disregarded the law's wording. Instead, the BIA limited participation in the Indian employment preference to people with "one-fourth or
more degree Indian blood" *and* membership in a federally recognized tribe.

A white BIA employee sued, claiming that the Indian preference
amounted to illegal racial discrimination. When the case reached the
Supreme Court, the court ignored the IRA's classification of nontribal
members who were at least one-half racially Indian as Indians. Instead,
it endorsed the BIA's enforcement policy, finding that limiting the preference to tribal members made it a lawful political preference, not a
presumptively illegal racial classification. The court's only acknowledg-
ment of the BIA's "one-fourth Indian blood" requirement was a cryptic
allusion to the Indian classification having "a racial component."[5]

---

3.   *Cohen's Handbook of Federal Indian Law* (New York: Lexis-Nexis 2019), Vol. 1, sec. 3.03.
4.   Indian Reorganization Act of 1934, 25 U.S.C. § 479 (2006).
5.   Rice v. Cayetano, 528 U.S. 495, 519 (2000).

Critics of *Mancari* argue that contrary to the court's holding, adding a political classification (tribal membership) to a racial one (blood-quantum requirement) does not make the latter any less racial.[6] Nevertheless, the Supreme Court has consistently reaffirmed *Mancari's* holding.[7] After the court decided *Mancari*, the BIA issued new regulations that allowed people with "one-half degree Indian blood" to qualify as Indians for employment preferences, even if they were not members of a tribe. Over four decades later, and even though the Supreme Court had stated that a purely descent-based standard would be illegal, this racial credential remains sufficient to qualify for the BIA's Indian employment preference.[8]

Like the *Mancari* court, nineteenth-century jurists who noticed the anomalous treatment of Indians under federal law argued that Indian status was a political, not a racial, classification. Tribal Indians had "not [been] regarded as a portion of the population of the United States," one senator proclaimed during an 1866 congressional debate. Rather, they were citizens of "tribes...spoken of in the Constitution as...independent nations."[9]

An 1881 legal treatise concluded that if the United States destroyed tribal sovereignty and subjected Indians to federal and state law, it would not be possible to "form a special code for Indians" without violating the Constitution.[10] Instead, the government would have two choices. It could accommodate Indian customs when enforcing laws that applied to everyone, but that could undermine those laws. Or it could refuse to accommodate those customs, which would be unfair to the Indians and lead to conflict. Respecting tribal sovereignty allowed

---

6. Dawavendewa v. Salt River Project Agr. Imp. & Power Dist., 154 F.3d 1117, 1120 (9th Cir. 1998) ("employment preference" in *Mancari* was "based on a racial classification").

7. Moe v. Confederated Salish & Kootenai Tribes of Flathead Reservation, 425 U.S. 463, 479 (1976); Fisher v. Dist. Court of Sixteenth Judicial Dist., 424 U.S. 382, 390-91 (1976); United States v. Antelope, 430 U.S. 641, 646 (1977); Delaware Tribal Bus. Comm. v. Weeks, 430 U.S. 73, 84 (1977); Washington v. Wash. State Commercial Passenger Fishing Vessel Ass'n, 443 U.S. 658, 673 n.20 (1979); Rice v. Cayetano, 528 U.S. 495, 520 (2000).

8. See BIA's form BIA-4432 "Verification of Indian Preference for Employment." https://www.bia.gov/sites/bia_prod.opengov.ibmcloud.com/files/assets/public/pdf/Verification_of_Indian_Preference_for_Employment_in_BIA_and_IHS.pdf.

9. 39 Cong. Globe 571 (1866) (statement of Sen. Doolittle).

10. Wharton, Francis. 1881. *A Treatise on the Conflict of Laws* § 252 n.4 (Philadelphia: Kay and Brothers, Second edition).

the federal government to devolve responsibility for laws governing Indians, especially those living on reservations, to the Indian tribes.

Subsequent generations of policymakers have not consistently observed the distinction between (1) giving Indian tribes jurisdiction over their own members and (2) legislation that treats Indians differently because of their race. Like the BIA's employment preference program, many current federal laws and regulations define "Indians" in ways that are hard to characterize as anything but racial.[11]

The landmark 1934 Indian Reorganization Act ushered in the modern era of Indian law with an emphasis on tribal self-determination. The IRA defines Indians to include, in addition to tribal members, all "persons of one-half or more Indian blood."[12]

Many other statutes and regulations define the category "Indians" to include anyone "considered by the Secretary of the Interior to be an Indian for any purpose." The IRA's blood quantum-based definition of that term has therefore been incorporated into many other provisions of federal law.[13]

Some laws have unique definitions of Indian. The Indian Civil Rights Act (ICRA) requires tribal governments to respect the freedoms protected by the Bill of Rights. The ICRA defines "Indian" to include individuals who have "some" Indian blood—no percentage is specified, though most courts agree that one-eighth is the minimum—and who are "recognized" by others as belonging to a federally recognized tribe, regardless of formal enrollment.[14] BIA regulations issued in 2020 governing eligibility for federal education grants to Indian students define Indians as those with

11.   United States v. Bruce, 394 F.3d 1215, 1225 n.6 (9th Cir. 2005); *American Indian Law Deskbook,* § 2:7 (Eagan, MN: LegalWorks, 2020); Smith, Clay R. "'Indian' Status: Let A Thousand Flowers Bloom," *Advocate* (Idaho) 46, May 2003, 19.
12.   25 U.S.C.A. § 5129 (West); *American Indian Law Deskbook,* §§ 1.13, 2:7; see L. Scott Gould, "The Consent Paradigm: Tribal Sovereignty at the Millennium," *Columbia Law Review,* 96, No. 4 (May 1996): 832.
13.   Brownell, Margo S. 2001. "Who Is an Indian? Searching for an Answer to the Question at the Core of Federal Indian Law," *University of Michigan Journal of Law Reform* 34, No. 1: 287–88 ("the IRA criteria remain the underpinning of many BIA rules governing eligibility. This is the case because section 19 of the IRA applies wherever an 'Indian' is defined as any person who is 'considered by the Secretary of the Interior to be an Indian for any purpose,' a phrase that frequently appears in BIA regulations.").
14.   *American Indian Law Deskbook,* § 2:6.

tribal membership or who are "at least one-fourth degree Indian blood descendant of a member of an Indian Tribe."[15]

Other federal laws and regulations, while not always using overtly racial criteria such as blood quantum, also extend Indian status to many individuals who are not enrolled in recognized tribes. For example, federal regulations implementing the Native American Programs Act of 1974 define Indian as encompassing anyone "claim[ing] to be an Indian... who is regarded as such by the Indian community...of which he or she claims to be a part."[16] The regulations also define Indian to include any "*descendant* of a member of a[n]...organized group of native people... indigenous to the...United States,"[17] whether or not that group is federally recognized.[18]

Such capacious definitions of "Indian" (or occasionally "Native American") can be found not only in provisions of law that deal mainly with Indians, but also in broader federal legislation. For example, a law governing federal grants for "minority-serving" institutions of higher learning defines a Native American as "an individual who is of a tribe, people, or culture that is indigenous to the United States." Tribal membership is not required.[19]

Most of these definitions are the products of administrative decisions from the bowels of the federal bureaucracy. But Congress sometimes explicitly promulgates broad definitions of "Indian" that do not depend on membership in a federally recognized tribe. For example, the Indian Health Care Improvement Act of 1976 (IHCIA) defines Indian as including "descendant[s] in the first or second degree" of members of an "organized group of Indians."[20]

The Justice Department objected in 2006 to congressional reauthorization of the IHCIA. Justice expressed concern that the law's broad definition of Indians was unconstitutional. Congress ignored these concerns and reauthorized the law in 2010 as part of the Affordable

15. Code of Federal Regulations, 25 C.F.R. § 273.112(c).
16. United States v. Bruce, 394 F.3d 1215, 1225 n.6 (9th Cir. 2005); *American Indian Law Deskbook*, § 2:7.
17. Code of Federal Regulations, 45 C.F.R. § 1336.10 (emphasis added).
18. Native American Programs, 48 Fed. Reg. 55818-01. The regulations also explicitly include members of state-recognized tribes and their descendants. 45 C.F.R. § 1336.10.
19. 20 U.S.C.A. § 1067q(c)(6) (West); see also Rolnick, Addie C. "The Promise of *Mancari*: Indian Political Rights as Racial Remedy," *New York University Law Review* 86, No. 4 (Oct. 2011): 1016.
20. 25 U.S.C.A. § 1603(13) (West).

Care Act.[21] Congress adopted the same broad definition of Indian in provisions of the No Child Left Behind Act governing federal funding of Indian education initiatives.[22]

In 1987, the Department of Health and Human Services (HHS) sought to limit eligibility for its Indian health programs to members of federally recognized tribes.[23] HHS had previously defined Indians to include anyone regarded as an Indian by his or her community.[24] Congress preferred the latter definition and promptly required HHS to reinstate it.[25] This definition remains in force.[26]

Racial criteria also appear in federal laws defining Native Alaskan and Native Hawaiian status. The Reindeer Act imposes certain barriers to non-Alaskan Natives' participation in the reindeer industry. It defines Alaskan Natives as descendants of those inhabiting Alaska when it was ceded to the United States in 1867 (at which time the region's population was almost entirely indigenous[27]) and descendants of Canadian First Nations peoples who migrated to Alaska over the next seventy years.[28] People of any other descent cannot be Native Alaskans, no matter how many generations their families have lived in Alaska.

Similarly, the eligibility criteria for federal grants to organizations providing health services to Native Hawaiians is based on descent. The governing statute provides that "Native Hawaiian" means any individual whose "ancestors were natives of...the Hawaiian Islands prior to 1778"[29]—the year that Captain James Cook became the first European to visit the islands. The Alaska Native Claims Settlement Act declares

21. Marx, Kitty and Roberts, Jim. "DOJ White Paper Derails Reauthorization of IHCIA," Northwest Portland Area Indian Health Board, Oct. 9, 2006; Pub. L. No. 111-148, § 10221(a), March 23, 2010, 124 Stat 119, 935.
22. 20 U.S.C. § 7491(3).
23. Indian Health Service, 52 FR 35044-01; Clay R. Smith. 2003. "Indian Status: Let A Thousand Flowers Bloom," *Advocate* 46: 19.
24. 42 C.F.R. § 136.12(a)(2).
25. Pub. L. No. 100-713, § 719(a), 102 Stat. 4784, 4838 (1988).
26. 42 C.F.R. § 136.12(a)(2).
27. Daley, Patrick J. and James, Beverly A. 2004. *Cultural Politics and the Mass Media: Alaska Native Voices* (Champaign: University of Illinois Press), 24.
28. Act of Sept. 1, 1937, ch. 897, §15, 50 Stat. 902.
29. 42 U.S.C.A. § 3057k (West).

that Alaska Natives includes any US citizen who is "of one-fourth degree or more Alaska Indian…Eskimo, or Aleut blood."[30]

In the 1980s and '90s, the Supreme Court held that laws or government policies providing benefits or disadvantages based on racial classifications are only constitutionally permissible in limited circumstances.[31] Many observers thought this called into doubt the constitutionality of federal laws that treated people differently if the government classifies them as Indians. One lower-court judge predicted that "[*Morton v.*] *Mancari*'s days are numbered."[32] *Mancari*, however, has survived.

The post-*Mancari* Supreme Court has objected to only one law that classified people based on indigenous descent unrelated to tribal affiliation. In 2000, the court invalidated a Hawaiian state constitutional provision limiting the right to vote for officials of the state Office of Hawaiian Affairs to Native Hawaiians. The court concluded that the Native Hawaiian classification was not governed by precedents like *Mancari* that allow for "the differential treatment of certain members of Indian tribes." Congress, the court explained, had not "determined that native Hawaiians have a status like that of Indians in organized tribes."[33]

Some lower federal courts have insisted that laws that classify indigenous Americans based on descent rather than tribal membership are presumptively unconstitutional. In 1997, a federal appeals court ruled that the Bureau of Indian Affairs could not apply the Reindeer Act to bar non-Alaskan Natives from participating in the reindeer industry.[34] Another US court of appeals declared in 2004, "Government discrimination against Indians based on race or national origin and not on membership…in tribal groups can be race discrimination subject to strict scrutiny."[35]

Barely a year later, however, a different panel of judges on the same court clarified that not every definition of Indian that extends beyond tribal membership is a presumptively unconstitutional racial classification.[36] In *United States v. Bruce*, a criminal defendant appealed

---

30.   43 U.S.C.A. § 1602 (West).
31.   Adarand Constructors, Inc. v. Pena, 515 U.S. 200, 227 (1995).
32.   Williams v. Babbitt, 115 F.3d 657, 665 (9th Cir. 1997).
33.   Rice v. Cayetano, 528 U.S. 495, 514, 518 (2000).
34.   *Williams*, 115 at 664.
35.   Kahawaiolaa v. Norton, 386 F.3d 1271, 1279 (9th Cir. 2004).
36.   United States v. Bruce, 394 F.3d 1215 (9th Cir. 2005).

her conviction for violating a federal law governing crimes committed on Indian land. She argued that the government should have charged her under the statute applicable to crimes committed by one Indian against another. Even though the defendant was neither an enrolled tribal member nor eligible for enrollment, she had "one-eighth Indian blood;" lived and was born on an Indian reservation; "participate[d] in Indian religious ceremonies; …ha[d]…been treated at Indian hospitals; and…was 'arrested tribal' all her life."

The appeals court found that these considerations made her an Indian and granted her appeal. A dissenting judge retorted that enrollment, or at least eligibility to be an enrolled member, "may be constitutionally required to avoid equal protection problems." Otherwise, the judge noted, "enforcement of federal criminal laws would arguably be based on an impermissible racial classification," in this case partial Indian descent.

The majority in *Bruce* may have been right to brush aside the dissent's racial classification concerns. The defendant had deep social ties to a federally recognized tribe, and her designation as an Indian still was therefore arguably "political rather than racial in nature." Yet, as we have seen, the same cannot be said of many other federal laws' criteria for Indian status that turn on "descent," "blood," or other nonpolitical factors that are proxies for race.

Unlike the BIA preference in *Mancari*, which made tribal enrollment *necessary* to Indian status (even if it was not sufficient), many laws classifying Americans as Indians do not require tribal membership. Indeed, some do not even require affiliation of any kind with a tribal organization. These definitions have remained on the books without facing serious legal challenge. It's only a matter of time, however, before the Supreme Court considers whether it's constitutional for Congress to treat people who claim Indian status but have no tribal affiliation differently from other Americans.

In other contexts, an American's "official" ethnic identity is primarily a matter of self-reporting; this is not so for Indians. The government has specific rules dictating how citizens may prove to the satisfaction of the

BIA and other government agencies that they have the correct amount of Indian ancestry to qualify for various programs. To provide proof of one's blood quantum (and tribal affiliation, if any), the Bureau of Indian Affairs issues an official Certificate Degree of Indian Blood (CDIB). The BIA's website explains the rules for acquiring that certificate:

- Your degree of Indian blood is computed from lineal ancestors of Indian blood who were enrolled with a federally recognized Indian tribe or whose names appear on the designated base rolls of a federally recognized Indian tribe.

- You must give the maiden names of all women listed on the Request for CDIB, unless they were enrolled by their married names.

- A Certified Copy of a Birth Certificate is required to establish your relationship to a parent(s) enrolled with a federally recognized Indian tribe(s).

- If your parent is not enrolled with a federally recognized Indian tribe, a Certified Copy of your parent's Birth or Death Certificate is required to establish your parent's relationship to an enrolled member of a federally recognized Indian tribe(s). If your grandparent(s) were not enrolled members of a federally recognized Indian tribe(s), a Certified Copy of the Birth or Death Certificate for each grandparent who was the child of an enrolled member of a federally recognized Indian tribe is required.

- Certified copies of Birth Certificates, Delayed Birth Certificates, and Death Certificates may be obtained from the State Department of Health or Bureau of Vital Statistics in the State where the person was born or died.

- In cases of adoption, the degree of Indian blood of the natural (birth) parent must be proven.[37]

---

37.   Bureau of Indian Affairs, Certificate of Degree of Indian or Alaska Native Blood. Instructions.tps://www.bia.gov/sites/bia.gov/files/assets/public/raca/online_forms/pdf/Certificate_of_Degree_of_Indian_Blood_1076-0153_Exp3-31-21_508.pdf.

The Major Crimes Act

The Major Crimes Act gives federal courts exclusive jurisdiction over many criminal cases when the defendant is an Indian. The act often results in stiff federal criminal penalties for illegal acts that state courts would treat less harshly.

The statute does not define "Indian"; to determine Indian status, courts apply the *Rogers* test, named after an 1845 Supreme Court case. Rogers was a citizen of the United States of European heritage who became a member of the Cherokee Tribe. Federal authorities charged him with committing a crime against an Indian. He objected that existing federal law did not apply to crimes committed by one Indian against another. The Supreme Court, however, ruled that Rogers was not an Indian for federal jurisdictional purposes. To be considered an Indian, the court concluded, a defendant must have both tribal recognition, which Rogers had, and Indian ancestry, which he did not.

The *Rogers* test has created long-term ambiguity on two fronts. First, it's not clear what percentage of Indian ancestry suffices to be considered an Indian. In one case, a court found one-eighth Indian ancestry sufficient;[38] in another, three thirty-seconds.[39] According to at least one federal court of appeals, this ancestry need not derive from an ancestor who was a member of a federally recognized tribe, so long as that ancestor was an Indian.[40]

Second, the meaning of tribal recognition is not clear. Courts agree that it does not require tribal membership. They consider such factors as whether the government recognizes the individual's eligibility for services reserved to Indians; whether the individual resides on a reservation and participates in Indian social life; and whether he has publicly identified as an Indian.

Three years after *Mancari*, the Supreme Court considered several criminal defendants' constitutional challenge to being charged in federal court under the Major Crimes Act. The defendants claimed that the

---

38.   United States v. Bruce, 394 F.3d 1215 (9th Cir. 2005).
39.   United States v. Stymiest, 581 F.3d 759, 762, 766 (8th Cir. 2009).
40.   United States v. Zepeda, 792 F.3d 1103, 1113 (9th Cir. 2015).

governments' classification of them as Indians was race-based and thus presumptively illegal. The court disagreed and upheld their convictions. The court seemed to consider it crucial that the defendants were found to be Indians because they were members of the Coeur d'Alene Tribe, not because of their race.[41] What will happen when a defendant who is not a member of an Indian tribe appeals a Major Crimes Act conviction to the Supreme Court remains to be seen.

The Cherokee Freedmen Descendants

While federal definitions of Indian are problematic, classification problems also arise because many federal laws defer to the Indian tribes' membership policies in determining who is legally Indian. These policies create some anomalies.

For example, some tribes require patrilineal descent from a member of the tribe to claim membership. Other tribes require matrilineal descent. An individual therefore can have two fully Indian parents, both of whom are members of their respective tribes, grow up and live on a reservation, and not be *legally* recognized as Indian because he qualifies for membership in neither tribe. Meanwhile, someone who has minimal Indian ancestry and lives his life as a white person with no connection to tribal culture may have the legal status of Indian if his ancestral tribe has lenient descent rules.

Relying on tribal membership policies for Indian status proved especially problematic in the contentious battle between the Cherokee tribe and the descendants of "Cherokee Freedmen"—former black slaves held by the Cherokee before the Civil War.[42] On the eve of the war, almost a quarter of the Cherokee Nation's population was enslaved.[43]

Cherokee law established a racial hierarchy similar to those of Southern legal systems.[44] The tribe's 1827 and 1839 constitutions

41. United States v. Antelope, 430 U.S. 641, 646-47 (1977).
42. Inniss, Lolita Buckner. 2015. "Cherokee Freedmen and the Color of Belonging," *Columbia Journal of Race & Law* 5: 106-07.
43. Ray, S. Alan. 2007. "A Race or A Nation? Cherokee National Identity and the Status of Freedmen's Descendants," *Michigan Journal of Race & Law* 12, No. 2: 425.
44. "Declaration by the People of the Cherokee Nation of the Causes Which Have Impelled them to Unite their Fortunes with those of the Confederate States of America," Oct. 12, 1861 ("The Cherokee people had its origin in the south; its institutions are similar to those of the southern States, and its interests identical with theirs.").

excluded persons of "the African race" from "the rights and privileges" of tribal citizenship, as well as from "any office...under [the Cherokee] Government."[45] During the Civil War, the Cherokee initially allied with the Confederacy[46] but soon repudiated both this alliance and the institution of slavery, which the tribal council voted to prohibit in 1863.[47]

Following the Union victory, the Cherokee signed a treaty with the federal government in 1866 that "forever abolished slavery." The treaty provided "all the rights of native Cherokees" to the Cherokees' former slaves who lived in the tribe's territory or who returned to it within six months, and their descendants.[48]

The Cherokee Freedmen's struggle for equality within the Cherokee Nation, however, was just beginning. Just a few years after signing the 1866 treaty, Cherokee leadership adopted measures to exclude the Freedmen from various benefits of tribal citizenship. This provoked rebukes from Congress, which passed multiple laws aimed at safeguarding the Freedmen's treaty rights.[49] The federal Court of Claims ruled in 1895 that the Freedmen and their descendants were entitled to an equal share in the distribution of proceeds from sales of tribally owned land.[50]

The Freedmen's situation improved around the turn of the twentieth century. Under Cherokee law, the Freedmen and their descendants enjoyed some civil rights and access to tribal courts. They could serve on juries, hold elected office, and use school facilities—though efforts by the Freedmen to assert their rights still met sporadic resistance from tribal policymakers.[51]

Freedmen descendants' participation in tribal civic life reached a new peak in the early 1970s when Congress restored the Cherokee Nation's right to elect its own officials.[52] The Freedmen descendants

45.   1827 Constitution of the Cherokee Nation Art. III § 4; 1839 Constitution of the Cherokee Nation Art. III § 5.
46.   "Declaration by the People."
47.   "Cherokee Nation and Freedmen: A Historical Timeline," *Cherokee Phoenix*, Sept. 27, 2017.
48.   Treaty with the Cherokee art. 9, July 19, 1866, 14 Stat. 799.
49.   Ray, "A Race or a Nation?" 404–410.
50.   Whitmire v. Cherokee Nation, 30 Ct. Cl. 138 (1895).
51.   Sturm, Circe. 2002. *Blood Politics: Race, Culture, and Identity in the Cherokee Nation of Oklahoma* (Oakland: University of California Press), 174–78.
52.   Ray, "A Race or a Nation," 41; Pub. L. 91-495, 84 Stat. 1091 (1970).

participated in the elections. In 1975, the Cherokee adopted a new constitution that guaranteed Cherokee citizenship to descendants of Freedmen protected by the 1866 treaty.[53]

The 1975 Cherokee constitution proved to be a short-lived victory for the Freedmen descendants. Cherokee leadership soon began chipping away at their political rights. Around 1977, the tribe's voter and membership registration committees quietly adopted a policy that required all Cherokee to have a Certificate of Degree of Indian Blood (CDIB) from the Bureau of Indian Affairs to qualify for tribal citizenship or vote in tribal elections. This requirement excluded most of the Freedmen descendants because they lacked Indian ancestry. Cherokee officials vacillated on enforcement for several years. They sometimes waived the CDIB requirement for voting.

By the early 1980s, however, tribal leadership had decided to disregard the tribe's Constitution and its 1866 treaty with the federal government in favor of disenfranchising the Freedmen descendants.[54] Deputy Chief Wilma Mankiller argued that "membership in the Cherokee tribe...is for people with Cherokee blood." Principal Chief Ross Swimmer analogized the Indian blood requirement to the US Constitution's requirement that the president be a natural-born citizen.[55] Many Freedmen alleged that Mankiller and Swimmer's attitudes were self-serving; they sought to exclude Freedmen descendants from voting because that group was thought to be hostile to the duo.[56]

During the 1983 tribal elections, several Freedmen descendants, including prominent activist Roger Nero, were turned away at the polls. "We weren't allowed to vote because...we didn't have Cherokee blood," Nero explained, even though his birth certificate shows that he was born a citizen of the Cherokee Nation.[57] Nero and other Freedmen

53. Allen v. Cherokee Nation Tribal Council, No. JAT-04-09, 2006 WL 5940403 (Cherokee Mar. 7, 2006); Cherokee Nation v. Nash, 267 F. Supp. 3d 86, 109-10 (D.D.C. 2017).
54. Sturm, *Blood Politics*, 178-83.
55. Ibid.
56. Osberg, Molly. "The Long, Thorny History of the Cherokee Who Owned African Slaves," *Splinter*, Oct. 18, 2017. https://splinternews.com/the-long-thorny-history-of-the-chero-kee-who-owned-afri-1819655748; Sturm, *Blood Politics*, 183.
57. Sturm, *Blood Politics*, 178-81.

descendants then sued the tribe in federal court. The court, however, dismissed the case, finding that it lacked jurisdiction.[58]

Adding to the Freedmen descendants' woes, there is a "long-held Cherokee bias against dark skin." A tribal member observed that "Cherokees have always prided themselves in being a light-skinned people."[59]

Some opponents of citizenship for the Freedmen descendants insisted that their position had nothing to do with hostility to African Americans. As a tribal member told the media in 1984, "Whether they are white, black or red, if they've got the blood then they are tribal members." A Freedmen descendant, however, rejoined that the tribe's definition of "Indian" was "exclusive if the hyphenated Indian is black and inclusive if the hyphenated Indian is white."[60]

As the Cherokee leadership gradually excluded Freedmen descendants from political life, they simultaneously relaxed blood-quantum rules to extend citizenship to many white-identifying individuals with minimal Cherokee ancestry. Today some Cherokee citizens are as little as 1/4,096 Cherokee by descent.[61] Thus, the tribe during this time "became progressively whiter" while also "rid[ding] itself of most of its black citizens."[62]

The Tribal Council adopted legislation in 1992 formally codifying the requirement of "proof of Cherokee blood" for tribal suffrage and citizenship.[63] The Freedmen descendants continued fighting to vindicate their political rights. In 2006, after years of litigation in tribal court, a group of Freedmen descendants prevailed before the Cherokee Nation's highest tribunal. The court held that the Tribal Council's law denying the Freedmen tribal citizenship and voting rights violated the 1975 Constitution.[64]

58.   Nero v. Cherokee Nation of Oklahoma, 892 F.2d 1457 (10th Cir. 1989).
59.   Sturm, Blood Politics, 244.
60.   Ibid., 169, 179.
61.   Sturm, Circe. August 2014. "Race, Sovereignty, and Civil Rights: Understanding the Cherokee Freedmen Controversy," Cultural Anthropology 29, No. 3: 583.
62.   Sturm, Blood Politics, 179, 184; see also Nagle, Rebecca. "Cherokee Nation Adopted Racism from Europeans. It's Time to Reject It," High Country News, Jul. 10, 2020.
63.   11 C.N.C.A. § 12; see also Cherokee Nation v. Nash, 267 F. Supp. 3d 86, 110 (D.D.C. 2017).
64.   Allen v. Cherokee Nation Tribal Council, No. JAT-04-09, 2006 WL 5940403 (Cherokee Mar. 7, 2006).

The 2006 ruling, however, prompted a backlash from some segments of Cherokee society. They launched a campaign to amend the tribal constitution to supersede the court's decision and again deny citizenship to the Freedmen. Central to the campaign were concerns about the distribution of benefits among tribal members. As a mass email circulated by supporters of the amendment forebodingly asked, "Do you want non-Indians…using your Health Care Dollars? …getting your Cherokee Nation scholarship dollars? …making your Housing wait list longer?"

A former Cherokee deputy chief likewise disparaged the Freedmen's push for political equality, opining, "I think they want some of the goodies that are coming our way."[65] And many Cherokees, in the words of then-Principal Chief Chad Smith, "believe[d] the freedmen did not help during the last hundred years to rebuild the Cherokee Nation and should not at this late time reap any benefits that Cherokees have earned."

A Freedmen descendant rejoined, "If the freedmen have not participated in building up the nation so far, it's because they haven't been allowed to." Moreover, the Freedmen ancestors involuntarily built up the nation as slaves.[66] The tribe's deputy chief asserted that the federal government forced the Cherokee to accept the Freedmen "to punish us. We are trying," he proclaimed, "to rectify this."[67]

Racial bias fueled support for the amendment. A Cherokee Nation employee warned in a widely circulated letter, "Don't let black freedmen back you into a corner…. They will suck you dry…. PROTECT CHEROKEE CULTURE FOR OUR CHILDREN. FOR OUR DAUGHTER[S]…FIGHT AGAINST THE INFILTRATION."[68]

In a 2007 referendum, tribal members voted by a nearly three-to-one ratio to amend the Cherokee Constitution to restrict tribal citizenship to

65. Geller, Adam. "Past and Future Collide in Fight over Cherokee Identity," *USA Today*, Feb. 10, 2007.
66. Hales, Donna. "Cherokee Chief Not Ready to End Fight to Keep Out Freedmen," *Muskogee Phoenix*, Mar. 16, 2006. https://www.aaanativearts.com/cherokee-chief-not-ready-to-end-fight-to-keep-out-freedmen.
67. Ray, "A Race or a Nation," 397 (quoting Chavez, Will. "Freedmen Debate Spreads to Communities, Cherokee," *Cherokee Phoenix*, Aug. 2006).
68. Sturm, "Race, Sovereignty," 583.

those who could show proof of Indian blood based on the Dawes Rolls, a century-old census of residents of the Indian Territories. This requirement disqualified the Freedmen descendants once again.[69] And this time, the Cherokee Supreme Court upheld the amendment against a challenge by the Freedmen descendants.[70]

The Freedmen descendants, meanwhile, were battling the Cherokee Nation in federal court, arguing that their disenfranchisement was illegal. For years, the litigation moved slowly through the judicial system as the parties battled over peripheral legal issues.[71] By the late 2000s, however, the Freedmen Descendants' plight had begun to attract broad national attention.

In response to the 2007 amendment to the tribal constitution, twenty-six members of the Congressional Black Caucus signed onto a document questioning the referendum's "validity, legality, as well as the morality."[72] Two African American members of Oklahoma's legislature wrote an open letter denouncing the amendment for enshrining a "racist-based" tribal citizenship regime.[73] Congresswoman Diane Watson introduced a bill that would have eliminated all federal funding for the Cherokee Nation until the tribe "recognize[d] the basic civil rights of the Cherokee Freedmen."

In 2011, the Department of Housing and Urban Development, citing similar concerns over the Freedmen's disenfranchisement, froze $33 million in federal aid to the Cherokee Nation pending an investigation.[74] That same year, the BIA wrote a letter to Cherokee leadership condemning the tribe's denial of citizenship to the Freedmen

---

69. Cherokee Nation Registrar v. Nash, No. SC-2011-02, 2011 WL 8843901 (Cherokee Sup. Ct. Aug. 22, 2011).

70. Ibid.

71. Joint Motion for Order Setting Briefing Schedule for Summary Judgment on Core Issue and Staying Case on all Other Matters, Cherokee Nation v. Nash, 267 F. Supp. 3d 86 (D.D.C. 2017) (No. 13-01313). https://turtletalk.files.wordpress.com/2013/09/2013-09-13-joint-motion-for-order-setting-briefing-schedule-for-summary-judgment-on-core-issue-and-staying-case-on-all-other-matters.pdf

72. Chavez, "Voters Amend Cherokee Constitution."

73. "Cherokee Chief Criticized for Stance on Freedmen," Indianz, Apr. 6, 2006. https://www.indianz.com/News/2006/04/06/cherokee_chief_6.asp.

74. Casteel, Chris. "Lawmaker Wants to Eliminate Funding for Cherokee Nation," The Oklahoman, June 22, 2007. https://oklahoman.com/article/3069097/lawmaker-wants-to-eliminate-funding-for-cherokee-nation.

descendants as a violation of the 1866 treaty with the United States.[75] Such external pressure eventually led the tribe to agree in late 2011 to temporarily give the Freedmen descendants full rights of tribal citizenship pending resolution of the ongoing federal lawsuit.[76]

In 2013, the tribe and the Freedmen descendants agreed to seek a judicial ruling on the Freedmen descendants' political rights.[77] In 2017, Judge Thomas Hogan of the DC federal district court sided with the Freedmen descendants. Judge Hogan's detailed opinion explained that "the 1866 Treaty guarantees that extant descendants of Cherokee freedmen shall have 'all the rights of native Cherokees,' including the right to [Cherokee] citizenship."[78]

Counsel for the Freedmen descendants called the decision "a wonderful victory" for the approximately 2,800 descendants of Cherokee slaves who, as parties to the lawsuit, "regained their identities as equal citizens in their Nation."[79] Also victorious were the estimated twenty-five thousand others whom the decision made eligible for Cherokee Nation membership.[80] The tribe declined to appeal the ruling, giving the Freedmen descendants a major victory in their 150-year struggle to vindicate their rights to full membership in the Cherokee Nation.[81]

75. Letter from Larry Echo Hawk, Assistant Sec'y for Indian Affairs, US Dep't of the Interior, to S. Joe Crittenden, Acting Principal Chief, The Cherokee Nation (Sept. 9, 2011), https://www.indianz.com/News/2011/09/12/bia090911.pdf.
76. O'Toole, Molly. "Cherokee Tribe Reaches Agreement to Reinstate 2,800 "Freedmen,'" Reuters, Sept. 20, 2011.
77. Joint Motion for Order Setting Briefing Schedule for Summary Judgment on Core Issue and Staying Case on all Other Matters, Cherokee Nation v. Nash, 267 F. Supp. 3d 86 (D.D.C. 2017) (No. 13-01313). https://turtletalk.files.wordpress.com/2013/09/2013-09-13-joint-motion-for-order-setting-briefing-schedule-for-summary-judgment-on-core-issue-and-staying-case-on-all-other-matters.pdf
78. Cherokee Nation v. Nash, 267 F. Supp. 3d 86, 90 (D.D.C. 2017).
79. Chavez, Will. "Hembree Won't Appeal Federal Freedmen Ruling," Cherokee Phoenix, Aug. 31, 2017. https://www.cherokeephoenix.org/Article/index/11548; "Cherokee Nation Accepts Court Ruling and Welcomes Freedmen for Citizenship," Indianz, Sept. 5, 2017. https://www.indianz.com/News/2017/09/05/cherokee-nation-accepts-court-ruling-and.asp.
80. Dekker, Michael. "Cherokees Begin Processing Freedmen Descendants for Tribal Citizenship," Tulsa World, Sept. 8, 2017. https://tulsaworld.com/news/state-and-regional/cherokees-begin-processing-freedmen-descendants-for-tribal-citizenship/article_555b6279-79fe-5571-b2a2-c88bb2005f2d.html.
81. Chavez, "Hembree Won't Appeal."

The Indian Child Welfare Act

Native Americans have suffered a long history of abusive practices in which Indian children were taken from their families and sent either to boarding schools or to white adoptive families. In 1978, Congress enacted the Indian Child Welfare Act (ICWA).[82] The act was a response to the "alarmingly high percentage" of Indian children who were being removed from their homes and placed with non-Indian adoptive parents.[83] A House of Representatives report criticized "[t]he wholesale separation of Indian Children from their families."[84]

At the time, as many as 25 to 35 percent of all Indian children were removed from their families and placed in foster, adoptive, or institutional care—five times the rate of non-Indian children. Neither children nor their parents typically had legal counsel. The cases often did not go through any formal adjudicatory process, relying instead on voluntary waivers of parental rights obtained by social workers.[85]

ICWA was enacted against this backdrop. Congress sought to "promote the stability and security of Indian tribes and families by the establishment of minimum Federal standards for the removal of Indian children from their families and the placement of such children in foster or adoptive homes which will reflect the unique values of Indian culture."[86]

ICWA applies whenever an Indian child is subject to a state court child custody proceeding. This includes foster care placements, terminations of parental rights, preadoptive placements, and adoptive placements. Under ICWA, when an Indian child subject to custody proceedings resides or is legally domiciled on a reservation, tribal courts have exclusive jurisdiction. When an Indian child is a ward of a tribal court, the tribe retains exclusive jurisdiction, regardless of the residence or domicile of the child. Even when an Indian child does not live on

82.   25 U.S.C. §§ 1900-1963.
83.   25 U.S.C. § 1901.
84.   H. R. Rep. No. 95-1386 at 9 (1978).
85.   Ibid.
86.   25 U.S.C. § 1902.

a reservation and a proceeding is initiated in a state court, the court must transfer the proceeding to the tribal court absent good cause or an objection by either parent.

Unfortunately, in practice ICWA often fails to protect children deemed Indian under the act. For example, for non-Indian families, parental rights can be terminated for sufficiently abusive behavior proven by "clear and convincing" evidence. Indian children, by contrast, cannot be removed from their parents unless the government can prove "beyond a reasonable doubt," based on expert witness testimony, that the child is in critical danger.

Rules enacted by the Bureau of Indian Affairs under the ICWA also require the government to make heroic efforts to reunite children with their abusive parents, efforts far beyond what is required for non-Indian children. The result is that Indian children are much more likely to be returned to abusive homes and get abused again than are non-Indian children.

The most controversial aspect of ICWA is likely its rules that severely inhibit the placement of Indian children in need of adoption into non-Indian adoptive homes. Essentially, the law privileges the interests of a child's tribe, and of Native American demography in general, over the interests of the child.

In state court proceedings involving children defined as Indians, ICWA creates a three-tiered hierarchy of placement preferences for adoptive homes. ICWA gives first preference to members of the child's extended family, second to other members of the Indian child's tribe, and third to other Indian families from different tribes. After these preferences have been exhausted, a court may place an Indian child for adoption in a non-Indian family. Additionally, ICWA ensures an active role for tribal governments by granting tribes a right to intervene in state court proceedings involving any child who is eligible for membership in the tribe.

ICWA does contain a "good cause" exception to this framework. Courts, however, have interpreted this exception narrowly, often overriding birth parents' wishes for their children and prioritizing tribal control. In *Mississippi Band of Choctaw Indians v. Holyfield*,[87] the Supreme Court held that tribal jurisdiction extended to twin children whose Indian birth parents wanted a non-Indian couple to adopt them. When their child was born, the birth parents lived two hundred miles from their tribe's reservation. The parents thought this would be sufficient to escape ICWA's grant of exclusive tribal jurisdiction over children domiciled on tribal land.

Within a month of their births, the twins were turned over to the Holyfields, their white adoptive parents. The parents' tribe intervened. Ultimately, the Supreme Court granted jurisdiction to the tribe because the children were legally domiciled on the reservation, even though they had never been there. By the time the court's ruling was issued, the twins had spent three years with the Holyfields as their adopted children. But as the court candidly acknowledged, ICWA is more about preserving tribal power than ensuring the well-being of individual children.[88]

This sort of case might be of limited interest if ICWA applied only to children who were tribal members and have two Indian parents who identify with that tribe. The law could then be understood as a somewhat-overbroad political concession to the sovereign rights of the Indian nations—especially given the history of government officials removing Indian children from their families on dubious grounds.

In fact, however, the act defines "Indian child" to include all unmarried persons under eighteen years old who are either (a) a member of a tribe or (b) eligible for membership in a tribe and the biological child of a member of an Indian tribe. The result is that children born hundreds or thousands of miles from a reservation—indeed, who never set foot on a reservation—may fall within ICWA rules if they meet a tribe's membership requirements and have at least one biological parent who is a member of the tribe. Why a child with, say, one Chinese American parent and one parent who is a member of an Indian tribe—who may

87.   430 U.S. 30 (1989).
88.   Similarly, a leading supporter of ICWA concedes that the law's purpose "'is ultimately to maintain the survival of the tribe through the retention of its members-not to protect children." Quoted in Sandefur, Timothy. "Treat Children as Individuals, Not as Resources (Cato Unbound, Aug. 1, 2016). https://www.cato-unbound.org/print-issue/2102 (quoting Matthew L.M. Fletcher).

have little or no cultural connection to the tribe—is deemed by ICWA an Indian rather than Asian, Chinese, biracial, mixed, or "just American" has never been articulated.

Even parents who are willing to relinquish their tribal membership cannot escape ICWA's jurisdiction over their children. In a 2016 case, the Oklahoma Supreme Court held that the Cherokee Nation's interest in moving a child from a non-Indian foster home to an ICWA-compliant one outweighed both birth parents' wishes.[89] This was so even though one parent was not an Indian, and the Indian parent had filed paperwork to unenroll from the tribe.

This case was particularly egregious because although the foster mother was not a member of the Cherokee Nation, she had significant ties to the tribe. At the time of the proceedings, she had been in a relationship with a member of the tribe for several years. She also worked for the tribe for several years. But despite her familiarity and respect for the tribe and its culture, the Cherokee Nation won and took the child from the foster mother.

More generally, cases applying ICWA show that, in practice, Indian status functions like a racial category; decisions rest more on children's genetic makeup than their cultural background. As noted, ICWA pins jurisdictional considerations on a child's membership (or eligibility for membership) in a tribe. Federal law leaves tribes to define their own criteria for membership,[90] and many tribes have done so through blood- quantum requirements, tying eligibility to an individual's percentage of Indian ancestry.[91] For example, the Navajo Nation, headquartered on the largest reservation in the United States, imposes a one-fourth blood-quantum requirement.[92] Some tribes impose no minimum blood-quantum requirement; a prospective member need only establish descent from a recognized member of the tribe.[93]

---

89. In re M.K.T., 368 P.3d 771 (Okla. 2016).
90. Santa Clara Pueblo v. Martinez, 436 U.S. 49, 72 n.32 (1978).
91. Spruhan, Paul. 2006. "A Legal History of Blood Quantum in Federal Indian Law to 1935," *South Dakota Law Review* 51, No. 1: 1 ("for membership in a tribal nation, a person generally must possess a threshold amount of Indian or tribal 'blood,' expressed as one-half, one-quarter, or some other fractional amount.").
92. Navajo Nation Frequently Asked Questions. https://www.navajo-nsn.gov/contact.htm.
93. Cherokee Nation Tribal Registration Frequently Asked Questions. https://www.cherokee.org/all-services/tribal-registration/frequently-asked-questions/.

The Supreme Court put some minor limits on the ICWA's scope in the infamous "Baby Veronica" case.[94] Veronica was born to an unmarried non-Indian mother and a father who was a member of the Cherokee Nation. While the mother was pregnant, the parents separated. The father agreed to relinquish his paternal rights. During her pregnancy, Veronica's birth mother decided to put Veronica up for adoption. She contacted a prospective adoptive couple through an adoption agency. The couple supported the birth mother emotionally and financially throughout the remainder of her pregnancy and were in the room when Veronica was born. The adoptive father even cut the umbilical cord.

A few days after her birth, the adoptive couple started adoption proceedings. Veronica's birth father signed papers stating he was not contesting the adoption. He later testified that he did not understand what he had signed. The day after signing the papers, he contacted an attorney and intervened in the adoption proceedings.

Veronica was only 3/256 Cherokee by descent, but because she was eligible for membership in the tribe via her father, Veronica fell within ICWA's definition of "Indian child." When the trial began, Veronica was two years old. She was living as the daughter of the adoptive couple, who kept Veronica in contact with her birth mother. The trial court ultimately ordered Veronica, then twenty-seven months old, to be taken from the only family she had ever known and turned over to her birth father, whom she had never met.

The Supreme Court reversed the order. The court reasoned that because Veronica's birth father never had custody, and he and the birth mother never married, he was not a "parent" within the meaning of ICWA.

The court argued that it would be absurd to read the ICWA in such a way that "a biological Indian father could abandon his child *in utero* and refuse any support for the birth mother...and then could play his ICWA trump card at the eleventh hour to override the mother's decision and the child's best interests." This would "put certain vulnerable children at a great disadvantage solely because an ancestor—even a remote one—was Indian."

94.   Adoptive Couple v. Baby Girl, 579 U.S. 637 (2013).

The Baby Veronica ruling left unresolved a broader issue. Under the ICWA, a child who has no ties to a tribe or its culture, and has one non-Indian parent, can be deemed an Indian. The law, meanwhile, does not apply to a child with no Native American ancestry adopted as an infant by members of an Indian tribe and given tribal membership. ICWA, in other words, effectively treats Indian status as a racial category, and that creates a constitutional problem.

The constitutionality of the ICWA eventually will reach the Supreme Court. A recent case, still working its way through the court system as of this writing, may be the trigger. Non-Indian adoptive and foster parents who took in children covered by the ICWA sued to have the ICWA declared unconstitutional. Several states acting through their attorneys general are collaborating with the plaintiffs.

The challengers argue that the ICWA adopts a race-based classification of children deemed Indian by the law. The federal government, the plaintiffs added, cannot articulate a "compelling interest" for such a racial classification, which the Constitution requires for race-based decision-making. Indeed, to the extent the government's interest is in aiding children, the law does the opposite. The ICWA overrides states' typical "best interests of the child" standard in custody matters in favor of the perceived interests of the general Indian population.

A federal district court in Texas agreed and held the ICWA unconstitutional.[95] A panel of three judges on the Fifth Circuit Court of Appeals, however, reversed.[96] The panel ruled that the ICWA was not a race-based law. The court reasoned that because the law required one parent to be a member of a federally or state recognized tribe, "Indian" was a predominately a political classification, as in *Mancari*, not a racial one.

In an unusual move, the full Fifth Circuit Court of Appeals vacated the ruling. It ordered that the case be reheard by all judges on the circuit to reconsider the ruling. The full court issued a complicated ruling agreeing that the ICWA's definition of "Indian child" is a political classification and therefore not unconstitutional.[97] The majority concluded that *Mancari* stands for the broad proposition that if "legislation that

95. Brackeen v. Zinke, 338 F.Supp.3d 514 (N.D. Tex. 2018).
96. Brackeen v. Bernhardt, 937 F.3d 406, 414 (5th Cir. 2019).
97. Brackeen v. Haaland, 994 F.3d 249 (5th Cir. 2021) (en banc).

singles out Indians for…special treatment can be tied rationally to the fulfillment of Congress' unique obligation toward the Indians," the statute "will not be disturbed."

A vigorous dissent argued that under Supreme Court precedent, it was unclear whether the ICWA Indian child classification should be understood as based on race. Regardless, the dissenters argued, the law was unconstitutional because "it did not rationally further federal obligations to tribes."

The dissenters gave three reasons for their conclusion. First, ICWA creates separate standards for Indian children that extend beyond internal tribal affairs and intrude into state proceedings. Second, the law applies to children who are only eligible for tribal membership but are not and may never become tribal members. The Indian tribes have no special interest in who has custody of such children, so the federal government can have no related obligations. Finally, the ICWA was intended to help Indian parents who did not want their children adopted outside their tribe. In practice, however, the ICWA allows tribes to intervene in custody proceedings against the parents' explicit wishes.

The *en banc* court, meanwhile, divided evenly on the question of whether the ICWA was unconstitutional to the extent it gives a custody preference to Indians who are members of a different tribe than the child whose custody is being determined. The federal government argued that many tribes have deep historical connections with each other. The plaintiffs rejoined that many tribes are entirely culturally distinct. Moreover, tribes that do have historical ties, such as the Hopi and Navajo, were often enemies.

The Supreme Court may very well decide to review this case. If it does so, its ruling not only will determine the constitutionality of the ICWA but also will give the court an opportunity to reconsider its holding in *Mancari*.

CHAPTER SIX
The Strange Career of Government-Mandated Racial Categories in Scientific and Medical Research

The standardized racial and ethnic categories developed in Statistical Directive No. 15 in 1977 (see Chapter One), came with an explicit warning these "classifications should not be interpreted as being scientific or anthropological in nature."[1] And indeed, the classifications have no valid scientific or anthropological basis. Yet the Food and Drug Administration (FDA) and the National Institutes of Health (NIH) require medical researchers to classify study participants by Directive 15 categories.

Participants are classified as Hispanic or non-Hispanic, and then "American Indian or Alaska Native," "Asian," "Black or African American," "Native Hawaiian or Other Pacific Islander," or "White." The researchers must then report study results sorted by those categories. Scientists have grown accustomed to using these classifications despite their lack of scientific validity.[2]

Directive 15 categories have unique problems, but scientists have pointed out a range of more general problems with using common racial categories in scientific and medical research. First, the phenotypes we associate with the different races, such as skin color and facial features,

---

1. Directive No. 15, Race and Ethnic Standards for Federal Statistics and Administrative Reporting, 43 Fed. Reg. 19,260 (1978).
2. Braun, Lundy et. al. September 2007. "Racial Categories in Medical Practice: How Useful are They?" *PLOS Medicine* 4, no. 9: 1425.

"simply do not correlate with data from the whole genome."[3] They also "do not correlate well with biochemical or other genetic characteristics."[4]

Variations in genetic differences between populations are roughly proportional to geographic distances among them.[5] Race is correlated with geographic distance among groups but is not coextensive with it. As one geneticist explains, "The take-home message is that [genetic] variation is continuous," and "is discordant with race."[6]

Additionally, there is no known example of polymorphism (genetic variation) found exclusively in any particular "racial" group.[7] An editorial in *Nature Biotechnology* drolly comments, "Pooling people in race silos is akin to zoologists grouping raccoons, tigers, and okapis on the basis that they are all stripey." [8]

Biomedical studies do occasionally show that race is correlated with a particular medical outcome. But these studies may be picking up the results of sociological differences, such as socioeconomic status, cultural habits, and diet, not genetic differences.

These studies, moreover, do not start from neutral premises. Rather, the "crucial failing of all biomedical research dealing with race" is that it begins with the presumption that race is relevant and then looks for information to corroborate this presumption.[9]

In the past, race may have been more useful as a crude proxy for genetic heterogeneity.[10] However, as DNA testing has become more

---

3.   Garte, Seymour. Sept.-Oct. 2002. "The Racial Genetics Paradox in Biomedical Research and Public Health," *Public Health Reports* 117, no. 5: 221; Cooper, Richard S. et al. March 20, 2003. "Race and Genomics," *New England Journal of Medicine* 348: 1166-70.
4.   Williams, D.R. 1997. "Race and Health: Basic Questions, Emerging Directions," *Annals of Epidemiology* 7, no. 5: 333.
5.   Kittles, Rick A. and Weiss, Kenneth M. September 2003. "Race, Ancestry and Genes: Implications for Defining Disease Risk," *Annual Review of Genomics and Human Genetics* 4: 38.
6.   Rotimi, Charles N. 2004. "Are Medical and Nonmedical Uses of Large-Scale Genomic Markers Conflating Genetics and 'Race'?," *Nature Genetics* 36, no. 11: S43-47.
7.   Kittles and Weiss, "Race, Ancestry, and Genes," 38.
8.   Editorial. 2005."Illuminating BiDil," *Nature Biotechnology* 23 (2005): 903.
9.   Perez-Rodriguez, Javier and de la Fuente, Alejandro. 2017. "Now Is the Time for a Postracial Medicine: Biomedical Research, The National Institutes of Health, and the Perpetuation of Scientific Racism," *American Journal of Bioethics* 17, no. 1: 41.
10.   Kahn, Jonathan. 2012. *Race in a Bottle: The Story of BiDil and Racialized Medicine in a Post-Genomic Age* (New York: Columbia University Press), 18 (noting that some supporters of using race in biomedical research acknowledge that it's a "crude surrogate," but claim that it's a stepping-stone to a future in which medical treatment will be individualized based on genomic factors).

available and much less expensive, race is a poor substitute for looking at discernible human genetic differences.[11] Rather than focusing on race, critics argue, researchers should look for the genetic markers that cause a treatment to be more effective or dangerous in certain populations. Those insights can then be applied on an individual rather than group basis.

Meanwhile, predictions that using racial data in biomedical research would be a temporary expedient until DNA testing became cheaper and better have been proven wrong. Since the NIH and FDA mandates began, the presence of racial data in medical studies has skyrocketed, despite major advances in DNA technology.[12]

Only a dwindling minority of scientists believe that race as popularly understood has medical salience.[13] But even if those dissenters were correct, the specific Directive 15 classifications mandated by the FDA and NIH are too arbitrary and indeterminate to be useful.[14]

First, researchers using the Directive 15 classifications have no consistent, reliable way of identifying subjects' race or ethnicity. Researchers rely primarily on self-identification, but self-identification is notoriously unreliable and variable. One-third of people report a different ethnicity or race a year after an initial interview.[15] Americans' self-identified race on census forms often varies from decade to decade.

When research subjects choose not to self-identify, some laboratories assign them a race based on surname and residence.[16] Some researchers classify anyone with a Spanish surname as Hispanic "until proven otherwise."[17] To say the least, this does not produce consistently reliable results.

---

11.   Kittles and Weiss, "Race, Ancestry, and Genes."
12.   Kahn, *Race in a Bottle*, 38.
13.   For example, Burchard, E. G. et al. 2003. "The Importance of Race and Ethnic Background in Biomedical Research and Practice," *New England Journal of Medicine* 348: 1170-1175. Risch, Neil et al. 2002. "Categorization of Humans in Biomedical Research: Genes, Race and Disease," *Genome Biology* 3, No. 7: 1-12.
14.   Osborne, Norman G. and Feit, Martin. 1992. "The Use of Race in Medical Research," *Journal of the American Medical Association* 267, no. 2: 275.
15.   Polednak, A.P. 1989. *Racial and Ethnic Differences in Disease* (New York: Oxford University Press, 1989).
16.   Janet K. Shim, et al. 2014. "Race and Ancestry in the Age of Inclusion: Technique and Meaning in Post-Genomic Science," *Journal of Health and Social Behavior* 54, No. 4: 504-18.
17.   Hun, M. and Megyesi, Mary S. 2008. "The Ambiguous Meaning of the Racial/Ethnic Categories Routinely Used in Human Genetics Research," *Social Science Medicine* 66, No. 2: 349.

Racial classification of this sort has become ingrained within scientific research. One scientist reports that he and his colleagues "just sort of use [racial classifications] blindly."

This scientist notes using the Directive 15 categories is contrary to the scientific method: "If we were laboratory scientists and we were developing assays, we wouldn't just use the assay somebody else came up with some other purpose. We would develop our own assays and test them and figure out what the coefficients of variability are and the properties of that assay before we applied them in experiments."[18]

Directive 15's racial categories mask vast genetic differences within each category. The Directive 15 white category includes everyone from Scots to Greeks to Moroccans. Within the group classified as white, DNA studies find that people from the Middle East can be divided into four separate populations, and Europeans divided into eight separate populations.[19] The white category is of "little value in gauging ethnicity or race" in a way that could be scientifically useful.[20]

People of black African descent, another Directive 15 classification, are highly genetically diverse, much more so than Europeans.[21] A category based on black African origin cannot adequately "capture the complexity of migrations, artificial boundaries, and gene drift" in Africa.[22]

Somalis, for example, "are genetically more similar to people in Saudi Arabia than they are to people from other parts of Africa." Saudis, meanwhile, are "White" under Directive 15 classification rules but are closer genetically to Somalis than to Norwegians. Most Ethiopians, whom Directive 15 categorizes as Black/African American, belong to the same genetic cluster as Ashkenazic Jews and Armenians.[23]

One justification for classifying study participants by race is that people of African descent metabolize drugs at a different rate than do other groups. Yet, the prevalence of gene variants that affect metabolism of different drugs varies widely among different African populations.

18.   Shim, et al., "Race and Ancestry."
19.   Roberts, Dorothy. 2011. *Fatal Invention: How Science, Politics, and Big Business Re-create Race in the Twenty-first Century* (New York: New Press), 66.
20.   Bhopal, et al.
21.   Rotimi, "Are Medical and Nonmedical Uses," 54.
22.   Braun, et. al, "Racial Categories," 1424.
23.   Roberts, *Fatal Invention*, 159.

For example, a gene variant involved in metabolizing codeine and antidepressants is found in 9 percent of Ethiopians, 17 percent of Tanzanians, and 34 percent of Zimbabweans. An allele that predicts severe reactions to a particular HIV drug is found in 13.6 percent of Masai in Kenya, 3.3 percent among the Kenyan Luhya, and 0 percent among the Yoruba in Nigeria.[24] Knowing only that someone is of African descent does not provide useful information about that person's ability to metabolize drugs.[25]

Most of members of the Directive 15 African American classification are descendants of American slaves. They rarely can pinpoint their origin within Africa and in any event, they are not asked to.

Assume a clinical drug study shows that its use creates a mildly elevated risk for African Americans. The finding, if valid, could result from a major risk to a small minority of research subjects who inherited genes from a particular African ethnic group. Or the reaction could reveal a much broader mild extra risk generalizable to people of West African descent.[26]

Similarly, research has suggested that African Americans are more susceptible to heart disease because of certain genes many share with West Africans. But one cannot properly assume that the same genetic variation exists in Americans whose ancestral roots are in Sub-Saharan or East Africa.

The Directive 15 category of Asian American, meanwhile, includes people with origins everywhere from the Philippines to the Indian subcontinent. There are vast differences just among the various ethnic groups from the Indian subcontinent. There are even greater differences between South Asians and East Asians. Genetic research suggests South Asians rarely have close genetic relationships to East Asians.[27] Mean-

---

24. Ibid., 160.
25. Braun, et. al, "Racial Categories," 1426.
26. Perez-Rodriguez and de la Fuente, "Now is the Time for a Postracial Medicine," 41.
27. Chaubey, Gyaneshwer. 2015. "East Asian Ancestry in India," *Indian J. Physical Anthropology and Human Genetics* 34, No. 2: 193-99; Metspalu, Meit et al. 2011. "Shared and Unique Components of Human Population Structure and Genome-Wide Signals of Positive Selection in South Asia," *American Journal of Human Genetics* 89, No. 6: 731-44; Moorjani, Priya et al. "Genetic Evidence for Recent Population Mixture in India," *American Journal of Human Genetics* 93, No. 3 (Sept. 5, 2013): 422-38; Yelmen, Burak et al. "Ancestry-Specific Analyses Reveal Differential Demographic Histories and Opposite Selective Pressures in Modern South Asian Populations," *Molecular Biology and Evolution* 36, No. 8 (Aug. 2019): 21628-42.

while, Filipinos, one of the largest groups classified as Asian Americans, are mostly of Austronesian ancestry.

Multiracial individuals present US researchers bound by the Directive 15 categories with additional difficulties. Most African Americans in the United States have some European or Native American ancestry.[28] "How white is white?" scientists asked in the *Journal of the American Medical Association*.[29] "Is a person who has only one grandparent of another race categorized the same as one who has one great-grandparent or two great-grandparents? What happens if two grandparents are white, one is black, and another is Asian?"[30]

The issue of multiracial subjects is not limited to self-identified African Americans. The average self-identified American Indian is of mostly European heritage. A significant number of self-identified whites in the United States have African or Native American ancestors.

Researchers account for individuals who self-identify as multiracial in scientifically arbitrary ways. One scientist, for example, reported that if a research subject self-identifies in multiple categories, "we say African-American trumps everything else. Then Hispanic then trumps everything else that's remaining. And then the Asian trumps everything else that's remaining. That's kind of what I think the standard thing that people do."[31]

Meanwhile, even scientists who are relatively sanguine about using race as a proxy for genetic variance acknowledge that the Hispanic category, as an internally multiracial category, is not scientifically coherent.[32] As discussed in Chapter Two, Hispanics "encompass nearly all possible combinations of African, Native American, and European ancestries."[33]

Further complicating matters, the genetic admixture varies geographically. Mexicans and Central Americans have more Native Amer-

28. Wright, Lawrence. "One Drop of Blood," *New Yorker*, July 25, 1994, 46.
29. Osborne and Feit, "The Use of Race in Medical Research," 275.
30. Ibid.
31. Shim, et al., "Race and Ancestry"; see also Yager, Rona et al. "Comparing Genetic Ancestry and Self-Described Race in African Americans Born in the United States and in Africa," *Cancer Epidemiological Biomarkers* 17, No. 6 (June 2008): 1334; Perez-Rodriguez and de la Fuente, "Now Is the Time for a Postracial Medicine."
32. Risch, et al., *Categorization of Humans in Biomedical Research*.
33. Katarzyna, Bryc et al. Jan. 8, 2015. "The Genetic Ancestry of African Americans, Latinos, and European Americans across the United States," *American Journal of Human Genetics* 96, No. 1: 37-53.

ican ancestry than average for Latin Americans; Puerto Ricans and Dominicans have higher levels of African ancestry; and Cubans and South Americans have more European ancestry.

There are also vast sociological differences among Hispanic groups. Data about urban Cuban Americans in South Florida cannot properly be used to understand health issues facing rural Puerto Ricans in Central Florida.[34]

Directive 15 describes the Hispanic/Latino category as an ethnicity and not a race. The FDA and NIH have never explained why they require researchers to classify study subjects and the data by Hispanic identity but not any other ethnicity.

Many other groups were historically far more endogamous and genetically isolated than Hispanics and therefore are more likely to have idiosyncratic reactions to medical interventions. The FDA and NIH do not, however, ask scientists to gather data about Ashkenazic Jews, Icelanders, Roma, Hungarians, or other ethnic groups.

Both agencies also require scientists to use Directive 15 categories in studies conducted outside the United States,[35] even though racial and ethnic categories are not consistent worldwide. Among the eight countries analyzed in one study, the number of categories used among researchers that correlate with American categories ranged from one to seventeen for "Asian," from three to twenty-four for "White," and from zero to twenty-eight for Black/African American. The relationship between the ethnic categories used abroad and Directive 15 categories "was highly complex."

Groups that American researchers are required to report in a single Directive 15 category sometimes have strikingly diverse genetic backgrounds. There is diversity among national groups but also within them. For example, the Malaysian population includes Malays, Indians, Chinese, and many non-Malay indigenous peoples.[36]

34. Hayes-Bautista, D. E. and Chapa, J. January 1987. "Latino Terminology: Conceptual Bases for Standardized Terminology," *American Journal of Public Health* 77, No. 1: 61-68.
35. Hsu, Paul et al. August 2019. "Racially Ambiguous Babies and Racial Narratives in the United States: A Growing Contradiction for Health Disparities Research," *Academic Medicine* 94, No. 8: 1099-1102.
36. Zhang, Frederick and Finkelstein, Joseph. July 2019. *Pharmacogenomics Perspectives in Medicine* 12: 107-22.

The upshot of all this is that using medical findings categories in a clinical setting that are based on Directive 15 classifications "may be of limited utility and potentially even damaging."[37] Some argue, however, that using them allows researchers to the study health disparities among populations that are primarily the product of cultural and sociological forces.[38]

This is a more persuasive rationale for using the Directive 15 categories than purported genetic differences. Nevertheless, data from Directive 15 categories can obscure more than they illuminate; there are vast differences in health measures among subgroups of the Directive 15 categories.[39]

For example, researchers found that 55 percent of "Asian" children in California had sufficient immunizations when they started kindergarten. But digging deeper into the data, the research found that only 21 percent of children of Southeast Asian descent had the requisite vaccines.[40] Making health policy for Southeast Asian children based on data from the broader Asian classification would lead to error.

Another study found that American-born and Haitian immigrant women had higher rates of cervical cancer than English-speaking Caribbean immigrants. Both immigrant groups had lower rates of breast cancer than their American-born black counterparts.

Six percent of Native American infants in New Mexico had low birth weight. Specific tribal rates, however, ranged from a high of 10.4 percent for the Mescalero Apache to a low of 1.8 percent for the Santa Clara Pueblo.[41] Knowing the "American Indian" rate in New Mexico would not properly guide a public policy response.

In the "Asian" category, people of Chinese descent have low rates of heart disease, while those of Asian Indian ancestry have high rates.

37.   Ibid.
38.   Kahn, *Race in a Bottle*, 193; Martin, Paul et al. 2007. "Reviving 'Racial Medicine'? The Use of Race/Ethnicity in Genetics and Biomedical Research, and the Implications for Science and Healthcare," (London: University of London): 1–16.
39.   Bhopal, Raj S. 2014. *Migration, Ethnicity, Race, and Health in Multicultural Societies* 2nd ed. (Oxford: Oxford University Press), 18.
40.   Williams, D.R. et al. 1994. "The Concept of Race and Health Status in America," *Public Health Reports* 109, No. 1: 26.
41.   Ibid.

In the South Asian subcategory of Asian, Bangladeshi men have high rates of smoking, while Sikhs have very low rates.[42] Studies on lung cancer or heart disease could not usefully generalize from either group to the entire South Asian population, much less to Asian Americans more generally.

One also cannot assume, as the public health literature often does, that Directive 15 minorities always have worse health outcomes than do whites. For example, Hispanics, Native Americans, and Asian Americans in California have significantly lower mortality rates and higher life expectancy than do non-Hispanic California whites.[43]

As Francis Collins, later director of the NIH, remarked, "We must strive to move beyond these weak surrogate relationships and get to the root causes of health and disease, be they genetic, environmental or both."[44] (Unfortunately, in his longstanding role as NIH director, Collins has not reformed NIH's own race-based research rules.)

Nonetheless, it may sometimes be useful to research health disparities among the Directive 15 categories, if only as a convenient way to try to identify possible inequities. If so, NIH and FDA should adopt specific classification policies for health disparity studies.[45] Current policy takes two separate concerns—health disparities that are a result of social forces, and genetic differences in medical response, respectively—and requires researchers to classify their subjects in the same way in both contexts.[46]

Another rationale for including race in scientific studies is to ensure minority populations are represented in those studies. This is thought to promote public confidence that medical researchers are concerned with the well-being of minorities.

42.   Bhopal, *Migration, Ethnicity, Race*, 18, 38.
43.   Hsu, Paul et al. 2018. "California and the Changing American Narrative on Diversity, Race, and Health, Health Equity," *Health Affairs* 37: 394.
44.   Collins, Francis S. 2004. "What We Do and Don't Know About 'Race', 'Ethnicity', Genetics and Health at the Dawn of the Genome Era," *Nature Genetics* 36: S15.
45.   Roberts, *Fatal Invention*, 106.
46.   Epstein, Steven. 2010. "Beyond Inclusion, Beyond Difference: The Biopolitics of Health." in *What's the Use of Race? Modern Governance and the Biology of Difference*, eds. Ian Whitmarsh and David S. Jones (Cambridge, MA: MIT Press), 67.

Pursuing this goal has its downsides, however. Researchers who need to meet goals for minority participation might unduly pressure potential minority subjects. Moreover, considering race in scientific research may "encourage the belief that race is biological in its essence."[47]

There is also a circular element to the argument from public confidence. The louder public health researchers proclaim that studies without a strong representation of minority subjects will not be deemed trustworthy, the less likely members of minority groups will be to trust such studies.

Federal requirements for using race in medical research may also inhibit scientists from studying specific issues. A researcher with no interest in studying possible "racial" differences in outcome is nevertheless required to report his results by Directive 15 racial categories.

Imagine a researcher who is considering launching a scientific investigation of the genetic origins, if any, of violent crime. This researcher has to worry that the results could show that a genetic marker associated with violent tendencies is more common in one or more Directive 15 minority groups.

Such a finding could give aid and comfort to racists. It could also be a career-ending faux pas, even if the data is not very robust and is susceptible to multiple interpretations. For both reasons, risk-averse researchers may avoid the topic, rather than undertake the research and be obligated to report results by race.

Moreover, using race in medical research inevitably encourages medical doctors to take their patients' race into account in diagnosis and treatment. While some doctors may do so only in the most scientifically justified and narrow ways, others may unconsciously resort to stereotype, resulting in medical mismanagement.[48]

Especially troubling, doctors sometimes base treatment decision on algorithms that suggest treatments work less for minority populations, especially African Americans. The algorithms often steer doctors away from treating minority patients as aggressively as white patients.[49]

47.   Epstein, Steven. 2007. *Inclusion: The Politics of Difference in Medical Research* (Chicago: University of Chicago Press), 11, 95.
48.   Witzig, Ritchie. October 15, 1996. "The Medicalization of Race: Scientific Legitimization of a Flawed Social Construct," *Annals of Internal Medicine* 126, no. 8: 678.
49.   Vyas, Darshali A. et al. July 11, 2020. "Hidden in Plain Sight–Reconsidering the Use of

The underlying data themselves are often of dubious validity. But beyond that, the way they are used in algorithms assumes, typically without evidence, that the data are picking up differences in genetic response to medical interventions.[50]

Yet another problem with using race in medical practice involves the gaps between people's self-perceptions of ethnic identity and how others perceive them. Emergency physicians often provide healthcare to individuals who are unconscious or otherwise nonresponsive. These patients cannot state their ethnic background, so their physicians decide based on appearance. But appearances can be deceiving.

A study by the National Center for Health Statistics found that 5.8 percent of people who identify as African American were perceived as white by census interviewers. The same study found that one-third of self-identified Asians and 70 percent of self-identified Native Americans were perceived by census interviewers as being white or black.[51] In another study of people who self-identified as Native American, 95.9 percent were classified as white by funeral directors on their death certificates, 4.1 percent as black, and none as Native American. Interviewers classified 61 percent of self-identified Native Americans as white and 37.8 percent as black.[52]

Meanwhile, any potential gains from using race in clinical practice must be weighed against the risks of alienating patients by labeling them by race. Some patients object to or are deeply suspicious of such labeling.[53] One expert who argues that "race, if used with care and attention, can produce valuable results" also cautions that "used carelessly, casually, or clumsily, it can blow up in your face."[54]

The need to satisfy FDA and NIH rules can also slow down important biomedical research, ultimately costing lives. In fall 2020, Moderna announced it was slowing enrollment in its clinical trial of

Race Correction in Clinical Algorithms," *New England Journal of Medicine* 383, no. 3: 874–82.
50.   Ibid.
51.   Wright, "One Drop of Blood."
52.   Hahn, Robert A. Truman, Benedict I. and Barker, Nancy D. January 1996. "Identifying Ancestry: The Reliability of Ancestral Identification in the United States by Self, Proxy, Interviewer, and Funeral Director," *Epidemiology* 7, No. 1 (Jan. 1996): 78.
53.   Witzig, "The Medicalization of Race."
54.   Kahn, *Race in a Bottle*, 24.

a COVID-19 vaccine to ensure it had sufficient minority representation among study participants. As thousands of people worldwide
were dying of COVID-19-related ailments, Moderna CEO Stéphane
Bancel made the remarkable assertion that diversity in research subjects
"matters more to [Moderna] than speed."[55]

NIH director Francis Collins later revealed that Moderna was
not acting autonomously but rather under his direction.[56] He told
Moderna that it needed to recruit more "people of color" (i.e., people
other than non-Hispanic whites), before NIH would acknowledge the
vaccine's safety.

Collins said this even though there was no reason to believe that
the vaccine would have a different safety and efficacy profile based on
ethnicity. Even if there had been reason for such concern, the broad,
crude Directive 15 categories Moderna was required to use would not
be a scientifically valid way of finding such differences. The "Hispanic"
category, with a primarily European genetic base with large admixtures
of Indigenous and African ancestry, is a particularly scientifically arbitrary category to use in this context.

Collins's goal seems to have been to get Moderna to more closely
match the Directive 15 profiles of its research subjects to the American
population. But if he had legitimate safety or efficacy concern for one
or more minority groups, the goal should have been to ensure that
there was enough representation of each group to get statistically valid
results. There is no *scientific* reason to be trying to match each group's
percentage of the population.

Indeed, Collins told National Public Radio that his underlying
concern was not about vaccine safety and efficacy. Rather, he believed
that if the vaccine trial participants had not represented American
demographic categories, the public would have distrusted the vaccine.
But this concern is circular. If it's true that Americans would not "trust"
a vaccine because its research subjects were not sufficiently "diverse,"

55. "Moderna Slows Coronavirus Vaccine Trial Enrollment to Ensure Minority Representation, CEO Says," CNBC, Sept. 4, 2020. https://www.cnbc.com/2020/09/04/moderna-slows-coronavirus-vaccine-trial-t-to-ensure-minority-representation-ceo-says.html.
56. "Moonshot in the Arm," *Planet Money*, Nov. 5, 2021. https://www.npr.org/
     transcripts/1053003777.

that is largely because the government insists that vaccines will not be deemed trustworthy unless they have been tested on a diverse population—as defined by the unscientific Directive 15 categories.

Francis, in other words, was not just responding to concerns about vaccine safety and efficacy for particular minority groups. Rather, his agency, NIH, is helping to create and then exacerbate such concerns. By contrast, non-Directive 15 minority groups, including ones that have unique genetic signatures after centuries of isolation and in-marriage, such as Ashkenazic Jews, remain blissfully unconcerned that they are not specifically represented in vaccine trials.

Given all the scientific and policy problems with requiring researchers who work with human subjects to use Directive 15 racial categories in reporting their results, it's worth exploring how this came to be.

Well into the twentieth century, medical researchers paid little attention to the racial and ethnic makeup of the subjects of medical studies. In the post-civil rights era researchers did not intentionally exclude members of minority groups from being study subjects.[57] But few researchers were concerned if their subjects were overwhelmingly white men.

Scientists assumed that the efficacy or safety of a pharmaceutical product or medical intervention would be the same across demographic groups. Meanwhile, researchers often relied on traditional social, professional, and educational networks to find research subjects for clinical studies. Members of minority groups were substantially underrepresented in these networks and therefore as participants in medical studies.[58]

The initial wave of criticism of the status quo came primarily from advocates for women's healthcare. Women, advocates noted, are biologically different from men. By relying primarily on male subjects to determine safety and efficacy, researchers might miss important differences in how women respond to a variety of medical interventions.[59]

Civil rights groups initially hesitated to demand representation for racial groups in medical research. The existence of clinically significant

57. Epstein, Steven. 2010. "Beyond Inclusion, Beyond Difference: The Biopolitics of Health," in *What's the Use of Race? Modern Governance and the Biology of Difference,* eds. Ian Whitmarsh and David S. Jones (Cambridge: MIT Press), 64.
58. Epstein, *Inclusion,* 51.
59. Roberts, *Fatal Invention,* 104-05.

biological differences among racial groups was hardly obvious. Indeed, suggesting such differences exist might play into racial prejudices.

Furthermore, African Americans were underrepresented in clinical studies for understandable reasons. Because of the mainstream medical community's history of racism, African Americans were reluctant to participate in medical research. Many African Americans distrusted the medical establishment and feared that researchers would treat them as expendable guinea pigs.[60] African Americans often took a cautionary lesson from the infamous Tuskegee experiment. Black men were allowed to die slowly from curable syphilis so that researchers could observe the disease's progression.

Persistent disparities in health outcomes between whites and minority groups, especially African Americans, persuaded activists that medical researchers should gather data aggregated by race. They hoped this data would help pinpoint relevant health disparities and create more avenues for the study of solutions.[61]

Reformers believed that African Americans underrepresentation in medical studies was due to "misguided protectionism" and "false universalism."[62] Misguided protectionism meant that after horrors like Tuskegee were revealed, white researchers saw medical studies as something to protect minorities from.

False universalism, meanwhile, was the unproven assumption that white men were similar enough to everyone else that the results of medical research on them could be extrapolated to everyone else. Critics contended that because members of certain minority groups had worse health indicia than whites, health researchers should be studying proportionally more members of those groups than whites, not fewer.[63]

The case for attending to race in medical research was bolstered by early studies, noted previously, suggesting that genetic differences

---

60. "Because some members of these [minority] and other groups perceive that race and ethnicity data have never been used to their advantage, they may be unwilling to cooperate with data collectors." Use of Race and Ethnicity in Public Health Surveillance: Summary of the CDC/ATSDR Workshop, https://www.cdc.gov/mmwr/preview/mmwrhtml/00021729.htm. See also Epstein, *Inclusion*, 62.
61. Epstein, *Inclusion*, 11; Roberts, *Fatal Invention*, 104.
62. Epstein, *Inclusion*, 62.
63. Ibid.

among racial groups led them to metabolize many pharmaceutical drugs differently. Such differences could result in varied effects on diverse populations. Advocates for minority health therefore "increasingly expressed reservations about medical treatments that had only been tested on white populations."[64]

As groups representing women and minority groups increasingly sought more "inclusion" and "representation" in medical research, they mixed and matched four different goals.

> **(1)** Statistical representation: Groups should be included in medical research according to their approximate percentages of the US population.

> **(2)** Social visibility: Both researchers and research subjects should reflect American "diversity."

> **(3)** Political voice: Researchers should ensure that their research addresses the needs of less-advantaged groups.

> **(4)** Symbolic representation: Medical researchers must be allies in ensuring that society understands the medically related problems facing various social groups.[65]

In 1986, in response to pressure by members of Congress concerned about minority health, NIH issued guidelines urging the inclusion of racial and ethnic minorities in medical research. These guidelines were not communicated well to the research community and had little impact.

In 1988, the FDA issued guidance explaining how researchers seeking approval for new drugs should analyze clinical study data.[66] The guidance emphasized the importance of reviewing safety and effec-

---

64. Ibid., 73.
65. Ibid., 89.
66. Food and Drug Administration, US Department of Health and Human Services, "Guideline for the Format and Content of the Clinical and Statistical Sections of New Drug Applications," July 1988, https://web.archive.org/web/20030409070109/https://www.fda.gov/cder/guidance/statnda.pdf.

tiveness data from clinical studies for population subsets, and specified race and ethnicity as relevant subsets.

Meanwhile, advocates for more minority representation were energized by an article in the *Journal of the American Medical Association*. The authors found that of thirty-five clinical studies reviewed, twenty did not include any African American participants. In most of the other studies, the percentage of African American participants was substantially lower than the African American population of the local area where the study took place. Notably, a relatively small percentage of subjects in AIDS research studies were African American or Latino, even though members of both groups disproportionately suffered from the AIDS virus.[67]

In 1993, women's health advocates persuaded Congress to take up legislation requiring federally funded researchers to enroll more women in medical studies. As the legislation proceeded through Congress, the Congressional Black Caucus persuaded the sponsors to add the phrase "and minorities" to the bill's language about women. No significant consideration was given to whether purported racial differences were analogous to male-female biological differences.[68]

The new law required federally funded clinical studies to enroll minorities as subjects and to "examine differential effects of such groups." The law's requirements were vague. For example, it did not specify which minority groups should be included or how membership in those groups should be determined.

Medical researchers expressed concern that the law would require them to provide statistically significant results by race for every minority group in every study. Recruiting enough subjects of each group to make this possible would have been extremely expensive and time-consuming. [69]

NIH responded to these concerns by issuing regulations clarifying that presenting such data was only necessary when previous studies suggested that results would vary by race. Otherwise, NIH advised,

---

67. Epstein, *Inclusion*, 6.
68. Roberts, *Fatal Invention*, 107.
69. Ibid., 105; Sally L. Satel, "Can Science Survive Research by Quota?," *USA Today Magazine*, Sept. 1994: 76.

researchers should report any racial differences they came across.[70] NIH also unofficially waived the minority-recruitment requirement for individual studies if the "overall research portfolio" for the relevant condition or therapy was sufficiently representative of minority groups.[71]

Nevertheless, the law "introduced politically derived race categories into science."[72] Critics contended that the law was based on a "dubious biological assumption: that races...differ so fundamentally that data from one group cannot be applied to another."[73]

Some major pharmaceutical companies embraced the new rules.[74] They wanted to avoid criticism that their drugs may not be suitable for the entire population. These companies also hoped that some therapies that showed no benefit to the general population might show positive results for a particular ethnic group. The therapy could then be approved by the FDA for use by that group.[75]

The heart disease drug BiDil is a famous example of this phenomenon. BiDil showed no clinically significant effects in the general population. In a post hoc analysis, however, it showed a positive effect in African American research subjects. The FDA agreed to approve BiDil only for use by patients of African descent. This decision remains controversial two decades later. According to critics, the FDA's decision rewarded scientifically invalid data dredging.[76]

In 1997, HHS Secretary Donna Shalala announced that Directive 15 categories should be used in HHS-funded and sponsored data collection and reporting systems.[77] The announcement was not legally binding, but it was a harbinger of regulations to come.

---

70. NIH Guidelines on the Inclusion of Women and Minorities as Subjects in Clinical Research, 59 Fed. Reg. 14,500 (1994).
71. Roberts, *Fatal Invention*, 114.
72. Catherine Lee and John D. Skrentny, "Race Categorization and the Regulation of Business and Science," *Law and Society Review* 44, Nos. 3-4, 2010: 631.
73. Benjamin Wittes and Janet Wittes, "Group Therapy," *New Republic*, April 5, 1993, 16.
74. For an extensive discussion and critique bio-pharmaceutical companies' support and pursuit of race-based research, see Kahn, *Race in a Bottle*.
75. Roberts, *Fatal Invention*, 67.
76. Paul Martin, et al. 2007. *Reviving 'Racial Medicine'? The Use of Race/Ethnicity in Genetics and Biomedical Research, and the Implications for Science and Healthcare* (London: University of London), 1-16.
77. Memorandum Issued by HHS Sec. Donna Shalala on October 24, 1997, https://aspe.hhs.gov/policy-statement-inclusion-race-and-ethnicity-dhhs-data-collection-activities.

Also in 1997, Congress required the FDA to study issues surrounding women and minorities' participation in clinical research. The following year, the FDA issued its so-called "Demographic Rule." This required companies submitting drug applications for FDA approval to tabulate participants in clinical trials by race and other factors.[78]

The FDA recommended that participants in clinical trials be asked to identify their racial group by Directive 15 categories. Companies were also instructed to pay attention to study data showing "clinically meaningful" differences between racial groups. "Minor differences" lacking medical significance, however, could be ignored.[79] The FDA suggested strategies companies might use in translating clinical data about ethnic groups in other parts of the world into data usable in FDA drug approval applications.[80]

In 1999, HHS issued a report recommending that any statistical work within HHS's purview use the Directive 15 categories. Researchers could break down the categories further if this would allow the aggregation of the different subcategories back into the Directive 15 categories.[81] The report offered no scientific justification for requiring researchers to use categories in medical research that were created for an entirely different purpose.

In 2001, the NIH required NIH-funded scientists to collect racial and ethnic data about study participants using the Directive 15 data.[82] Adopting the Directive 15 categories complied with HHS's 1999 recommendation. It also relieved NIH (and later FDA) of having to come up with and defend novel racial and ethnic categories that would surely have been controversial.

---

78. Investigational New Drug Applications and New Drug Applications, 63 Fed. Reg. 6854 (Feb. 11, 1998),
79. Ibid.
80. E5 Guidance on Ethnic Factors in the Acceptability of Foreign Clinical Data, prepared under the auspices of the International Conference on Harmonisation of Technical Requirements for Registration of Pharmaceuticals for Human Use (ICH) 63 Fed. Reg. 31,790 (1998).
81. "Improving the Collection and Use of Racial and Ethnic Data in HHS," https://aspe.hhs.gov/report/improving-collection-and-use-racial-and-ethnic-data-hhs.
82. "Policy on Reporting Race and Ethnicity Data: Subjects in Clinical Research," https://grants.nih.gov/grants/guide/notice-files/not-od-01-053.html; Lee and Skrentny, "Race Categorization," 632.

The NIH did not request public comments before issuing this policy, and the policy received very little attention. No scientific organization, health advocacy group, or government official publicly commented.

NIH rules apply to late-stage, large-scale phase 3 trials. Researchers must check whether previous studies suggested clinically important racial/ethnic-based differences in the expected effects of the intervention being studied. If such differences are apparent, the phase 3 trial design must address them.

For example, let's say existing evidence suggests that African Americans may respond differently than average to a given intervention. The phase 3 clinical trial must be designed to show both whether the intervention works for the nonblack population and (separately) whether it works for the black population.

Even when prior studies suggested no significant ethnic or racial distinctions, NIH encourages inclusion of racially diverse research subjects and analysis of data by racial/ethnic group. This way, researchers could engage in "valid analysis" of the effects on various groups. To avoid requiring scientists to recruit large numbers of subjects from every minority group, however, researchers were not required "to provide high statistical power for these comparisons."[83]

NIH-funded researchers who carefully identify study participants by more scientifically salient criteria still must aggregate their findings into the approved Directive 15 categories. Researchers must do so even if the subsamples of each group are too small to have statistically significant results and even when race has nothing to do with the purpose of the studies.[84] As one critic has noted, the "NIH policy is a de facto mandate to insert race as a relevant biologic statistical variable in all medical research."[85]

Meanwhile, NIH revised its standard grant application form to include a chart on which investigators must enter their study recruitment targets by race and ethnicity. Once funding is approved, NIH requires

---

83. Ibid., 633.
84. Epstein, *Inclusion*, 106.
85. Rodriguez and de la Fuente, "Time for a Postracial Medicine," 42.

investigators to submit annual reports demonstrating that the demographics of study participants are consistent with the original plan.

The requirement to use the Directive 15 categories led to difficulties in finding subjects and reporting them accurately. This was particularly true for clinical trials conducted outside the United States, where people's racial self-identification often does not match Directive 15 categories.[86] Researchers were encouraged to allow subjects to use the local vernacular to identify themselves. However, the researchers were also required to translate and aggregate the subjects' responses into the culturally insensitive or irrelevant Directive 15 categories.[87]

In 2003, the FDA issued draft guidance on the collection of racial and ethnic data in clinical trials. This guidance stated that regulated parties should use the Directive 15 categories.[88] The agency recommended using more detailed race and ethnicity categories "when appropriate to the study or locale," but only in addition to the Directive 15 categories. The FDA approved one modification for foreign research subjects. It permitted scientists undertaking research abroad to replace "Black or African American," which sounds strange to non-Americans, with "Black, of African Heritage."[89]

The FDA invited comments on its draft guidance, and it received hundreds of them. Most were identical products of a letter-writing campaign from civil rights groups that supported the guidance.

The most prominent endorsement of the guidance from a scientific or medical organization came from the American Medical Association (AMA), which represents US physicians.[90] The AMA argued that using the Directive 15 categories in medical research would ensure consistency across studies in government and industry, lead to improved evaluation of possible differences in the safety and efficacy of drugs across different

86.   Epstein, "Beyond Inclusion," 66.
87.   Ibid.
88.   Draft Guidance for Industry on the Collection of Race and Ethnicity Data in Clinical Trials for FDA Regulated Products, 68 Fed. Reg. 4,788 (2003); "Draft Guidance for Industry, Collection of Race and Ethnicity Data in Clinical Trials," 2003 WL 24014190, January 23, 2003.
89.   Ibid.
90.   Scotti, Michael. Comment on Collection of Race and Ethnicity Data in Clinical Trials for FDA Regulated Products, Draft Guide, Mar. 3, 2003.

population groups, and help scientists recognize useful variables in health responses and outcome that correlate with race and ethnicity. The AMA cautioned that it supported using the Directive 15 categories only "until more scientifically rigorous standards are available."[91]

By contrast, comments from pharmaceutical and biomedical company representatives were overwhelmingly negative, sometimes brutally so. Several respondents noted the absence of a scientific basis for utilizing the Directive 15 categories. A DNAPrint Genomics representative argued that the Directive 15 categories would not "consistently confer the most accurate information about a subject's genetic or cultural heritage...particularly if reliance is made exclusively on self-reporting."[92]

Judith Molt of AstraZeneca observed that Directive 15 categories do not match scientific/anthropological categories. "The whole concept of 'race,'" she explained, has been superseded by "a new understanding of the human genetic code." We have learned "that the genetic differences between two person [sic] of the same race or ethnicity is just as great as between two persons of different race or ethnicity." Conclusions derived from using the Directive 15 categories to analyze study data would therefore be unreliable. The result of relying on those conclusions, Molt warned, would be decreased patient safety. [93]

Gillian Woollett of the Biotechnology Industry Organization explained that Directive 15 categories "pre-date the work of the Human Genome Project, and reflect social, not scientific, categories." While such categories might be useful for studying national demographics or when trying to discover how health policy affects minority communities, "They are not suitable for scientific analyses of ancestry.... It is not reasonable," Woollett concluded, "for FDA to expect sponsors of clinical trials to label persons by their 'ethnic' background when such a label will not provide meaningful scientific data."[94]

91.   Ibid.
92.   DNAPrint Genomics to FDA, Feb. 4, 2003.
93.   Molt, Judith. Comment on Collection of Race and Ethnicity Data in Clinical Trials for FDA
      Regulated Products, Mar. 27, 2003.
94.   Woollett, Gillian. Comment on Collection of Race and Ethnicity Data in Clinical Trials for
      FDA Regulated Products, Mar. 28, 2003.

Alice Till of PhRMA emphasized that the proper the evaluation of safety and effectiveness requires science-based data and analysis. The Directive 15 race and ethnicity categories, however, are not based on science. If race and ethnicity categories must be used to gain knowledge about subpopulations, Till suggested, the categories "should be scientifically based."[95]

Several commenters disputed the FDA's contention that gathering medical data based on Directive 15 categories would lead to racially customized medical treatments. Woollett argued that the links between causal outcomes of racially customized treatments are tenuous and anecdotal at best. Moreover, the "categories proposed are, simply, too crude to be used as an accurate measure of drug effect assessment." She suggested the FDA encourage emerging technologies that could offer far more precision by isolating particular genetic factors that may be more prevalent in some races, but aren't "racial."[96] Similarly, a DNAPrint Genomics' representative suggested that rather than requiring researchers to use unscientific Directive 15 categories, the FDA should encourage genetic research to find scientifically salient ways of classifying research subjects.

A Merck spokesperson reminded the FDA of the "extensive international component" to pharmaceutical development. Using Directive 15 categories, he contended, was not "feasible when considered on a global basis for international clinical trials."[97] Several companies and industry organizations called attention to the International Conference on Harmonization (ICH) Guideline Document E5. Document E5 had standardized how to account for "ethnic factors" in research around the world.[98]

Jenny Peters of Pharmacia Corp. pointed out that understandings and definitions of race and ethnicity vary worldwide. The required use of Directive 15 categories would make it difficult to make useful comparisons across countries. She noted, for example, that the Hispanic/Latino

95.   Till, Alice. Comment on Collection of Race and Ethnicity Data in Clinical Trials for FDA Regulated Products, Mar. 28, 2003.
96.. Woollett, Comment.
97.   Letter, Merck to FDA, 26 March 2003.
98.   International Conference on Harmonization, Ethnic Factors in the Acceptability of Foreign Clinical Data, Feb. 5, 1998. https://www.ema.europa.eu/en/documents/scientific-guideline/ich-e-5-r1-ethnic-factors-acceptability-foreign-clinical-data-step-5_en.pdf.

classification is unique to the US. Peters added that the categories don't make sense anthropologically. For example, while Spaniards are Hispanic per Directive 15 guidelines, they are culturally and genetically closer to the French than to Mexicans.

Till emphasized that definitions of race and ethnicity vary across developed countries. Requiring American researchers to use Directive 15 categories inhibits scientists from making useful comparisons across countries. Shoehorning American racial and ethnic categories into vastly disparate cultures, Till added, would lead to problems. For example, subjects in Japan might not take study questions seriously if asked whether they were of Hispanic descent.

Undeterred by these comments, the FDA published its final Guidance on Collection of Race and Ethnicity Data in Clinical Trials.[99] As in the draft guidance, the FDA recommended using the Directive 15 categories for data collection. The FDA acknowledged that these categories have no scientific basis. The agency asserted that the categories are nevertheless relevant to governmental objectives such as monitoring and mitigating public health disparities among groups. Using the Directive 15 categories, the FDA asserted, would make it easier to identify and evaluate any differences in the safety and effectiveness of medical products in population subgroups.

The FDA noted that "differences in response to medical products have already been observed in racially and ethnically distinct subgroups of the U.S. population." But the FDA never explained why it chose the Directive 15 classifications. Subgroups within these classifications ("white" Finns vs. "white" Ashkenazic Jews, or Indigenous "Hispanics" vs. "Hispanics" of European descent) may have genetic differences that are more medically salient than differences among Directive 15 groups.

Heterogeneity within Directive 15 categories renders race-based medicine not just useless but counterproductive for many individuals. Studies purporting to discover an "Asian" biological reaction to a medi-

---

99.   2005 FDA Guidance: Collection of Race and Ethnicity Data in Clinical Trials (September 2005).   https://web.archive.org/web/20090710151540/http://www.fda.gov/downloads/RegulatoryInformation/Guidances/ucm126396.pdf.

cation cannot provide useful information across the entire, genetically diverse, Asian category.

For example, the FDA has noted that "slower enzyme metabolism (CYP2C19) has been observed in persons in the United States of Asian descent as compared to Whites and Blacks." But the Directive 15 Asian category includes a vast array of ethnic subgroups. Asian study participation subjects of any study can be East Asians, South Asians, Filipinos, or any combination of those groups. These groups are primarily of Asian, Caucasian, and Austronesian genetic ancestry, respectively.

By characterizing some Directive 15 groups as "races," the FDA implicitly endorsed the notion that traditional American racial taxonomy identifies scientifically distinct entities, something few geneticists believe. And in encouraging researchers to rely on "racial" or "ethnic" self-identification, the FDA ignored the instability of self-identification over time.

Self-identification can also be arbitrary from a genetic perspective. For example, an individual of primarily European descent may self-identify as "Hispanic" based on one distant Mexican grandparent who was primarily of Spanish descent, while his sister may self-identify as white. Most self-identified American Indians and African Americans are of partial European heritage, even if they self-identify only as a member of the minority category.

In any event, the FDA recommended that study participants self-report race and ethnicity. If a subject proved unwilling or unable to respond, researchers were told to request the information "from a first-degree relative or other knowledgeable source."

Researchers are permitted to collect race and ethnicity data beyond the Directive 15 categories. The FDA recommended that if researchers do so, they should use subcategories developed by Health Level Seven (HL7). HL7 is an organization that creates "interoperability standards for health care and health related information." Like the Directive 15 codes, however, the HL7 codes have no scientific basis; there is no plausible scientific justification for classifying individuals as "Cuban," "La Raza," or "South American."

The FDA made one minor concession to concerns regarding the incongruities of using American racial categories abroad; it permitted researchers who work in foreign countries to substitute "Black" for "Black or African American." This is still problematic, however, as the category is intended for people of African descent. Some groups considered black in their home countries and who may self-identify as black, such as Australian Aborigines, are not of African origin.[100]

In 2016, the FDA revisited its guidance on using race in clinical trials. The agency made one significant change for domestic studies; if researchers wanted to gather more granular ethnic or national origin data than the Directive 15 categories provide, they were no longer directed to the HL7 categories. Instead, the FDA referred researchers to the 2011 HHS Implementation Guidance on Data Collection Standards for Race, Ethnicity, Sex, Primary Language, and Disability Status.

Based on the HHS guidance, the FDA gave the following example for what researchers should ask:

Are you Hispanic, Latino/a, or of Spanish origin?
(One or more categories may be selected.)

a. _____ No, not of Hispanic, Latino/a, or Spanish origin

b. _____ Yes, Mexican, Mexican American, Chicano/a

c. _____ Yes, Puerto Rican

d. _____ Yes, Cuban

e. _____ Yes, Another Hispanic, Latino/a or Spanish origin

---

100. Hammerschmidt, Dale E. 1999. *Journal of Laboratory Clinical Medicine* 133, No. 1:11.

What is your race? (One or more categories may
be selected.)

a. _____ White

b. _____ Black or African American

c. _____ American Indian or Alaska Native

d. _____ Asian Indian

e. _____ Chinese

f. _____ Filipino

g. _____ Japanese

h. _____ Korean

i. _____ Vietnamese

j. _____ Other Asian

k. _____ Native Hawaiian

l. _____ Guamanian or Chamorro

m._____ Samoan

n. _____ Other Pacific Islander

The FDA provided no rationale for accounting for (most) Hispanics
and (most) Asians by country of origin but not doing the same for
whites or blacks. Most likely, the FDA was again shoehorning categories established for nonscientific purposes into scientific research.
For research conducted outside the United States, the only change was
modifying the "Black" category to "Black, of African heritage."

FDA rules continue to require sponsors of studies on new drugs to report the total number of subjects initially planned for inclusion in the study, the number recruited to the study by race and other demographic criteria, and the number of each group that participated to completion. Researchers must present a summary of safety and effectiveness data by race and an analysis of whether modifications of dose or dosage intervals are needed for specific subgroups.

As Steven Epstein, author of *Inclusion: The Politics of Difference in Medical Research*, notes, "There are many ways of representing the dispersion of biological or genetic differences within the human population. So it was not foreordained that medical and political categories will come to be aligned."[101]

Two factors led the FDA and NIH to impose unscientific racial categories on researchers. The first is bureaucratic inertia and risk-aversion. The Directive 15 categories were in use by HHS and the rest of the federal government, so those were the easiest, and least controversial, categories to adopt.

The second factor is that the categories have sociological salience. Though still imprecise, the categories may have utility for studying the causes of disparities in health outcomes.

Even if so, the FDA and NIH should not demand reliance on these categories in determining the safety and efficacy of medical interventions.[102] Not only is there no scientific rationale for requiring the use of Directive 15 categories in biomedical research, doing so is counterproductive; "The use of race as a proxy is inhibiting scientists from doing their job of separating and identifying the real environmental and genetic causes of disease."[103]

---

101. Epstein, "Beyond Inclusion," 70.
102. Ellison, George T.H. et al. September 2007. "Racial Categories in Medicine: A Failure of Evidence-Based Practice?" *PloS Medicine* 4, No. 9: e287.
103. "The Unexamined Population," *Nature Genetics*, 36, No. 1 (2004): 53.

CONCLUSION
Where Do We Go from Here:
The Separation of Race and State?

G overnment bureaucrats operating with little public scrutiny created the familiar legal classifications for American racial and ethnic groups. The categories often draw arbitrary and inconsistent distinctions among groups and sometimes verge on incoherence.

Office of Management and Budget Statistical Directive No. 15, which dates to 1977 with only minor subsequent amendments, is by far the most important government classification scheme. Directive 15 categories came with the official, explicit caveats that the classifications "should not be interpreted as being scientific or anthropological in nature" and should not be "viewed as determinants of eligibility for participation in any Federal program."[1] Those caveats were ignored, and the Directive 15 classifications became entrenched in American law and culture.

Official and racial ethnic classifications in the United States are self-fulfilling. The classifications encourage people to think of themselves as members of racial and ethnic categories that were invented or at least officially established and promoted by the government.[2]

For example, fifty years ago few Americans thought of themselves as Hispanic or Asian American; neither term was in common use, nor

---

1. Directive No. 15, Race and Ethnic Standards for Federal Statistics and Administrative Reporting, 43 Fed. Reg. 19,260 (May 4, 1978).
2. Wright, Lawrence. "One Drop of Blood," *New Yorker*, July 25, 1994.

was there much intergroup solidarity among the national origin groups within those categories.[3] The fact that many Americans self-identify with those categories is mostly a result of the government officially adopting these classifications in Directive 15.

Government-endorsed and imposed racial and ethnic categories encourage people to organize themselves politically by those categories.[4] This can help disfavored minority groups find a political voice to express valid concerns. It also, however, can also lead to gratuitous societal divisions. Such divisions pose special risk to the long-term welfare of minorities; after all, they are *minorities* in a democracy in which majority sentiment typically prevails.

In a country in which white supremacy was a governing ideology for most of its history, one should not be blasé about the risks inherent in identity politics. The horrendous history of racial classifications in places like Nazi Germany and South Africa should give further pause.

And yet Americans do tend to be blasé. The "white" classification should be much more controversial than it is. The United States classifies over two hundred million people with wildly diverse national origins and ethnicities, as white, part of "a single government-created pseudo-race."[5] The groups encompassed within the white label differ dramatically in ethnicity, socioeconomic status, geographic concentration, religious beliefs, appearance, and so on.

Despite this internal diversity, the white classification is based on the implicit assumption that people classified as white have common interests distinct from those of their fellow Americans. People who may otherwise have primarily self-identified as Greek, Irish, mixed, Catholic, gay, Texan, "just American," and so on are frequently requested to check a box identifying themselves as white and are therefore encouraged to think of themselves as white. The result is increased racial

---

3.   Even today, most people classified as Asian American reject that label, and most Hispanics prefer a national origin designation, such as Mexican American. Mora, G. Cristina. 2014. *Making Hispanics: How Activists, Bureaucrats & Media Constructed a New American Identity* (Chicago: University of Chicago Press), 7–8; Pew Research Center, The Rise of Asian Americans. http://www.pewsocialtrends.org/2012/06/19/the-rise-of-asian-americans; McGowan, Miranda Oshige. 1996. "Diversity of What?" *Representations* 55: 133.

4.   Ibid.

5.   Lind, Michael. "The Future of Whiteness," *Salon*, May 29, 2012.

consciousness among Americans classified as white. This development has, ironically, occurred at the same time Americans are intermixing more than ever.

Many progressive social theorists applaud increasing white racial consciousness. They believe that there will be a progression from increased white racial consciousness, to getting white Americans to acknowledge their "white privilege," to white Americans developing a "collective critical consciousness" that will make them allies in eradicating racism.[6] After all, what could go wrong with encouraging white racial identity? A lot, though the theorists in question are generally oblivious to the risks. Contrary to their optimistic projections, increased white racial consciousness encourages ethnonationalism, nativism, and other manifestations of intolerance, adding fuel to ideological fires that are increasingly threatening liberal democracy worldwide.[7]

There is an especially significant risk of a chauvinistic backlash in the US because the government combines assigning people an official white identity with the exclusion of those classified as white from benefits provided to those without legal whiteness. And indeed, rising white identity consciousness has already had significant, and broadly negative, political consequences in the United States.[8] Not surprisingly, though contrary to the predictions of the social theorists mentioned above, racially conscious whites are much more likely than other whites to believe themselves to the victims of minority groups' political gains. They are also much more likely to support racist political action, that is, political action meant to specifically advance white people's interests.[9]

So, what should be done about racial classifications by the government in the United States? One option would be to follow the example

---

6.   For an example of the vast literature with this theme, see Collins, Christopher S. and Jun, Alexander. 2020. *White Evolution: The Constant Struggle for Racial Consciousness* (New York: Peter Lang).

7.   Kaufmann, Eric. 2019. *Whiteshift: Populism, Immigration, and the Future of White Majorities* (New York: Henry N. Abrams).

8.   Sides, John and Tesle, Michael and Vavreck, Lynn. 2018. *Identity Crisis: The 2016 Presidential Campaign and the Battle for the Meaning of America* (Princeton, NJ: Princeton University Press); Thompson, Jack. "What It Means to Be a 'True American': Ethnonationalism and Voting in the 2016 U.S. Presidential Election, *Nations and Nationalism* 27, No. 1 (January 2021): 279-297.

9.   Jardina, Ashley. 2019. *White Identity Politics* (New York: Cambridge University Press).

of some countries with multiethnic populations, most famously France, that outright refuse to classify their citizens by race or ethnicity. The prevailing wisdom in such countries is that official race or ethnic classifications are divisive and undermine common national identity. Common national identity, meanwhile, is seen as a key to social solidarity and societal stability.

The argument in favor of a French-style solution is buttressed by the "almost comically arbitrary" nature of America's official racial categories when they are used in ways not intended or anticipated by those who created them.[10] Given, for example, that the categories came with the caveat that they are not based on science or anthropology, one could hardly expect them to be anything but arbitrary when used in biomedical research.

There would, however, be an important downside to totally failing to officially distinguish among racial and ethnic groups in the United States. Without such classifications, it would be much more difficult for the government to detect and try to redress discrimination.

While highly imperfect, the standard racial and ethnic categories are generally good enough for their original intended main purpose: monitoring discrimination by the government, government contractors, mortgage lenders, educational institutions, employers, and so on against minority groups that have been subject to the most severe and pervasive discrimination. Controversy over the salience of statistical disparities for showing discrimination is well beyond this book's scope. But to the extent it's useful and proper for the government to monitor and try to remedy such disparities, using the current categories is broadly defensible.

The categories would be even sounder for discrimination-monitoring if a few glaring anomalies were eliminated. For example, South Asians should not be in the same category—Asian American—as East Asians. One can easily imagine an institution with an ingrained bias

10. Schuck, Peter H. 2003. *Diversity in America: Keeping Government at a Safe Distance* (Cambridge, MA: Harvard University Press), 164; Omi, Michael. 1997. "Racial Identity and the State: The Dilemmas of Classification," *Law & Inequality* 15: 16; Wright, Lawrence. "One Drop of Blood."

against people of Asian Indian descent but not, for example, Chinese descent, or vice versa. Classifying groups that are so different in the same category will tend to obscure discriminatory patterns more than illuminate them.

Beyond discrimination-monitoring, just as the United States has managed religious diversity via the separation of church and state, it could similarly manage ethnic diversity via the separation of race and state. The late Justice Antonin Scalia argued for this rule, constitutionally enforced. Scalia declared in one judicial opinion that "in the eyes of government, we are just one race here. It is American."[11]

Scalia's proclamation has been extremely controversial because he made it while arguing that government affirmative action preferences based on race are unconstitutional. However, as we shall see, the government can pursue the most prominent goal of affirmative action, redressing the present effects of historical discrimination against African Americans, without resorting to racial classification.

Below, I discuss four major areas in which government-imposed racial classifications are used: biomedical research, sociological research, minority business enterprise preferences, and higher education preferences. In each area, the current racial classification scheme is a poor match for achieving the government's underlying goals, and indeed using the categories is often counterproductive. Between that and the inherent dangers of dividing the country by race and ethnicity, use of racial and ethnic classification should be abandoned in these contexts.

Biomedical Research

For the reasons discussed in Chapter Six, the FDA and NIH should stop requiring biomedical researchers to classify research participants by scientifically unjustifiable government-dictated racial and ethnic classifications. At best, requiring the use of these classifications in biomedical research is a wasteful distraction and has inhibited researchers from discovering and using much more productive ways of classifying research subjects. At worst, using these classifications promotes an

11. Adarand Constructors, Inc. v. Pena, 515 U.S. 200, 239 (1995) (Scalia, J., concurring in part and concurring in the judgment).

unsound racialism in science and medicine. This creates a high risk of encouraging junk science and expert quackery (or "quackspertise") about race and its scientific salience, with potentially disastrous consequences. Vital research is already being slowed by researchers' need to satisfy the FDA by having "enough" members of official minority groups as research subjects. This is happening even though the official racial and ethnic classifications have no valid scientific basis, and the FDA has never tried to show otherwise.

Sociological Research

Doing away with racial categories in favor of more precise classifications would also be appropriate in the context of monitoring the economic, social, and educational progress of various groups. The government's categories are too broad and internally disparate to provide sufficiently granular data to be very useful. Nevertheless, the government, most prominently the Census Bureau, uses the official classifications in its studies of the American population.

Consider the widely disparate national origin groups that make up the Asian American category. Chinese, Japanese, and Indian Americans, all relatively large groups, on average are thriving economically. Burmese, Laotian, and Bangladeshi Americans, all relatively small groups, on average are not. In the aggregate, data for Asian Americans looks positive. The needs of the less successful groups therefore tend to be ignored.

Similarly, the growing population of African and Caribbean immigrants and their descendants—10 percent of the black population of the United States was born abroad—distorts statistics for the African American category. The immigrant-derived black population has substantially higher average income and educational achievement than black descendants of American slaves. African Americans with one white parent also are socioeconomically advantaged relative to the overall African American cohort.[12] Grouping all people of African

---

12.   Brown, Kevin. 2014. *Because of Our Success: The Changing Racial and Ethnic Ancestry of Blacks on Affirmative Action* (Durham, NC: Carolina Academic Press).

descent together gives a misleading impression of socioeconomic conditions across the entire African American population.

The Hispanic category presents additional complexities for researchers. Not only do Hispanics come from many different countries and have varying degrees of European, African, indigenous, and even Asian ancestry, but many people with Hispanic ancestry do not identify as Hispanic. According to one study, only 21.4 percent of individuals with Mexican ancestry on only one side of their family check the Hispanic box on the census; only 5.6 percent of individuals whose most recent ancestor from a Spanish-speaking country immigrated five generations ago self-identity as Hispanic.[13]

Better educated and wealthier people of Hispanic descent are more likely to assimilate out of Hispanic identity. They are therefore less likely than other people of Hispanic descent to check the Hispanic box on the census and other forms. Statistics based on self-reported Hispanic identity therefore will understate the socioeconomic progress of the Hispanic-origin population.

The white category, as noted above, also includes people from a wide range of ethnicities, religions, and cultures. Sixty years ago, mass poverty among white Appalachians was an issue of great national concern.[14] Appalachians still struggle with low median incomes and widespread unemployment, and the opioid epidemic hit their region particularly hard. The scope of their problems is obscured, however, because government statistics place them within the much broader non-Hispanic white category.

For the same reason, we have relatively little data on the collective welfare of other "white" groups considered marginalized before official racial and ethnic classifications took root in the late 1970s. This includes, for example, Hasidic Jews, Cajuns in the Southeast, and French Canadians and Portuguese in New England. Government entities such as the federal departments of Education, Justice, and Labor do not distinguish these groups from other whites in the statistics they collect.

13.   Duncan, Brian and Trejo, Stephan J. *Ethnic Identification, Intermarriage, and Unmeasured Progress by Mexican Americans*, http://www.nber.org/chapters/c0104, 235.

14.   Harrington, Michael. 1962. *The Other America* (New York: MacMillan).

Minority Business Enterprise Preferences

Businesses owned by African American descendants of slaves (ADOS) were the original primary intended beneficiaries of minority business enterprise (MBE) preferences. Nevertheless, members of all minority groups became equally eligible for these preferences, even though the Directive 15 classifications came with the specific warning that they should not be used to determine eligibility for government programs.[15] Those eligible for MBE preferences include people whose ancestors did not suffer from generations of discrimination in the US. Rather, they "arrived in the United States after passage of the Civil Rights Act of 1964—Sri Lankans, Vietnamese, Colombians, to name only a few."[16]

Most MBE preferences now go to businesses owned by members of official minority groups who are not descendants of enslaved Americans. The ADOS population is dwarfed demographically by the combined population of Hispanics, Asian Americans, Native Americans, and black immigrants from Africa and the Caribbean and their descendants.[17] The non-ADOS groups not only outnumber black Americans but on average have more of the economic, educational, and social capital needed to obtain government contracts.

The gap between the primary original intention to help ADOS and the actual beneficiaries of MBE preferences is destined to grow. Immigration from Africa, Asia, and Latin America continues. Meanwhile, intergroup marriage rates among Hispanics, Asian Americans, and Native Americans are much higher than among African Americans. Under current rules and norms, anyone with partial Asian or Hispanic ancestry going back at least to one's grandparents and perhaps indefinitely can claim membership in those groups. Americans of mixed

15.   Graham, Hugh Davis. 2002. *Collision Course: The Strange Convergence of Affirmative Action and Immigration Policy in America* (New York: Oxford University Press), 289.
16.   Skrentny, John D. "Affirmative Action and New Demographic Realities," *Chronicle of Higher Education*, Feb. 26, 2001.
17.   Skerry, Peter. 1989. "Borders and Quotas: Immigration and the Affirmative-Action State," *Public Interest* 96: 88–89.

ancestry are generally willing to shift their self-identified racial or ethnic status to whatever currently benefits them.[18]

Within a generation or two, a large majority of Americans will be eligible for MBE preferences. If almost everyone is eligible for affirmative action preferences, they cease being meaningful. Limiting MBE preferences to fewer people may be the only way the preferences can be saved.[19]

All this suggests that to the extent MBE preferences continue, the government should limit them primarily to the original intended beneficiaries, ADOS. Members of recognized Indian tribes who live on and perhaps very close to reservations, a much smaller demographic, should also be included.

Such a limitation would have several advantages. First, ADOS and residents of Indian reservations are the two American groups whose ancestors suffered the most by far from state and private violence, oppression, and exclusion, with continuing reverberations today.[20]

Second, the categories of African American descendants of slaves and Native American residents of reservations have objective, definable boundaries, limiting the arbitrariness of the categories. Using these categories would also limit, though admittedly not eliminate, opportunities for fraud and misrepresentation.

Finally, government-granted preferences to people based on their racial or ethnic category raise constitutional, ethical, and practical concerns. But neither descent from American slaves nor membership in an Indian tribe and residence on an Indian reservation is a racial category, as such. Black Americans born in Africa would no longer qualify for MBE preferences, nor would a Los Angeles resident who has one Native American great-grandparent.

Americans rarely police (or desire to police) their fellow citizens who self-identify as members of a racial or ethnic minority group.

---

18.   Lee, Jennifer and Bean, Frank D. 2010. *The Diversity Paradox: Immigration and the Color Line in 21st Century America* (New York: Russell Sage Foundation), 191.

19.   Ibid., 193 ("if all groups are subject to discrimination, then in effect none are, at least when it comes to finding practical policy solutions").

20.   Prewitt, Kenneth. 2013. *What Is Your Race?: The Census and Our Flawed Efforts to Classify Americans* (Princeton: Princeton University Press), 102.

Limiting MBE preferences to ADOS and residents of Indian reservations would get the government out of the business of determining and sometimes rewarding individuals' racial identity. The government could be largely "color-blind" while retaining the ability to redress the lingering harms from state-sponsored racism.[21]

With a limited pool of affirmative action benefits, and an ever-increasing percentage of Americans potentially eligible for such benefits, another option would be to screen Americans for specific racial characteristics that leave people vulnerable to discrimination. The cautionary model in this context is Brazil. Brazil has set up race tribunals to determine the race of every applicant for a government job. One Brazilian state, looking for objective measures of race, issued guidelines about how to measure lip size, hair texture, and nose width to determine African descent.[22] Few Americans want official race tribunals, much less ones that work like that.

Affirmative Action in Higher Education

The only purpose for which the Supreme Court permits university-level affirmative action is to enhance the "diversity" of a school's student body for the benefit of all concerned. In inventing this doctrine in the *Bakke* case in 1978, Justice Lewis Powell had in mind a college admissions office that wanted to admit applicants who would add racial and ethnic diversity to the crop of musicians, athletes, scholars, artists, actors, and other groups colleges recruit.

Yet the way colleges go about achieving racial and ethnic diversity makes little sense if diversity per se is the objective, as opposed to using diversity as a subterfuge while pursuing other objectives. First, many elite schools try to match their percentage of minority students from various groups with their respective percentages of the appli-

21.   On opposition to color-blindness as an appropriate goal, see Gotanda, Neil. 1991. "A Critique of 'Our Constitution is Color-Blind,'" *Stanford Law Review* 44: 1-67; Lopez, Ian F. Haney. 2011. "Is the 'Post' in Post-Racial the 'Blind' in Colorblind?" *Cardozo Law Review* 32: 822, 831.
22.   "For Affirmative Action, Brazil Sets Up Controversial Boards to Determine Race," *NPR,* Sept. 29, 2016.

cant pool or other demographic baseline. Approximately one-half of 1 percent of the American population identifies as Native American, compared to 18 percent as Hispanic. In an entering class of, say, one thousand, the one hundred and eightieth Hispanic student surely does not make the class more ethnically diverse than would the sixth Native American.

Moreover, universities often give little or no consideration to the fact that members of official minority groups "may have no interest whatsoever in the culture popularly associated with the group."[23] An applicant who checks the Hispanic box and inherited the name Lopez via her Mexican great-grandfather, but otherwise has no cultural connection to Mexico or to Mexican Americans, does not add to a school's cultural diversity simply because she meets the official definition of Hispanic.

Meanwhile, the relevant official minority categories are themselves internally ethnically diverse, often radically so. A small college with ten Indian, ten Chinese, four Korean, three Pakistani, three Vietnamese, two Thai, two Nepalese, two Japanese, and two Filipino American students is surely more ethnically diverse than its same-sized counterpart with twenty Chinese and eighteen Indian American students. Current classification norms, however, would tell us only that both schools have thirty-eight Asian American students and are equally diverse.[24]

The white category, like the Asian American category, covers a tremendous amount of ethnic, cultural, linguistic, and religious diversity. A Yemeni Muslim student may add significant religious, ethnic, and cultural diversity to a campus. For campus affirmative action purposes, however, admissions offices classify her as just another white student. The same is true of an Egyptian Copt, a Hungarian

---

23. Hollinger, David A. 2000. *Posthnic America: Beyond Multiculturalism* (New York: Basic Books, Second edition), 180.
24. It "would be ludicrous to suggest that all [students classified as 'Asian'] have similar backgrounds and similar ideas and experiences to share." Such a "crude" and "overly simplistic" racial category cannot possibly capture how "individuals of Chinese, Japanese, Korean, Vietnamese, Cambodian, Hmong, Indian and other backgrounds comprising roughly 60% of the world's population" would contribute to diversity on a college campus. Fisher v. University of Texas, 136 S. Ct. 2198, 2229 (2016) (Alito, J., dissenting) (quoting Brief for Asian American Legal Foundation et al. as Amici Curiae).

Roma, a Bosnian refugee, a Scandinavian Laplander, a Siberian Tatar, a Bobover Hasid, and their descendants. The only exception arises if a white applicant has Spanish-speaking ancestors and therefore qualifies as Hispanic. This seems entirely arbitrary if a student body with diverse backgrounds is the goal.

Those who qualify for the African American category also are not culturally uniform. A descendant of American slaves who grew up in a working-class, majority-black neighborhood in Milwaukee does not contribute to diversity in the same way as a child of an African diplomat who grew up in toney DC suburb, nor as a black-identified applicant with multiracial ancestry who grew up in a small town in Montana. Yet they all fall into the same diversity category.

The Native American category is also extremely internally diverse. This classification includes everyone from a resident of the impoverished Hopi reservation with an unbroken line of Hopi ancestry to an applicant who grew up with no Native American cultural knowledge or experience, has fair skin, blond hair, and blue eyes, but inherited Cherokee tribal membership via a distant Cherokee ancestor. Surely, these applicants would make very distinct contributions to a campus' ethnic diversity. Classifying them both as generic Native Americans obscures those distinctions.

Fraudulent and exaggerated claims of Native American identity have been rampant in law school admissions, which suggests they are also rampant in admission to other university programs. Researchers discovered that for a given cohort of law school graduates, there was a massive disparity between those who listed themselves as Native American lawyers on the census (228) and the number of self-identified Native Americans who graduated law school over that same time period (2,610).[25] In other words, over ten times as many people claimed to be Native American when they applied to law school than identified themselves as Native American lawyers once they graduated.

In response, the American Bar Association urged law schools to require applicants claiming American Indian status to provide proof

---

25.   Clarke, Jessica A. 2015. "Identity and Form," *California Law Review* 103: 805.

of tribal citizenship or other evidence of Native American identity.[26] The Coalition of Bar Associations of Color passed a broader resolution demanding that law schools crack down on "academic ethnic fraud."[27]

The best way forward for schools truly interested in attracting a diverse group of students would be to cease relying on crude government-imposed racial and ethnic classifications as a proxy for genuine diversity. As in the MBE context, affirmative action preferences, if pursued, should be limited to African American descendants of slaves and members of American Indian tribes who live on reservations. The goal of such preferences would not be diversity, but the righting historical injustices that have modern reverberations, and helping to bring marginalized groups into the American mainstream.[28] There is a risk, however, that the Supreme Court would hold that the ADOS and Indian reservation resident categories are proxies for racial classifications and therefore presumptively unconstitutional.

The Judicial Role:
Is the Current Classification Regime Constitutional?

The default response by the government to questions raised about the arbitrariness of the current classification regime and its enforcement has been almost total inertia. The relevant racial and ethnic categories have barely changed over the decades.

I am not optimistic about the prospect of legislative or administrative reform, especially in the context of affirmative action preferences. Experience around the world shows that affirmative action categories almost always expand rather than contract, as more and more groups

---

26. House of Delegates Resolution No. 102, ABA (Aug. 7–8, 2011), perma.cc/PGY4-NXM7.
27. Hu, Elise "Minority Rules: Who Gets to Claim Status as a Person of Color?" *NPR*, May 16, 2012. https://perma.cc/YZY7-N53P.
28. Ford, Richard Thompson. 2005. *Racial Culture: A Critique* (Princeton: Princeton University Press), 97–98 (policies "should focus on eliminating status hierarchies, while generally leaving questions of cultural difference to the more fluid institutions of popular politics and the market"); Rubenfeld, Jed. "Affirmative Action," *Yale Law Journal* 107 (Nov. 1997): 472. ("In fact, the true, core objective of race-based affirmative action is nothing other than helping blacks. Friends of affirmative action, if there are any left, should acknowledge this objective, and they should embrace it—in the name of justice.").

lobby to be get affirmative action preferences and then lobby to protect those preferences.

Courts, however, may intervene by finding the current classification scheme, or at least elements of it, unconstitutional. No case has yet addressed the question of whether Americans have a right to choose their racial and ethnic identity, regardless of official government classifications and definitions. Americans increasingly have the right to choose their gender identity, raising the question of whether the government may lawfully refuse to recognize someone's racial and ethnic self-identity.

Meanwhile, arbitrary racial classification is traditionally treated very suspiciously by the Supreme Court. So far, only a few lawsuits have raised challenges to the arbitrariness of the official racial and ethnic categories and, in those cases, lower courts have mostly been deferential and upheld the categories. The categories have not, however, been immune from judicial criticism. Most recently, Judge Amul Thapar of the United States Court of Appeals for the Sixth Circuit, writing about a federal small business program, noted that "individuals who trace their ancestry to Pakistan and India qualify for special treatment. But those from Afghanistan, Iran, and Iraq do not. Those from China, Japan, and Hong Kong all qualify. But those from Tunisia, Libya, and Morocco do not…. It is indeed 'a sordid business' to divide 'us up by race.'"[29]

The Supreme Court and lower courts of the vast majority of jurisdictions have not weighed in on whether official racial categories are unconstitutionally arbitrary, in whole or in part. We lack firm judicial precedent, for example, on whether in pursuing affirmative action the government may include Filipinos, Bangladeshis, and Mongolians in the same category despite their vast differences, or whether the government may arbitrarily draw the lines for the Asian American category at the western borders of Pakistan and China.

In future cases, courts might be especially troubled that the Asian American classification is disfavored by most people who come within the category. The category also matches the pseudoracial and anthropo-

---

29.   Vitolo v. Guzman, 999 F.3d 353 (6th Cir. 2021).

logical category used to exclude Asians from immigration and citizens earlier in United States history.

There is, admittedly, something to be said for using past discriminatory policies as a baseline for current categorization. But many of the nationality groups currently classified as Asian American had little or no interaction with American law until well after discriminatory immigration and citizenship laws had been reformed or repealed. And there is a strong argument that we should not encourage the persistence of the racist classifications of a bygone era, even for remedial purposes. The argument becomes even stronger in the context of well-documented allegations that some universities discriminate against applicants classified as Asian American because members of that group are deemed overrepresented in the student body.

Meanwhile, there is no consensus on how to define the Hispanic/Latino classification or whether there is any non-arbitrary, constitutionally proper way to do so. As one court has noted, "There is no agreed working definition of Hispanic persons since they may be of different races and may have very different cultural, religious and geographic origins."[30]

As discussed in Chapter Two, some decisionmakers have relied on the literal official definition of Hispanic to conclude that anyone with Spanish-speaking ancestry can properly assert a Hispanic identity. Other courts and agencies have concluded that for affirmative action purposes, only individuals who likely suffered discrimination due to their Hispanic background qualify. Hispanic status therefore depends on factors such as Spanish fluency, appearance, surname, and community ties. Meanwhile, two federal appellate courts have issued opposing rulings on whether the government may provide preferences to white Americans of European descent who have Spanish-speaking ancestry but not to any other demographic group the government deems white.[31]

---

30. Concrete Works of Colo., Inc. v. City and County of Denver, Colo., 86 F. Supp. 2d 1042, 1069 (D. Colo. 2000), rev'd, 321 F.3d 950 (10th Cir. 2003).
31. Builders Association of Greater Chicago v. County of Cook, 256 F.3d 642 (7th Cir. 2001) (unconstitutional); Peightal v. Metropolitan Dade County, 940 F.2d 1394 (11th Cir. 1991) (constitutional).

*   *   *   *

The internal American struggle between the desire to maintain official racial classifications to redress harm from racism and wanting to eliminate them as unconstitutional and antiliberal continues. My fellow law professors, particularly those writing from a Critical Race Theory perspective, often start with the presumption that racial division inevitably will be a permanent part of the American landscape.[32] I disagree.

Many American interethnic conflicts have faded into distant memory. This includes relatively obscure intergroup friction, such as Germans versus Scandinavians in the Upper Midwest and clashes between Basque shepherds and ranchers of other ethnicities. It also includes better-known antipathies, such as anti-Chinese agitation in the American West and tensions between ascendant Irish Americans and the Anglo establishment in East Coast cities.

Bitter and sometimes violent hostility to non-Protestant religious groups that once marked American life has also faded.[33] This includes anti-Mormon violence in the 1800s and the hostility toward Catholics that led to a vigorous rebirth of the Ku Klux Klan in the 1920s. These conflicts have only faint echoes today and seem faintly ridiculous to most Americans.

Hopefully, Americans also will one day look back on today's racial divisions and accompanying tensions as a faintly ridiculous vestige of a less sophisticated, enlightened, and tolerant past. How the US government handles racial classification will be a decisive factor in whether that outcome comes to pass. Law played a significant role in establishing racial divisions in the United States, and law (or its absence) can play a significant role in either maintaining or abolishing, or at least severely mitigating, those divisions.

32. Bell, Derrick. 1992. *Faces at the Bottom of the Well: The Permanence of Racism* (New York: Basic Books).
33. Moore, R. Laurence. 1987. *Religious Outsiders and the Making of Americans* (New York: Oxford University Press).

ACKNOWLEDGMENTS

For their comments, suggestions, and research leads, the author thanks Nadia Ahmad, Charles Barzun, Jonathan Bean, David Boaz, Lillian Bernstein, Natalie Bernstein, Stanley Bernstein, Joshua Braver, Jack Chin, Jessica Clarke, Steven Epstein, Mike Gonzalez, Jeremy Kessler, Julian Ku, Lars Noah, Chris Newman, George La Noue, Christopher Ogolla, Walter Olson, Zvi Rosen, Michael Rosman, David Schleicher, Peter Schuck, John Skrentny, Ilya Somin, John Sullivan, John Tehranian, Sean Trende, and Alexander Tsesis.

Special thanks to Daniel Greenberg for volunteering his much-appreciated editorial assistance with the manuscript.

Sigal Bernstein was a constant source of encouragement, suggestions for improvement, and love.

Scalia Law School librarian Robert Willey was indefatigable in tracking down needed sources, especially obscure ones, despite the limitations imposed by the pandemic.

Aaron Gordon, Garrett Snedeker, and Emily Yu provided very helpful research assistance.

The author benefitted from a small grant from the Institute for Humane Studies at George Mason University that helped pay for research assistants.

Scattered portions of this book, especially Chapter One, originally appeared in somewhat different form in David E. Bernstein, "The Modern American Law of Race," *Southern California Law Review* 94, No. 2 (2021): 171–250. A shorter, preliminary version of Chapter Six was published by the *Yale Journal on Regulation* as part of an online symposium on racism in administrative law, https://www.yalejreg.com/nc/two-decades-ago-the-fda-and-nih-mandated-the-use-of-race-to-categorize-subjects-and-report-results-in-medical-and-scientific-research-they-oversee-it-was-a-huge-mistake-by-david-e-bernstein.